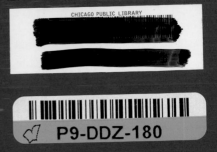

DANCING SPIRIT

DANCING SPIRIT

AN AUTOBIOGRAPHY

JUDITH JAMISON

WITH HOWARD KAPLAN

DOUBLEDAY

New York   London   Toronto   Sydney   Auckland

FRONTISPIECE
In Talley Beatty's *Toccata*. *Author's personal collection*

PUBLISHED BY DOUBLEDAY
a division of Bantam Doubleday Dell Publishing Group, Inc.
1540 Broadway, New York, New York 10036

DOUBLEDAY and the portrayal of an anchor
with a dolphin are trademarks of Doubleday,
a division of Bantam Doubleday Dell Publishing Group, Inc.

Review of *Cry* copyright © 1971
by The New York Times Company.
Reprinted by permission.

Excerpts from the journals of
Alvin Ailey reprinted by
permission of Allan Gray, executor,
the estate of Alvin Ailey.

Excerpt from *Dance* magazine,
July 1972, © 1993 *Dance*
magazine, reprinted by permission.

Book design by Marysarah Quinn

Library of Congress Cataloging-in-Publication Data

Jamison, Judith.
Dancing spirit: an autobiography / Judith Jamison with Howard Kaplan.
p.   cm.
1. Jamison, Judith.   2. Dancers—United States—Biography.
3. Afro-Americans—Biography.   4. Alvin Ailey American Dance Theater.
I. Kaplan, Howard, 1960–   .   II. Title.
GV1785.J26A3   1993
792.8′028′092—dc20
[B]   93-25480
CIP

ISBN 0-385-42557-0

November 1993

10   9   8   7   6   5   4   3   2   1

First Edition

FOR ALVIN

To all those dancers who hold high
the great African-American artists
who gave and are still giving,
so that we may continue
to have this place in the sun.

ACKNOWLEDGMENTS

Grateful acknowledgment to: Michael, Annie, Peter, and Andrew Ahearn, Dr. Laurie Bauman, Laura Beaumont, Ken and Caroline Brody, Cheryl McClenney-Brooker and Moe Brooker, Donald Byrd, Masazumi Chaya, Pamela Cooper, Chloe and Carter Deas, Timothy DeBaets, Garth Fagan, Vivianne Ford and the Priesthood, Ellis Hazlip, Patricia Jacobs, John Charles Jamison, The Jamison Partners, Denise Jefferson, Michael Kaiser, Nancy Kalodner, Dr. Francis C. Kempf, Dr. Albert Knapp, Annie Leibovitz, Morton and Georgette Levy, Lili Cockerille Livingston, Marc Manigault, Shahida Mausi, Dr. Richard Mendes, Milton Myers, Dr. Jeanne Noble, Michael Peters, Sathi Pillai, Dr. Robert L. Polk, Ken Rubenstein, Robert T. and Helen Summers, Liz Thompson, and Sylvia Waters.

Howard Kaplan wishes to acknowledge the contribution and support of John Blee.

PROLOGUE

When in doubt, turn . . .

In 1967, during my third season with the Alvin Ailey American Dance Theater, the State Department sent us on a nine-country tour of Africa that started in Addis Ababa, Ethiopia, and took us down to Madagascar and across the continent. The year before, we danced at the First World Festival of Negro Arts in Dakar. All I had known of Africa up to this point were the distortions Hollywood had showed me, and the limited paragraphs in my history books. Those images were wrong. In my travels through Africa, the truth was almost too much to absorb. The diversity and beauty of the continent hit me in the face, in the spirit, and in the heart. I was overwhelmed by the differences between the people, in color, in the way they carried themselves, in the clothes that they wore, in the music, the rhythms, the art. I was fascinated to know that there were Ghanians who looked like my uncle Charles.

In each country I was drawn to the marketplaces, the landscape, the diversity of everyday life unfolding before me. I very much wanted to be identified as being from somewhere on the continent. I wanted to be identified with *somebody*, to see something in that bone structure that said, "You're from here, your ancestors are from here." I was hungry for that identification. It wasn't until I got to Accra that I saw people who could have been related to me. In Senegal, I was told that I looked like a member of the Peul tribe. My coloring was very much like theirs, as were my facial features. I was tickled when I learned that the Peul were nomadic. It was perfect. *They were gypsies, so was I.*

Mom and Dad in Fairmount Park for a holiday picnic. *Author's personal collection*

CHAPTER 1

"And Still I Rise . . ."
Maya Angelou

My father's hands, rough from work, were gentle when he taught me how to play the piano. His long, tapered fingers, callused from wood and metal carpentry, brought an exquisite touch to Rachmaninoff, one of his favorite composers. I would arch my hands over the keyboard as he placed my fingers on the notes, the piano lamp lighting us softly.

My father taught me work and beauty, the lessons of his hands. Deep within, I've always felt that complement of opposites: body and soul, solitude and companionship, and in the dance studio, contraction and release, rise and fall.

The contraries of looking back while moving ahead pull at me now; I was taught to look forward. In many African-American families that I know the elders do not sit down with their children and grandchildren and speak of the past. I was raised in that tradition. Children were not privy to adult information—that branch of my family tree was always out of reach.

When I was asked to make a family tree in junior high school, Mother and I sat at the dining-room table with pen and paper. She made a lovely tree, but there were few names on it. I became angry that my family could not trace our ancestry as far back as we should have been able to. The tree went no further back than to my great-grandparents.

To this day, I still want to know. I want to see something, hold an heirloom, hear a name. I know I can't see a picture. I've seen pictures of my paternal grandmother, Abigail, and I look at her and smile because I see myself all over her. I'm also supposed to resemble my maternal great-grandmother, but I've never seen what she looked like. She had scars on her back from being beaten as a slave in the South because she was a strong-headed woman; she needed to have an attitude to survive. Some Black families are able to trace their families more than others. Some can actually go back to Africa, but not the Jamisons.

A tree puts down its roots before it sends its shoots up and out. My parents, born and raised in the South, met and settled in the North. I'm moved by contraries, by opposites, the strength that was my mother's eyes, the beauty of my father's hands.

To get to Orangeburg, South Carolina, you drive eighty miles north-west from coastal Charleston, pass through the towns of Summerville and Holly Hill, over paved roads my father once walked when he was a boy and they were dirt. Orangeburg, first settled in 1704, was named for William, Prince of Orange, son-in-law of the former King James II of England. On the map the distance between Charleston and Orangeburg is only a few inches, the marks resembling the facial lines of a person who has lived a long time. If it's summer, the blacktop highway swells with heat; if it's winter, it's pretty much the same. I'm trying to find out more about my family name but the records here are incomplete. The only Jamison listed is a General Jamison who owned slaves, but it doesn't necessarily mean that my name came from his farm or plantation. In many counties, freed slaves wanted new names, and would take the name of the family down the road or whoever might have turned toward them with any kindness.

My father, John Henry Jamison, was raised in the segregated South, in Orangeburg, one of five children born to Abigail and Charles Jamison—Theodore, Charles Jr., Henrietta, Herbert, and Dad. When my father was six years old, Grandfather Charles, an engineer at the linseed oil mill and a carpenter, died suddenly, leaving the family devastated and destitute. Grandmother and Henrietta moved up north shortly after, leaving my father and his brothers with a family friend until Abigail could afford to send for them.

Once Grandmother Abigail was settled in Philadelphia, she took care of people, which is something I've always done, especially for dancers. When Jesse Summers came up north from Orangeburg, she took him in. Eventually, he and my aunt Henrietta would marry and have eleven children, ten boys and one girl, my cousin Helen. Aunt Henrietta passed away in 1953.

My father had to do everything he possibly could to make a living. Nothing was given to him. Work was a requirement. As a boy he hauled cakes of ice into the homes of people who could afford an icebox. Ten cents for fifty pounds of ice that lasted two days. He hauled coal for people without furnaces, to burn in their cast-iron stoves. His brother Charles worked in the local bakery. Two loaves of bread cost ten cents, a dozen eggs fifteen.

The South had separate drinking fountains marked "Black" and "White," separate benches, separate restaurants, separate lives. When my father traveled north it was in a segregated train. African-Americans were supposed to "walk a straight line," and to live double lives. The reality was the duality of their survival. Photos of young Black men hanged in Augusta and Atlanta served as indelible reminders.

My great-uncles raised pigs, hogs, and sugarcane on their farm outside Orangeburg. They made their own syrup. Horse was the mode of travel. One uncle had a black patent leather surrey, the "farmer's Cadillac" that seated four and was pulled by jet-black horses with coats so shiny my dad said he could almost see his own reflection.

Orangeburg was a resort for Northerners who wintered in large, breezy homes, and a college town, with both Claflin College and South Carolina State College, which was founded in 1896. Education was stressed in the South at the time, although most farmers had only a grade-school education. Booker T. Washington emphasized the importance of education, so did my grandparents as well as my father and mother.

My mother, Tessie Belle Brown, was also raised in the South, in Bartow, Florida, daughter of Annie May and Timothy Brown. My great-grandfather, Jethro Brown, owned a candy store. I did not know my great-grandparents, and have only recently learned some stories of their lives from Mrs. Allie Whetstone, my mother's sister. When Mother and Allie were children, Great-grandfather would invite the girls into his store and offer them anything they wanted, so naturally they would stuff their pockets with sweets. Later, when he ran into his son, he'd say, "*Your* kids ate ten cents' worth of *my* candy." In other words, pay up! Great-grandfather, I'm told, was a very tall, distinguished-looking man.

My great-grandmother would be very careful about the boys who used to visit her girls, Annie May and Great-aunt Cora. When she cleared her throat in the next room, no later than nine o'clock, it meant, "Boys go home, you should be in bed. Get out of here."

My maternal grandfather, Timothy Brown, studied at Morehouse College, which was established in 1867 as the Augusta Institute by Richard C. Coulter, an escaped slave. In 1913 the Institute became Morehouse College, a Black, all-male, four-year liberal arts college. It would become famous for graduating Dr. Martin Luther King, Jr.

In time, both my parents would leave the South and move to Pennsylvania. They would attend the same church, Mother Bethel African Methodist Episcopal, the oldest Black church in the country, organized by Pastor Richard Allen in 1787, when he walked out of his old, segregated church. *That's* how Mother Bethel started. My parents met in choir. On May 3, 1938, Tessie Belle Brown and John Henry Jamison were married by Reverend Van Buren of Camden, New Jersey, and set up house in West Philadelphia.

Mom and Dad in the Mother Bethel A.M.E. choir. Mom's top row, second from right, and Dad's second from right, bottom row. *Author's personal collection*

*   *   *

When I was six years old I was tall, lean, and long-legged. At ten I could walk down the street and see over everybody's head. I loved being last on line in elementary school and peeking at what was happening up front. I don't remember being little or having to look up at people. I think I was born five feet ten. It's not that I felt especially tall. I was wondering when everybody else was going to catch up.

I had my mother and Marion Cuyjet, my first ballet teacher, as examples of women who stood erect and carried themselves proudly. It amazed me that anybody *schlumped* or didn't walk completely straight. I didn't have to walk around with a ruler in my back. I was in dance class all the time and even I had to be "pulled up." Marion Cuyjet always used to say, "Give me a nice *looong* line." While Marion was telling everybody to lengthen, I was already there. I had that advantage.

I've always felt blessed to look the way I look, to have the bones I have and the richly dark brown skin. Thank God for my mom and dad. I was a skinny kid with knobby knees and slender fingers. Mother said that when I was born I had the longest fingers and the *longest* legs. She didn't say, "Here's a musician or here's a dancer." She knew that if she didn't get her energetic daughter out of the house and into some kind of constructive direction, that *she* would not be able to live.

My parents had the good sense to channel my energy and put me in dancing school, because I was driving them *crazy*. When they brought me home from the hospital to our house on Folsom Street, West Philadelphia, I shared a room with my brother, John Henry Jamison, Jr., who was three at the time. I was so noisy and restless I would not let him sleep. "Get this loud baby out of my room," he told our mother. I was hyperactive with energy that went on forever. I used to jump in bed at night. Dad said I wore out a couple of cribs that way. I knew I wasn't supposed to be doing it. I don't know if they let me or simply looked the other way. When they were sufficiently worried about my behavior, they took me to the pediatrician. He told my parents that I was overly energetic, but not to worry, I'd soon grow out of it. But I haven't. I still have that kind of energy. Jumping takes place in another arena now.

I don't remember a time when I wasn't moving. When I was a toddler in our Folsom Street house, I tested out my newly learned walk and fell down the stairs. Mom ran several blocks to the hospital with me in her arms.

I was a "why, why, why?" kid, always asking my parents, why this or why that? Back then, I was a child with a lot of energy who ran around and wore my parents out. For a time I was *so* wound up, I'd do things backward. Mom would send me to the store and I'd ask for "tissue toilet" instead of toilet tissue. Once when she asked me to put a stamp on a letter, I placed it on the wrong side. It was a bill that had to be paid, and Mom was upset that I had wasted a stamp.

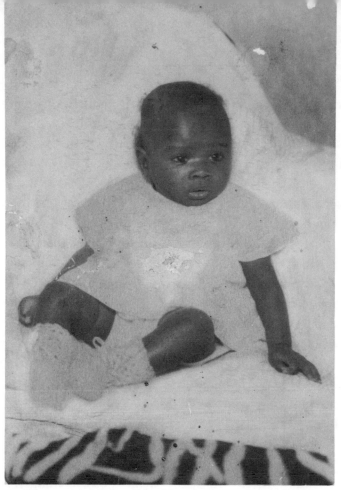

Future member of the Alvin Ailey American Dance Theater.
Author's personal collection

To this day, I have a hard time sitting still unless I'm really tired. I can't sit still for a very long time because everything hurts. But that's normal, because I've been in extraordinary motion my entire life.

When I was five years old we moved to Germantown, a racially mixed community, and a step up from our old neighborhood in West Philadelphia. The streets were tree-lined. As African-Americans began to buy homes there, white flight came into existence. Germantown was a blue-collar community. Above Germantown was Mount Airy, where the doctors and lawyers and bankers lived. Way at the top was the neighborhood of Chestnut Hill, but the stone mansions and estates were not open to Black families when I was growing up.

As part of Dad's job as a sheet-metal engineer, he installed fountain equipment in bars, soda shops, and drugstores. One day he brought home a malted milk machine and a "Pepsi-Cola Hits the Spot" stainless-steel display. I punched a button and it played the Pepsi jingle. At the time of our move, we packed Dad's work truck, made trips back and forth between the two houses until one was empty and the other was filled. I held our cat, Kit-Wit, firmly on my lap in case she had second thoughts about the move. The old house on Folsom Street was a row house with a front porch. The house no longer exists. The bumpy street was paved with steel-gray stones a foot across and a foot deep. On this ballast, our milk was delivered by a horse-drawn cart. The milk came in marvelous bottles that were sealed with a paper lip you pulled up to open. Inside, the cream floated on top like thick, sweet clouds.

The night before the move, I had a nightmare: our house was hitched to wheels and it rolled so far away from me that I could not keep up. Every time I got close enough to touch it, it rolled farther away. But I know where the night images were coming from: the horse-drawn milk cart had pulled its way from the morning delivery to my evening sleep. The constant sound of wooden wheels clacking over on cobblestones spun its way from the street into my increasingly empty bedroom.

The Philadelphia into which I was born on May 10, 1943, was the city of the great African-American migration, and my early years, following World War II, saw an increase in the Black population as many African-Americans moved from the South to the North. The civil rights movement had yet to gain its strength and the desegregation of schools was over ten years away with the Supreme Court's 1954 decision of *Brown v. The Board of Education of Topeka, Kansas*. However, the Black community in Philadelphia was becoming empowered and created social programs that addressed its particular needs. Organizations such as the Philadelphia Urban League and the

National Association for the Advancement of Colored People were prominent. The Philadelphia *Tribune* was America's oldest Black newspaper. In addition, the Black churches became crucial in addressing not only the spiritual needs of its congregants, but also their social and civic requisites.

Culturally, Black Philadelphia thrived. Heritage House, founded by the visionary Dr. Eugene Wayman Jones, was one of the most prominent cultural institutions in the Black community, sponsoring the annual Christmas cotillions, where I would dance. Musician Raymond Smith had founded both the Philadelphia Concert Orchestra and the Dra Mu Opera Company, which not only provided Black Philadelphia with extraordinary performances, but created opportunities for talented African-American performers. Essie Marie Dorsey, who almost single-handedly brought classical dance to Black Philadelphia, and nourished the talents of my first ballet teacher and mentor, Marion Cuyjet, was the opera company's first ballet director.

I had a great time growing up in Philadelphia. My parents, who loved classical music and opera, tried to expose my brother and me to all the cultural institutions of the city. Philadelphia was full of wonderment for me as a child, full of people interested in artistic expression. It was that way then and it was that way when I attended the Philadelphia Dance Academy in the early 1960s, and that way when I returned in 1988 with my own dance company, the Jamison Project.

We did most things as a family. There was not a place in Philadelphia with any kind of culture we did not explore. We walked everywhere, to the zoo, to the art museum, where we saw exhibits from Africa, China, and India. I loved to visit the Rodin, a jewel of a museum, with the sculptor's *Thinker* in the courtyard. I'd sit across from him and wonder . . . *what was on his mind?*

We went to the theater, heard opera, went to church, attended plays. We didn't have a television until 1953. Then, we'd sometimes watch the Friday night fights sponsored by Gillette. Thursday night was peach ice cream night, Dad's favorite. Our first car came in 1957—a '53 Dodge. My brother learned to drive in that car. I couldn't take driver's education in school because I was always in dance class.

When I was growing up I wanted to live on the street that inter-

With Cousin Helen and Shep at the side of our house. *Author's personal collection*

sected Duval, Burbridge Street, where Mrs. Evans, my piano teacher, lived. There were many semiaffluent people on this street, living in big, old semidetached houses. Those with "real" money had their own separate homes.

It was natural for me to want to ride a bicycle, because I couldn't keep still, and walking wasn't giving me the motion I craved. My brother, Johnny, taught me how to ride my first bicycle, a twenty-six-inch Shelby. He'd rest his hand on the back of the seat until I caught my balance. The day he let go I sailed into the biggest tree on the block. The tire was completely bent out of shape. A car could not have knocked that tree down!

I used to roller skate around Duval Street. My first skates were metal and made a wonderful sound as I picked up speed. I had to lock myself into the skate with a key. If it wasn't tight enough, it would flop off and hit me in the ankle. *Ouch!*

A few blocks from my house was a home for unwed mothers, but I didn't find that out till I was late in my teens. When I was a child, it was just a big old gray house on Burbridge Street that fired my imagination, a house of gabled roofs and high wooden fences and a wooden gate that was shut tightly and reminded me of the gate in the *King Kong* movie. Even as tall as I was, I couldn't see inside. Now I can walk past it and see right in. I always had a vivid imagination about that house because I had seen too many "jungle" movies. There was a mystery about it. I thought some rather fantastic, otherworldly animals lived behind those gates.

Mother spoiled me from the time I was born until the day she died. She would not let me in the kitchen. I learned how to cook from my grandmother. My mother came into my room every morning and made my bed. After dance class, I'd be so "whipped" that Mother would massage my legs with cold cream and alcohol. She never told me, when I started dancing at the age of six, that I'd *have* to take class every day for the rest of my life.

I grew up with the feeling that there were good people and bad people, no matter what color. I remember Mom making that very clear. When anything racist would happen I could go home to her and she would reestablish the pride in my African heritage.

When I was a child I hated going shopping with Mother because I saw that she had to be constantly on her guard against people being absolutely familiar with her or ignoring her, or, as people were in those times and still are to this day, obnoxious about people of color coming into a fine store. To this day, one of my biggest peeves is when people who do not know me call me Judith or Judi. It's disrespectful, particularly in business. I think my feeling for this comes from the days when slaves were called by their first names to further strip away their remaining dignity.

My mother would speak the "King's English." There was never a curse word coming out of her mouth. If she had to "read" someone it would be precise, to the point, curt, and then she'd press on. She could look you in the eye and you knew you were right or wrong; she could do that with anyone. She didn't have to say a word, but if she did she would let you know beautifully and quietly; there was never any ranting and raving. Meantime, I would be hanging on her, going "I want this. I want that thing," as any insistent and spoiled child would be. But it was too late. There was dust on her heels because she would not put up with any kind of attitude or condescension. Eventually, I felt so much respect for her because she stood her ground. In her movements and to a certain extent in her speech, she was saying, "I'm a human being, too." I admire that in her now but as a kid I didn't understand what was going on.

I was a bit of a pouter, wearing my heart on my sleeve, but stubborn and determined. Whenever I was photographed as a child, Mother would say, "Smile," and I'd pout. I was bashful, which is hard to believe now. One day we took a ride to get soft ice cream. Usually Dad got out of the car to buy the ice cream, but on this day Mom turned around to face me and say, "Judith, now you get out of the car and get the ice cream." I was afraid to get out of the car. I cried and cried and came up with every excuse not to leave the car. But I didn't have a choice; Mom made the choice for me. I got out of the car and got the ice cream.

Mother was very, very formal. When the telephone rang, she would answer it with "Hello, Jamisons' Residence" right smack in the middle of whatever was going on in the house. She was articulate, eloquent, and was asked to give speeches for the church and teach creative dramatics in Philadelphia's Free Library System. She learned braille in order to work with the blind and she counseled young girls because she was appalled that children were having children.

I learned recently that my mother's dream was to become a concert violinist. She got more than she bargained for when I took up the violin in junior high and hit some sour notes during practice! I saw her express herself through calligraphy, but Aunt Allie told me recently that she would draw, or paint in oils, and tear her work up. She was famous for her meticulous placards. I can see the dining-room table cleared of supper dishes, Dad in the living room with a book and the record player on, Johnny teasing me about something, and Mom unfolding a fresh piece of paper and laying it out flat. I see her taking out her calligraphy pens, careful not to waste any ink and always using the pen's flat tip until it was worn down. She'd steady her right hand by slowly guiding it with the left. I can see her making signs for my school or church, her graceful hand moving steadily over the page. Once, she created a huge musical scale for my Sunday school class, careful to fill in all the notes, so that when it was stretched across the school's stage, the song could be read by the entire class.

Our house was built with bricks, heated with coal, and filled with love. Daddy stoked the fire at night and hopefully it was stoked well enough so that in the morning the embers were still lit, and all he needed to do was add a fresh layer of coal. Sometimes it would go out, but I *still* had to get up and into the bathtub to get ready for school. The tub was ice-cold and because we were trying to save water, the tub wasn't fully filled—only enough so that I could sit down and *freeze to death.* Mom would have the portable heater on, and a thick cotton towel to wrap me in, but it was still freezing!

Mom used to get mad at Dad because he would stoke the fire and then come upstairs and track soot through the kitchen. Usually, it was the time that she had just finished cleaning the kitchen, and she'd "throw" him one of her looks: *How could it have crossed his mind to cross the floor at that moment?*

I'd walk through the gated white picket fence, heavy with wisteria, to enter the house through the kitchen. Dad made almost everything by hand in our house at 220 Duval Street: the stainless-steel kitchen cabinets with a hammered diamond pattern, the dining-room table, and the credenza. When he came home from work, Dad washed with abrasive Lava soap to get the dirt out from under his nails. But he still had to go to the basement, shovel the coal, and then scrub his hands all over again. He still had to wake up the next day and do it all over again. Sometimes I don't know how my parents did it all . . . they loved us so much.

One of my earliest memories is of the sound of my father singing me to sleep. At seventy-nine, he's just as handsome as ever, standing a half inch taller than I. He had wanted to be a concert pianist and he taught me classical piano. My first lesson, with another teacher, was a total disaster because I came in knowing more than a beginning student would have known. I could play parts of Beethoven's *Pathé-tique* and *Moonlight* sonatas with the "tiredest" fingering you ever saw in your life, and I could get through them with great expression. I thought that Artur Rubinstein didn't know what he was doing; my father did. However, I found out later that he was my father's favorite pianist. My father's musical interpretations made the strongest impression on me, filled with depth and feeling. It was the same kind of compassion he had when he would sing "Lullaby and Goodnight" in his beautiful baritone voice.

When I became fascinated with airplanes—which could go a lot quicker than I could on my roller skates or bicycle—he took me to the Philadelphia International Airport to watch the planes take off and land. I was fascinated: how could an enormous steel bird fly so gracefully? I like the sound of very large engines, the grace of wings, the phenomenon of flight.

It's very much like a dancer, in control of a technique that frees you to fly . . .

At home we had the red velvet *Metropolitan Opera Book* and the *Victor Book of the Opera*, a gift from Aunt Allie and inscribed for my parents' seventh wedding anniversary, January 3, 1945: "To enhance your enjoyment of the finest art, and to add another pearl to your already long string of happiness." There was always music in our house. Milton Cross would introduce the Saturday matinee broadcasts from the Metropolitan Opera in New York City, "This is Milton Cross coming to you from the Metropolitan Opera . . ." I'll never forget that. Even now, I can hear that man's voice so clearly, with its intonation and rhythm.

Marian Anderson made a strong impression on me as a child. She was a handsome woman with a great carriage. She was our first African-American opera diva. I listened to her early recordings, which were not the best quality, but my God, what a voice, what a beautiful face, and what dignity. I was very aware of her history and the Daughters of the American Revolution not permitting her to sing in Washington in 1939. I never saw her sing live, but I did see her on television. The generations of African-Americans before me had to go through so much hell. She withstood so much racism and prejudice and did the groundwork for Leontyne Price, Grace Bumbry, Jessye Norman, and Kathleen Battle. It's an uphill battle for an opera singer, anyway. Opera singers usually have to go to Europe to make a name for themselves and are then perceived as overnight sensations when they sing at the Met. They have time; dancers do not. Opera singers' voices mature as they age, but dancers, they've got to hit it right away.

Sometimes my parents would turn the dial from the classical station and find big-band music. They were so adorable when they'd dance together. They were cheek-to-cheek. Johnny and I were so tickled just to watch them dance in the living room. We'd sit on the upholstered deep purple sofa and laugh and laugh.

My brother and I were surrounded by so much. Our parents were loving, patient, and able to lay down the kinds of rules and regulations that let us develop our own ideas, styles, and thoughts. My brother was my childhood buddy and I believed everything he told me. Johnny sat me down and convinced me that Arabian stallions had ivory bones which set them apart from other steeds. If an elephant can have ivory tusks, I thought, then why not an entire horse made of it? I believed Johnny and, of course, my brother was *always* right.

Johnny and I loved to put together model planes and ships, aircraft carriers and destroyers. The dining room smelled of airplane glue. I was too impatient to read the instructions, so even when I completed the model, there were still little pieces left over.

My brother would let me in his room only on Saturday morning, when Mom and Dad would go out shopping. We'd put on boxing gloves and play at sparring. The padded gloves were very thick and didn't hurt at all. I'd beat up on him real bad. I'd hit him and he'd hit me and it would be just the time that Mom and Dad were pulling up. I'd go crying and singing the blues. "He hurt me," I'd whine but my parents knew my little tricks. Poor Johnny, I used to wear him out!

Our parents gave us money to go to the movies to see triple features on Saturday at the Rialto in Germantown, or the Orpheum in West Philadelphia. Johnny used to eat up all of my Good & Plentys.

At home, we'd watch the early, very skinny Mickey Mouse on little 8mm reels. Our cartoons were so old Mickey Mouse had strings for legs. We projected them on the wall. We always looked at the same three. It was a real treat because we had to go through the ordeal of digging the projector out from the bottom of the hall closet. The cartoons were great, accompanied with old, funky cartoon music.

Johnny and I used to sled down Fairmount Park's Thomas Hill, which was a lot of fun, though it used to knock the wind out of me. I'd want to come home earlier than anybody else because my fingers and my toes would get so cold. But Johnny always wanted to stay out longer and play with his friends. I'd have to "hang" with him until he said that it was time. By the time we got home I was frozen stiff. Mother would run the cold water on my fingers and I can still feel that sting.

When I was a child I knew that I had whatever "spirit" there is in this world. It's difficult to name because I believe His name has been thrown all over kingdom come. I believe that this world was set about for us to enjoy and to love and to experience, and to have it all be, to a certain extent, unpredictable. Ever since I was a child I have believed that my life has been guided.

As I look back over the landscape of my childhood I see a house cloaked under the umbrella of the church—the warmth, receptiveness, faith, tradition, and all those good things the church represents. It's not that my life was centered around the church; my life was centered around as many things as my parents could present to me. For the years when we didn't have an automobile, we took public transportation to church—the number 53 trolley to Broad and Erie, then a subway to South Street station, and finally another trolley to Sixth and Lombard. I didn't think of it as an ordeal. It was part of our weekly routine.

Mother Bethel A.M.E. is our family church. It stands on the oldest parcel of U.S. land continuously owned by Blacks. It's had four buildings since its first structure, which began as a blacksmith shop at the end of the eighteenth century. Walking down the red-carpeted

Mom and Johnny in their Sunday best. Johnny's smile
makes me think they're on their way *home* from church.
Author's personal collection

stairs to the basement is like walking into another century. It's filled
with history. Richard Allen's tomb is down there, as well as his original
pulpit. The church was a focal point of the underground railroad,
helping escaped slaves in their struggle toward freedom. There's also
an old-fashioned wooden ballot box, in which a parishioner cast his
vote with either a white marble for "yea" or a black one for "nay." Too
many "nays" and you would have blackballed that candidate.

Part of the Black church is about color, about oratory, warm
feelings, and getting the Spirit. I could be involved in the pageantry of
the church or stare across the congregation under the vaulted ceiling
to the stained-glass window. Its colors filled my eyes like a kaleido-

scope. I stared so long at the Masonic symbol I imagined the pharaoh's face in the colored glass, the sunlight pouring through, my thoughts brought back to the service by the different choirs—spirit coming through their voices like the ribbons of sunlight through the mosaicked window. Opposite the pulpit, on the balcony, was a clock made in 1805, encased in wooden wings that would gently spread on the hour.

The ushers wore white gloves, one hand held behind their back, as the choirs paraded down the aisles of the church in their multicolored robes. For communion, the church became a ceremony of white, pure white like new paper about to receive the word. As an adult I understood the symbolism of communion. As a child, however, I had a hard time equating the grape juice and the wafer I was given with the blood and body of Christ.

My father sang in the church choir as well as with the family when we'd sit in our pew singing four-part harmony. In addition to Dad's baritone, there was Mom's soprano, Johnny's bass, and my alto. It was perfect harmony that blended with the entire church's singing. I was always too loud, especially in my school's choir. You could hear me above everybody else. I was told to cool it down, but I couldn't help it. It felt so good to sing with my full decibel power.

The Reverend Charles Stewart was one of my favorite pastors, filled with the spirit of the Holy Ghost. His strength was that he preached quietly, unlike the "fire and brimstone" ministers. Reverend Stewart began his sermons softly, and raised his voice gradually in a slow crescendo until it reached its full strength. I listened attentively because I didn't want to miss *a word*.

Every Wednesday I attended Bible school meetings for young people. It was not overtly religious and did not supplement Sunday school. *Nothing* could do that. Church began at eleven o'clock and ended at one, Sunday school lasted from two to three. That's what made the day so long. We wouldn't get home until late in the afternoon. In between church and Sunday school Johnny and I would walk down the street to Levi's for lunch. We didn't want to eat a full meal at the church, because we knew that Mom would have supper for us at home. At Levi's, the first soda fountain in town, we'd eat hot dogs and sip cherry "champagne" colas. The drink was so wonderfully overcarbonated that it tickled my throat.

Johnny and I knew how to "act" in public. We weren't loud. We only spoke when we were spoken to by an elder. We had respect for older people, like Mr. Wilson, the official church historian. He was over one hundred years old when he died. When he passed away, Mom became one of the historians of Mother Bethel.

That's the way the kids I knew grew up. We had that kind of discipline. There was no such thing as being taken to a store and running up and down the aisles screaming or knocking things over. We weren't squelched as children but we had a certain decorum that derived from respect for our parents, and from our knowledge that we were representing them wherever we went.

Mom would cook Sunday's dinner, which she sometimes prepared in the morning. She cooked every single meal. There was no such thing as going to a take-out place. And she cooked "real" food, black-eyed peas, chicken or turkey, potato salad, and so forth.

During holidays we'd alternate gathering at home and at Aunt Allie and Uncle Jim's. At Thanksgiving, there was a children's table and an adult's table. I sat at the children's table, which also held the desserts and the brown-and-serve rolls. It was a miracle that any of those rolls ever got to the main table because they were my favorite.

Grandfather would pray over the holiday table. Forever! You could have bounced the biscuits off of the wall before we were allowed to eat them. They were sitting there getting cold while my grandfather was praying. He would say such wonderful prayers, both short and long. If you had a question about the Bible you could either go to your concordance or go to Granddaddy. His prayers were usually sermons. He would read "loaves and fishes" and then expand on its meaning. Meanwhile, the biscuits were getting cold, the food was getting cold, and we still needed a formal blessing before we could eat. You could have been to church and back by the time all of the blessings had been recited.

Sometimes Aunt Allie and Mom used to take me to the movies, and if it was a musical with Ginger Rogers or Ann Miller, I'd imitate what I'd seen on screen. At least that's what Aunt Allie tells me. She says I used to spin around a lot and make *her* dizzy.

My mom and Aunt Allie were both very independent, but chose different ways to express that. Aunt Allie was more progressive as far as a single woman going out on her own. She was a career woman who studied social science at the University of Chicago, but returned home at the outbreak of World War II. She married Uncle Jim, a real character, but one who's "down" and earthy. He has absolutely no pretension. He would be the one to start risqué jokes until Aunt Allie would say, "No, Jim." Then my father would tell the jokes and laugh until Mom "threw" him one of her looks.

Grandma Annie and Granddaddy Timothy lived right next door to us on Duval Street—our houses were attached. We had no phone in those early years, so I'd knock on the wall to get my grandparents. Otherwise, I'd have to go outside even if it was freezing and there was snow on the ground.

My grandparents raised three children—Mom, Allie, and my uncle Sam, who was epileptic. Later, when I was an adult, I also learned that he was mentally handicapped. He had seizures, though not in front of me, because he was usually medicated. We had a distant relationship because he was frequently hospitalized. When he spoke, he'd stop mid-sentence and stare off into the distance. He might come into a room where Johnny and I were playing and just stare, then turn around and leave. He died very mysteriously, all alone. I learned only recently that he was not Granddaddy's son.

My grandfather's skin was pure black. If you see a light-skinned Black person, it's simply because we have so many variations. For some people, it's difficult to embrace those differences. When people try to blanket African-Americans in one group, you've got a problem. Our root is African, but we acknowledge that there are so many different influences culturally in our physical makeup—we come in many hues.

Grandma, who had an hourglass figure as a young woman, was four feet eleven, and heavyset when I knew her. I remember her being soft and warm. When I was little, I would sit on her lap. She smelled baby-sweet. I'd just curl right up into her. When she was ill and in the hospital close to her death, she had lost so much weight from cancer that you could see how beautiful her face actually was once the bone structure was more obvious. She was gorgeous, even in death.

My grandparents had a second house in Franklinville, New Jersey, which Granddaddy built by himself. At the time, that part of Morris Township had horse farms and a lot of cattle. Out in the country, Johnny used to practice driving in Granddaddy's truck—turn the throttle, step down on the starter, and it was ready to go. It was an old Ford farm truck with a flatbed to haul his tomatoes and other crops. Grandmother had chickens and other fowl and she'd just go in the backyard and grab one by the neck. When Johnny first started to feed the chickens, he'd throw the grain too close to his feet and they'd peck right through his Keds!

Mom and Dad created a homemade backdrop in our yard.

Author's personal collection

CHAPTER 2

Marion Cuyjet, my first dance teacher:

I remember the day Judi's mother came to register her at my first studio on 1310 Walnut Street. Judi was tall. She looked like she was nine years old. She was six. We were rehearsing the Swan Lake *overture for our recital, and Judi and her mother stood to the side of the studio, watching and admiring the dancers. Judi's mother said to her, "You'll be doing that one day, Judith." I was so excited by her that all my husband and I talked about on Saturday nights, the only night I had dinner home, was Judi. Did you see that? Did you see her extension? Judi. Judi. Judi.*

When I was a child I had three parents, Mom, Dad, and Marion Cuyjet, my mentor. I began my first dance classes at the age of six at the Judimar School of Dance under her tutelage. I always called her Miss Marion and I still do. She created a world for young Black children that encompassed more than dance. It introduced us to life.

When I first met Marion she was as gorgeous as she is now, a most distinguished-looking woman with very fair skin and a shock of flaming red hair. She looked Caucasian and rented studio space that landlords would not rent to a person they thought was Black. Marion came from a mixed blood community in Delaware and was the first African-American to rent space in Center City, Philadelphia. She broke the color barrier and was constantly evicted once Black children were discovered on the premises; she had to move her school seven times. The landlords always found an excuse, in order to avoid civil rights infractions, but she insisted on teaching dance in Center City.

Marion had begun her dance studies at the age of fourteen with dance pioneer Essie Marie Dorsey, Miss Essie, who had studied privately with Fokine, as well as with Ruth St. Denis and Ted Shawn. There were so few opportunities for people of color in the arts that Mrs. Dorsey's accomplishments are greater for the fact that no one thought Black people could dance ballet. Not that long ago, the "ideal" ballerina was thought to have skin "the color of a freshly peeled apple." Black dancers were relegated to the nightclub and commercial arena. In order for her to succeed in concert dance, she, like Marion Cuyjet, had to rely on her fair skin in order to get a foot in the door.

Marion says that Mrs. Dorsey liked to come into class to fix our arabesques. From Miss Essie's Philadelphia studio, from the mid-1930s through the mid-1940s, came some of the most important figures in dance. In addition to Marion, John Hines, who also studied with Katherine Dunham and taught Dunham technique; Mary Hinkson, who became a leading dancer with Martha Graham's company; Joan Myers Brown, artistic director of Philadanco; and Sydney King, who teamed up with Marion Cuyjet to open the Sydney-Marion School of Dance. That collaboration only lasted for a few years and when it was disbanded both women opened their own schools, the Sydney King School of Dance, and the Judimar School of Dance in 1948, which Marion named by combining the first letters of her name with that of her daughter Judy.

On my first day at Judimar, Marion and John Hines took one look

Alice Mayes, Marion Cuyjet, and Juanita Jones. *Author's personal collection*

at me and argued about whether or not I belonged with the more advanced girls who were learning *Swan Lake*. Because of my height, John Hines wanted to put me immediately into the ballet, but Marion disagreed. She had established a progression for new students at Judimar. They knew the steps, knew each other, and had established a rapport. Marion photocopied pages from her books on French terminology so that we learned the proper ballet terms. When I look back on those early days, I realize that she was right. I had to achieve a certain amount of technical prowess before I could advance. I started at the beginning.

In Marion's classes you behaved and you acknowledged the fact that you were in a "holy" place. When you came into her studio you knew you were there to work and you came in wanting knowledge; you came in there wanting to be a sponge. You did not "mess around"; you did not drape your belongings across the barre. You entered ready to dance and you danced every class as if it were a performance. You danced to an imaginary audience. There was always a theatrical sense, even in our technique classes. Nothing was done statically. You wanted everything to involve your entire being, moving to the music.

Marion taught us that onstage we represented something larger than ourselves. I had learned that earlier in my house. Marion wore her ballet skirt—a Degas skirt with only one layer—and carried a big stick at her side, not to strike anyone but to keep the tempo. During class she'd walk slowly along the barre and gently give corrections. She would separate the knees if they were turned in by running the stick between the legs in order to make them turn out more. She wanted one leg to be slightly backward. "Dance out of that leg," Marion said. "Dance away from it." She might stop the lesson to light up a cigarette, take a good long drag, and then continue the class. She had such a carriage, such a demeanor, and such a *way* with language. I'm not sure my mom knew Marion's vocabulary. She would use colorful language for emphasis. As a child, it would put the fear of God in you.

Marion believed that dancers were not hybrid creatures dropped down from the clouds with no relation to the earth. She was a "whole human being" and wanted us, as dancers, to be as whole.

For my first recital at Judimar at the age of six, I danced to "I'm an Old Cowhand from the Rio Grande." I wore dungarees, a red-checked shirt like a tablecloth, and pink ballet slippers. Glissade (a slow, sliding step). Tendu (s-t-r-e-t-c-h-e-d). And a lot of little piqués (stepping into positions or turns on the supporting foot): piqué arabesque, piqué attitude, piqué turn upstage, piqué turn downstage, piqué this, piqué that. I remember being really frightened before the performance. To this day if I'm nervous before going onstage, I either yawn, which releases the tension, or I say absolutely nothing. Back then my mother, along with all the other mothers, was backstage trying to reassure me. But it was no use; she got no response. I went mute.

But I was fine, and Mother knew it. Once I got out onstage and started doing the steps I realized I couldn't see a thing under all the lights. I mean, *nothing*. But I knew there was an audience and I felt something special in the air.

I learned from a variety of people with exemplary posture and attitude. Marion Cuyjet moved differently from my mother, who moved differently from John Jones, who moved differently from Delores Brown Abelson, my second ballet teacher. Gradually, I came to understand how my body worked, how movement had to come organically. There was natural movement already in me.

At six I studied classical dance only, but by the time I was eight I was studying everything. I studied tap with Ann Bernardino, and acrobatics, which I didn't like very much and didn't take for very long. All through my dance career everyone thought that I had a very flexible back. In fact, my back is not flexible at all. I'm very strong through my middle and my thighs and my calves and my feet and my w-h-o-l-e body. But my back has never been high-arch flexible. Part of the magic of dance is that it can be illusory. And so, if you remember that my legs were very high and that my back went all the way down to the floor . . . it did! That's part of the magic of dance because dancers *are* performers.

When I was eight, Marion had me up on pointe, which even she would agree is a bit too early. Getting up on pointe was a weird

At age eight I was old enough to wear Dura-Toes in *Swan Lake*. *Author's personal collection*

sensation at first—I hung on for dear life. It hurts at first and my Dura-Toe Capezios felt like iron booties. But once I was up, it felt great and I could see everyone and *everything*—the story of my life!

What she called "primitive" classes then were really classes in the Katherine Dunham technique. I radiated toward this percussive sound. Drumming has always been very important to me because it is *Heartbeat*. The classes lasted for hours because nobody wanted to stop. Class would start with maybe three drummers. You'd turn around and there'd be five and then ten. The drummers, in the corner of the studio, sweated as the polyrhythms got increasingly complicated. It would be so hot, you could smell the heat. The drummers' muscles strained as they got deeper into the rhythm. The vibration from the drums would travel through the floor into our bare feet and up through our bodies. There were also intangible rhythms in the air. If we could "can it," we'd "sell it." It's impossible to simulate what happens at the moment when you're in the presence of great drummers. It was incredible. The door to the fire escape was opened. One drummer would drop out to get some air, while the other rhythms continued.

Sara Yarborough, Janet Collins, Dr. Pearl Primus, and myself. *Photograph © Jack Mitchell*

*   *   *

When I was ten anthropologist and dancer Dr. Pearl Primus came to Philadelphia to give a lecture-demonstration, where she first spoke and then danced. A lecture-demonstration gives the history of movement and brings it closer to home so that it does not become some inaccessible magical moment.

Dr. Primus, a graduate of Hunter College, studied briefly with Denishawn alumni Martha Graham, Doris Humphrey, and Charles Weidman. In 1959 President William Tubman of Liberia invited Dr. Primus to head the African performing arts center in Monrovia.

Dr. Primus's husband, Percival Borde, played the drums while she danced. She had great strength and a "fierce" jump. She was not the classical-ballet version of a dancer. She brought the Black woman's power and knowledge to the stage. She was the first performing anthropologist involved with traditional African movement. She had gone to the homeland, which impressed me as a ten-year-old, and I was blown away by her performance. Eventually, her dances would be included in the repertory of the Alvin Ailey American Dance Theater.

If you study dances from around the world you realize that the older the dance, the more natural the stance—before it became totally erect or turned out. The most extraordinary thing to realize is that the basis of your movement, historically, is coming from a very "primitive" tradition. If you look at dances that have been done for centuries in West Africa, then you'll realize that modern dance's foundation of contraction and release had a practical function. It wasn't used just for the beauty of the way it looked. Significantly, I'm told it was used because women wanted to strengthen their abdominal walls for childbirth.

I didn't have visions of sugar plum fairies dancing in my head. I'd cut out photographs from *Dance Magazine* and slap them on my wall, along with photos of movie stars like Bette Davis and Joan Crawford. My mother had seen Janet Collins dance, so I cut her photos out of the program. I knew she was the first Black ballerina at the Metropolitan Opera. "The wallpaper, the wallpaper," my parents cried at first, but I created a collage of people whom I admired—Alexandra Danilova, Frederic Franklin, Pearl Primus, Carmen de Lavallade, Tanaquil LeClercq, and prima ballerina assoluta Galina Ulanova. Ulanova had the oddest body, with a very wide rib cage like mine. It would distend in attitude, a position on one leg, with the other raised behind. I'm so glad I learned the Russian technique, years later at the Philadelphia Dance Academy, because I was trained in Cecchetti, which felt more restrictive.

Italian dancer and ballet master Enrico Cecchetti was born in 1850 and passed away in 1928. His technique emphasizes the five body positions and the seven kinds of movement. He became ballet master of the Imperial School in St. Petersburg, where his students included Pavlova, Nijinsky, Karsavina, and Kshessinska, and in 1909 the official instructor for Diaghilev's Ballets Russes. When he opened his London school nine years later his students included Massine, Lopokova, De Valois, Danilova, Dolin, and Lifar.

When I was ten Mom took me to see the Ballet Russe de Monte Carlo at the Academy of Music, and after the performance we went backstage to ask Alicia Alonso for her autograph. Onstage, she impressed me with her exquisite port de bras. Backstage, she wore a shawl around her shoulders and was in full makeup. Back then I didn't know that the stage makes you look larger than life. It puts weight on you, just as television and film do. I was stunned that she was as tiny as she was, that she wore so much makeup. From where I sat, in the top ring, it didn't look like she had much on at all. You learn to put more makeup on for a larger house and less for a smaller one. Miss Alonso wore incredible false lashes and the extreme kind of makeup Moira Shearer used in *The Red Shoes*, where the pencil lines extended past the eyes.

Marion had the good sense to know when to start sending dancers to other teachers, to supplement our learning. When I was ten I began studying with the English choreographer Antony Tudor and Madame Swoboda. Maria Swoboda was born in St. Petersburg at the turn of the century and began her studies at the Bolshoi Theatre at the age of fifteen. In the mid-1930s she and her husband opened a dance school in New York, which continued even after his death. In 1954 her school became the company school of the Ballet Russe de Monte Carlo.

Madame held her classes at the local YWCA. The minute we descended the stairway to the rehearsal studio, you could smell the chlorine from the swimming pool next door. The walls were wet as if from sweat. At this point in her life, Madame was rather austere, and wore dark glasses that hid the movements of her eyes. Her hair was pulled back into a tight chignon, and she always kept a cane by her side. She taught from a sitting position and "talked" the class.

A lot of the older teachers "talked" the classes. As a dancer, you knew your terminology so well you were expected to listen to a combination and then do it. A combination is a learned series of steps. You already have the vocabulary of ballet, or whatever technique you are studying, and a combination of those steps are put together. The class involves multiple combinations, from the pliés at the beginning to the big jumps and the grand battements at the end. You go from the barre to the center of the floor, unassisted by the ballet barre.

Antony Tudor had founded the Philadelphia Ballet Guild and taught in the suburb of Frankford. Before going to Tudor's studio I had private tutoring with a friend of Marion's to prepare for his classes. I would go to his house after church and hold on to the kitchen stove. Precisely, with maybe three exercises, he made sure that my feet were properly turned out, that I was using my full extension, that my posture was correct, my pliés precise, my tendus articulated properly. He was meticulous, and of course, I *loved* all the attention.

I adored Antony Tudor and admired his subtle and understated choreography—*Lilac Garden, Dark Elegies, Pillar of Fire.* Mr. Tudor had a cold exterior, but he was warm with a dry sense of humor. He was very erect, extremely straight-backed. His face was immobile; I don't remember him smiling at all. He reminded me of a bird perched on a high stool in front of the class. In the middle of a combination he might stop us cold, but he was always very calm. He would not demonstrate a combination but he would "talk" it. There were times when he asked me to the front of the room to demonstrate. I was ten years old in a class of adults. I approached the combination as a child, simply and directly, giving the exercise a certain naiveté. That was my advantage, that naiveté, which I cherish to this day—it makes me charge ahead. Of course, putting my head down and rushing forward has also gotten me in a *lot* of trouble.

I was so glad to have a teacher like Mr. Tudor because I had to think as well as move. We learned the Cecchetti system, which has extensive port de bras, the passages of the arms that go on and on like positions on a violin. Mr. Tudor would not move an inch unless you did something wrong, then the whole class would stop.

I remember one day he had stopped the class and I thought it was because we had all done something wrong. But he removed a piece of gum from under his chair and with his British accent and dry, dry sense of humor looked at his hand in disbelief and slowly said, "What is this?" He frowned into a look of disgust as if to say, "How dare this piece of gum enter my studio." Then we had to do the combination again from the beginning.

Years later, when we both lived in Manhattan and I was dancing with Alvin, I'd sometimes see him on the number 104 bus heading to Lincoln Center. He sat at the back of the bus and it was always a surprise to see him there. I'd say hello and he was always gracious, but I wasn't quite sure if he remembered me or not.

Delores Brown Abelson was my second ballet teacher and Marion's first prima ballerina. Delores came to Judimar at fourteen on scholarship, and began to teach the younger children. One summer Marion took her and some of the older students to class at Ballet Arts, at Carnegie Hall, two evenings a week. They shared a room at Tatum House, an East Side Y. "The students were dreadful, the teachers were wonderful," Delores said. In Vladimir Dokoudovsky's partnering class, the men had refused to dance with any of the women of color. Miss Cuyjet said, "OK, girls, we'll partner each other." Finally one man extended his hand to Delores.

Delores, Billy Wilson, Joe Nash, and I, plus a cast of thousands, danced at the annual cotillions, the debutante balls, where the cream of Black Philadelphia society made their debuts in their finery. Not me—I was in my dancing clothes! All the dance schools in Philadelphia came together to be represented, and thus elevated the prestige of the ballet. That's how I came to dance in one of Billy Wilson's *very* early works, when at seventeen he choreographed a part of *The Blue Venus*, one of the most successful of all the cotillions. The Blue Venus was a mystical creature who came once a year to bring blessings to a small Italian village. I danced the role of a convent girl.

Billy, who had been a student of Sydney King's as well as Antony Tudor's, was strikingly handsome and knowledgeable. I had a big crush on him. In the ballet Billy partnered Judy Cuyjet, while dancer and teacher Joe Nash partnered Delores Brown. Marion's business agent, Eddie Gaines, brought Joe to Philadelphia to teach her more advanced students. He stayed at Judimar from 1953 to 1956.

The cotillions were the first place I ever did four pirouettes on pointe. That was an accomplishment for me. I used to turn to the right very well. But at the cotillions I also discovered that I was an incredible left turner and able to do double tours en l'air to the left. I'll never forget Dr. Eugene Wayman Jones, the man who organized the annual cotillions. He was wonderful, and he was the first "colorful" man I had ever seen. He had the eccentric flair of Quentin Crisp. He dyed his hair a shade of reddish blond and wore it in an upsweep. His face was pure sculpture. He wore eyeliner, a little mascara, and a fine silk ascot to set it all off.

Billy, Delores, and Joe would go on to make their names in the dance world. At nineteen, Billy made his New York City debut in the City Center production of *Carmen Jones*, followed by appearances in *Bells Are Ringing* and *Jamaica*. When, like many African-Americans, he found little work in classical ballet, Billy moved overseas. He became principal soloist with the National Ballet of Holland, where he created the role of Othello in Serge Lifar's ballet *Le Maure de Venise*. People remember Billy for choreographing the Tony Award–winning musical *Bubbling Brown Sugar* and for his work on the public television show "Zoom." He created the ballets *Concerto in F* (to Gershwin's score) and *Lullaby for a Jazz Baby* for the Ailey company, and for our 1992 season he choreographed a wonderful tribute to honor Dizzy Gillespie's seventy-fifth birthday, *The Winter in Lisbon*. And yes, Billy is still fine!

Delores was the prima ballerina for the National Negro Opera Company's *Aida*. At seventeen she left Judimar and attended the School of American Ballet—the official school of the New York City Ballet—which had been established by Lincoln Kirstein in 1933. During the 1953–54 season, there were no African-Americans in the company, and only a handful in the school—Delores, Louis Johnson, Georgia Collins, and Arthur Mitchell, who joined New York City Ballet in 1956 and was promoted to soloist three years later. (Though Jerome Robbins selected Louis Johnson to appear in his 1952 New York City Ballet *Ballade*, Louis did not enter the company.) Delores joined Ballet Americana, which would change its name to the New York Negro Ballet. It was at one of Karel Shook's ballet classes that she met Alvin, and she first worked with him when Alvin auditioned a work for Balanchine's *Panamerica* evening. She joined Talley Beatty's company in the mid 1960s and danced the lead in *The Road of the Phoebe Snow* and "Rooftops" in *Come and Get the Beauty of It Hot.* She held the position of scholarship director at the Alvin Ailey American Dance Center from 1974 through 1981.

One day while she and Alvin were talking at the school, he turned to a student who was manning the reception desk and said, "Please tell my next appointment that I'm at the restaurant down the street." When Alvin walked toward the elevator, the student said, rather sharply, "I would if I knew who you were." At that, Alvin turned around, smiled, and said, "I'm Donald McKayle!"

At Judimar, the students in Joe Nash's senior class included Delores, Arthur Hall, John Jones, and Frances Jiminez. Like Delores, Frances joined Ballet Americana. Arthur had his own African dance company, which survived for more than twenty-five years. Mr. Nash had a fusion approach to his classes, teaching ballet, modern, and African movement, influenced, he said, by his teacher Syvilla Fort's Afro-modern classes. For Dave Garroway's initial "Today" program, Marion Cuyjet asked Mr. Nash to choreograph something. It was quite a spectacle, with cameras panning on dancers on the steps of the Museum of Art and on jazz musicians inside the museum. "It was historic," Mr. Nash said, "because it was the first use of Black dancers on television emanating out of Philadelphia." When Mr. Nash left Judimar, he danced with Donald McKayle in New York. Helen Tamiris, who had achieved fame for her 1937 ballet, *How Long, Brethren?,* gave Mr. Nash his first job in her production of *Show Boat* in 1946, along with Dunham dancer Talley Beatty. Choreographer Michael Kidd put Mr. Nash in his London production of *Finian's Rainbow,* and in 1951 he appeared in Tamiris's *Flahooley.*

When Mr. Nash stopped dancing, in 1958, he went to work for the National Council of Churches, later becoming the premier historian of African-American dance—an invaluable chronicler of our times.

Marion taught social graces when she would gather her students for tea dances, which were a little uncomfortable for me. But I knew that they were "part and parcel" of the Judimar routine. At Judimar, we had to stand apart from our partners, the man's hand on the woman's waist, and the woman's hand on the man's shoulder. I wore my tailored dress. At home, my brother taught me to social dance. He was up on the latest dances and so was I. We'd jump all over the place in our dungarees. It was "laid back" and comfortable.

Some of the young men Marion brought to the tea dances did not attend Judimar, but they were from "good" families. We didn't always have enough men, because it wasn't fashionable for boys to study dance back then. We were so formal that I was uncomfortable. Nine times out of ten I'd be looking over my partner's head because I was taller than almost everyone. That's not a delicious moment in one's life.

A lot of people ask me if as a child I felt awkward being so tall. The answer is no, because in dance class I always felt great. In grade school, too, I was fine. But when it came to something like social dancing my height made me uncomfortable. I didn't like the constrictions of the clothes. I was coming up in the crinoline era, when cinched belts were popular. I had a square kind of body with very long legs, so the cinch belt always made my waist look as if it were somewhere around my armpits. Plus, my figure didn't "dent in" with that stereotypically female curve, so whatever hips I had were behind me, not at my sides. But I had a great structure for jumping, and I could jump like a boy.

When I was fourteen I started to teach dance to nine-year-olds. I was a very strict teacher. I wouldn't put up with any nonsense. I treated them as adults. If they didn't respond, I didn't have the experience to know how to keep their attention. I was expecting too much from a nine-year-old because I was such a focused child. When it came to dance, nothing else mattered. It's taken me until the middle of my life to realize that everybody doesn't have the same kind of concentration. As a young person, it was a very parochial focus that worked for me.

At fifteen I made my formal debut as Myrtha, Queen of the Wilis, in *Giselle.* The Wilis were young girls who died before their wedding day and who, in the evenings, rose from the dead and lured their

As Myrtha in *Giselle*, top center. *Author's personal collection*

suitors through their lyric, but deadly, dance. I executed a lot of grands jetés. My jump was my forte, so the role was perfect for me.

I danced the lead role in *Peter Pan* and for my graduation from Judimar at seventeen I did the *Sleeping Beauty* pas de deux from the Petipa-Tchaikovsky ballet at Philadelphia's Town Hall. I had a problem at the big crescendo, the end of the third section of the pas de deux, when I had to get on pointe. I had to step piqué on the pointe shoe from a low position on the floor. I had to press up onto one leg, into attitude, hold it and balance. In rehearsal I held my balance *forever.* In performance, in my beautiful tutu, I let go of my partner, and balanced for less than a second. It was a great disappointment because I had worked on that for many hours. That was my final performance with the Judimar School of Dance. I wanted to hit the equivalent of a three-pointer, and I missed the shot! I was, and still am, a perfectionist. It was part of my agenda to hit that balance. When I didn't, I wasn't destroyed, but it was a letdown because I had worked so hard.

After eleven years at Judimar, I had learned vocabulary and steps. I had learned the beginnings of how to dance with the natural talent I had. But there was much, much more to come.

CHAPTER 3

I spent many evenings in my room listening to 45s and reading. My parents would be in the living room, reading the newspaper and doing what parents do. Johnny would be out playing cowboys and Indians. I grew up looking at Western movies and witnessed the degradation of the American Indian. In retrospect, I realize that I have also been guilty of watching Westerns without acknowledging that Native Americans have gone through the same madness as African-Americans. Isn't it extraordinary that sometimes the most offended have not seen others being offended?

I loved Walt Disney's *Fantasia* when I was a child. I remember seeing Leopold Stokowski in that film and thinking, "This is what conductors do. I like this." The film turned me on to the composers Bach, Stravinsky, and Mussorgsky, whose "Night on Bald Mountain" is animated with a marvelous beast at the peak of the mountain. The figure had such an incredible form. As a dancer I'd be looking at the contours of the body, and here I found a terribly focused and sensuous creature whose piercing eyes were aflame.

Stravinsky is funky like Bach, because his music is so percussive. He gets into the heart of the beat. It's syncopated and polyrhythmic. I love that, plus I can sing along with Bach. Try singing with Stravinsky! I always admired choreographers who've worked on "The Rite of Spring"—the score is so difficult.

In 1956, when I was thirteen, the film of *The King and I* was released. That was the first musical I remember seeing. I insisted that somebody in the house take me downtown so I could find a record store. I still have the extended-play 45s of *The King and I*, which include the soliloquy that is not in the film with Yul Brynner, *"All that bowing and kowtowing to remind you of your royalty, I find a most disgusting exhibition. I wouldn't ask a Siamese cat to demonstrate his loyalty by taking such a ridiculous position . . ."*

I know that soliloquy by heart because that's one of the things I used to recite in my room, with the door closed. I could memorize lyrics and tunes and sing along with the records, easily. My ear for music helped me with my piano and my violin. When it came to dance, the visual part of that kind of talent helped me to learn things very quickly. The way I could hear music and then sing it was the way I could see dance and then do it.

Spending so much time in my room caused Mom to worry about my reclusiveness. "You cannot stay in your room," she said. "You have to go out and see children your own age." But if I wasn't alone, I preferred the company of older people. I loved the special kind of wisdom that is acquired only with years.

Mom worried that I was in some kind of fantasy world, which in many ways I was. It enabled me to become the person I am today.

As a teenager I was so impressed with Leonard Bernstein's Young People's Concerts. I thought he was the most extraordinary conductor because of his style. His entire body *danced* so that the music moved the way he wanted it to move. I appreciated his lushness and I'd rather hear that than another conductor's abrupt coolness.

If I turned the music off, and just watched him, he was dancing. When I turned the music back on, what he was doing with his body was being translated into the music. If you look at a dancer in silence, his or her body will be the music. If you turn the music on, that body will be an extension of what you're hearing. I was very impressed that Leonard Bernstein made music accessible.

It's what Wynton Marsalis does with his jazz series for young people at Lincoln Center. I told him the reason people shy away from choreographing to jazz is because its structure is so complicated. He looked at me and said, "No, it isn't. If I sit you down for two hours or so, at least I can explain the structure, and it's not complicated. Don't think of it that way. It is multilayered and polyrhythmic, but complicated, no." Not if you have his genius, that is.

In terms of jazz musicians, if you hear a really good set it's because the musicians have jelled. They're playing as one organic unit with different branches. If you're onstage with artists you respect and you know they can go out there and "terrorize" the stage, it's a real energizer. It's a delight. You don't have to see them, you can *feel them.*

Mother was determined to give us the best education possible and she insisted on sending Johnny to the C. W. Henry School. He was the first Black child to attend that school, before graduating to Roosevelt and then Germantown High School.

When I started going to Henry School, Mom used to walk us every day, taking us in the morning and walking us home in the afternoon. Johnny held my hand. The police officer all the kids called "Charlie the cop" used to help us cross Lincoln Drive. Mother was always very "well heeled," despite the hilly Germantown streets. One day she realized that we had gotten way ahead of her and that was the last day she walked us to school. I missed the reassuring sound of her heels clicking on the Germantown pavement.

Sometimes when I came home from school for lunch Mom would

make me a sandwich and a bowl of Campbell's soup. I loved to float saltine crackers on top. We kept saltines in the house for my grandfather, who, after his stomach operation, could eat very few foods comfortably. Mom made bologna sandwiches on white bread with mayonnaise. I loved mayonnaise on white bread. I had a thing for mayonnaise. I had a thing for bread!

In social studies class when we learned about the Civil War, there was a minimal paragraph on slavery and the plight of African-Americans. The teacher read the text, looked at me, and said, "I'm sorry, that's all they have in here." At the time, I thought, "Well thanks, gee, I really appreciate it," because I knew much more had happened than was being revealed by the teacher. She feigned embarrassment that that's all there was in the book. Today, educators are constantly re-evaluating and correcting omissions of the African-American contributions to American history.

Even after school, there were still lessons to be learned. One day my friend Murray invited me to his house. I'll never forget the look on his mother's face. I must have been the first Black child who had ever crossed her threshold. I never got invited back and it wasn't because I had bad table manners. It was unspoken. It was called "the fifties."

I used to play with the guys in school not only because I was their height but because I was very strong, too. We used to have "killer" games of dodgeball. I could palm the ball as well as any boy, and when I released it, some pretty serious sparks flew!

I used to win all of the races in my gym class, that is, until a faster classmate showed up and passed me right by. I was so mad at no longer being quickest that when I ran my next race, I hit the finish line and a brick wall at the same time. I walked away from the wall and the next thing I knew I was on my knees. I broke one arm and strained the other. Hospital interns slapped plaster of paris all over that arm until it was pretty thick. It didn't occur to me to call home, because I was in a state of shock, but inside I remember feeling worried that my mother did not know where I was. When I got home and opened the door, Mom didn't look too bad, though I'm sure on the inside she was worried sick.

When my doctor took the cast off and I was on the number 53

trolley heading home, the once broken arm kept rising by itself. The release of the weight was the strangest sensation. My arm was doing its own dance.

I learned violin from scratch in the Philadelphia school system. At one point when I missed a few classes, and the teacher had taught a more advanced position, I knew what the note was supposed to sound like. Despite my limited knowledge of the instrument, I had a great ear, so I would get up to those positions any way I could. I played the violin in the All-Philadelphia Junior High School Orchestra and the All-Philadelphia String Ensemble.

In high school I studied eurythmics, a system originated by Émile Jaques-Dalcroze to teach rhythm through movement. Eurythmics looked like dance combined with mild gymnastics. There might have been a cartwheel or two, but no double back flips! It was an easy movement class, things the general high school population could do without too much training. We stood in a phalanx and I was positioned dead center at the point position of the triangle. Thirty other students stood behind me. With my classical training, it was a breeze.

When my eurythmics class was asked to perform with other classes from the Philadelphia schools at the Academy of Music, I was placed in the back row, in the corner, out of the way. I was upset because I knew I could do this the best. I felt that I was being put in the back row because I was Black. I knew I was good. There was no one on that stage doing this work better than I. I was angry, but I knew even then how to direct my anger. I've always known how to direct emotion into the dance.

In high school I was a member of the Hockey Club, the Basketball Club, the Glee Club, and Future Nurses of America, where we'd watch films of surgery that had been performed at the University of Pennsylvania. At home I practiced on my dolls—*I put the scalpel to them!* I thought it was fascinating to dissect frogs in science class— until I had a frog for a pet. Now I knew what was going on inside of him, literally. My perspective on him changed overnight when my teacher put a bounty on his green, rather bumpy little head. But I became less interested in *how* he moved, those inner intricacies, and more interested in the fact that he was a living creature and moved uniquely. He used to jump all over the place. Finally, he jumped out of his bowl and I couldn't find him for two days. Then he jumped out from behind the piano, and he was a dust ball with legs. I was "too through."

After graduating from Germantown High School, I did not want to go to college right away, though that was my parents' preference. Not going to college meant I had to go out and find a job. I would go to a job application knowing full well that I had no secretarial training whatsoever. In high school, there were two kinds of curriculums, academic and commercial. I was on an academic syllabus, which prepared students for college.

I applied for jobs and was told I'd be called if there was an opening. After that, I would go to the movies. There were never any calls, so I spent the year reading a lot and giving myself class at home. I felt that I was getting heavier because I was not taking a structured dance class every day. I went on a grapefruit and egg diet and lost a lot of weight. I spent many afternoons at the museums. It was a year of thought, contemplation, and *what comes next?* It was a time of floating. I was at a loss as to what to do. I did not know whether I was going to become a dancer. I did not think of dance as a career, but I knew that I missed taking class on a regular basis.

A year later, at the suggestion of Marion Cuyjet, I decided to attend Fisk University in Nashville, Tennessee. Marion knew Mabel Love, the head of the physical education department, and together they arranged a scholarship for me.

Mother had always been very "pulled up," knees together, white-gloved—very much a woman of her era. I didn't have to go to finishing school. I had my mother. At thirteen I was without an ounce of body fat, and my mother had me in a girdle. I had to get used to what I was going to wear as an older person, she said. Mother must have known that I was going to grow into a well-rounded girl, who was going to be a well-rounded woman. As a dancer I used to sit comfortably, a bit askew. If I had to "pull it up" and sit like a princess, then I did it, but that was part of a performance. I could do that if I had to. It used to drive my mother nuts when I wouldn't. It wasn't a natural part of me to be that pristine, because I was so used to the freedom and comfort of leotard and tights.

Mother objected to my wearing dungarees. She wanted her daughter to dress like a young lady. I did, until my late teens, when I rebelled, rather selfishly. I wanted to go shopping. I didn't want to wear any more of her handmade clothes. I was saying, "I want to do it *my* way." Mother made Johnny's clothes, too, until one day she came from the sewing machine with a pair of pants that had no back pockets. His friends teased him for days. He told her, "*Please* don't make me any more pants."

I didn't like "busy" clothes. Frills and I have never gone well together, unless they were on a tutu. Even then, I preferred simple costumes. In my later teens, I enjoyed dressing up and putting on the heels. Those heels were high when I was a teenager and they narrowed to points. I didn't know where my toes were. After my first couple of years with the Ailey company, my feet grew one full size. After having spent my life in ballet and pointe shoes, my feet just grew, because we started working in barefeet, "Mary Janes," and less restrictive footwear. For all I know, at five feet ten, I needed more foot for balance.

I dated a bit but didn't enjoy it very much. I went on dates with some very boring people. I didn't really get into guys until late because I was busy doing other things. Anyway, nobody really impressed me very much when I was a teenager. I had my crushes on people in school, but nothing ever came of those crushes.

I was also living in a situation where a lot of the time I was surrounded by people who were not Black, except at church. My focus was on music, dance, the arts, theater, and school. Nobody had much money, so going out to dinner was rare. I missed both the junior and senior proms. I thought it was a "hateful" idea in the first place. I didn't like dressing up, which carried right over into my college days. I was there for another purpose, though it wasn't clear to me at first

The adventurous one, Aunt Allie. *Author's personal collection*

what that purpose was. I was impressed by the fashionable girls, but even though I had arrived with new clothes, I didn't want to compete. Nor did I have the money.

In anticipation of my going to Fisk, Mom and Dad bought me a steamer trunk and Aunt Allie took me shopping for clothes. She took me to the large department stores downtown, Bonwit Teller and John Wanamaker. Jonathan Logan clothes were big at the time. I liked the plaids and the herringbones and the full pleated skirts. I always liked dense material, and the skirt we chose was very dense. There was a little collarless jacket that went with it. It was very Philadelphia conservative. There's one photograph taken of me outside church. I'm wearing gloves, my cloth coat with a fox collar, and my hair is in a bouffant. I'm wearing my pointed shoes and my ankle is slightly pronated in, just like my mother used to stand.

At Bonwit's, once we picked out one item, we were able to sit down while the salesperson did all the legwork to create an ensemble. We showed her the coat; next thing I knew I had a hat, gloves, and scarf to match. I had never experienced that kind of service before. I didn't know that wealthy people did that all the time. That isn't how we lived. Aunt Allie was able to expose me to a part of the world I had not known before.

It took twenty-four hours to get to Nashville by train. It was a real milk train, picking up passengers constantly. I'd get a glimpse of small towns through the window of my sleeper compartment. I had great illusions about the South and what was going on in the 1960s. The farther south I got, the more I felt I was about to descend into the lion's den. I kept looking out the window for the kinds of signs my father had experienced like "Whites Only, No Coloreds." I don't recall seeing any of that, but I kept my eyes peeled. I was ready to experience what I had seen in the media and read about. The trip, however, was uneventful.

I spent three semesters at Fisk University, in the flat landscape of Nashville, my first time away from home. I lived with a roommate in Jubilee Hall with all the other freshmen. She put Jergens lotion in her hair to condition it. At the time, I was setting my hair in rollers that were as big as Coca-Cola bottles, for a bouffant hairdo. *Very* sixties.

An old grand stairway led to the long corridors of wooden floors. I can still see the old oil painting of the Fisk Jubilee Singers, when they went to sing for the Queen of England. I became friends with a marvelous gospel singer named Stinny, who was from Troy, New York, and always dressed impeccably. When he wore dungarees they were ironed. He was very dark brown-skinned, which reminded me of my grandfather Timothy. Stinny was bald and so striking and different in the university setting that I radiated right toward him. I spent a lot of time in the chapel listening to the Fisk Jubilee Singers.

Mabel Love was the head of the dance club at Fisk. She had a very gentle voice, not quite the roar of Marion Cuyjet. We danced mostly jazz and popular routines in our socks and sneakers. I insisted on doing ballet and pointe work as well. During halftime at basketball games I danced on pointe. People thought I was totally nuts. But I was having a ball. I'd come out in my leotard and tights, walk out onto the shellacked floor, and do dances that I'd made up or dances in a group. I think I must have been all right because they kept letting me do it. They didn't know what to make of me at Fisk.

There was a small contingent of civil rights activists in the school, but for me, Fisk was a closed environment where I felt protected. Everything came to us. I saw my first foreign films here, *The Four Hundred Blows, Diabolique*, and *The Loneliness of the Long Distance Runner*. I attended a lecture by Dr. Linus Pauling. I heard John Browning play the piano, and I heard George Shirley sing.

When I called home, Mother began to notice a change in my voice. Southern accents are infectious. By the fourth or fifth telephone call, I had an easy, lazy drawl. My mother kept saying "Hello? Hello?" when she first answered, waiting for her daughter's old, familiar voice.

In the summer of 1964 I returned home to Philadelphia and began taking dance classes with Jean Williams. Jean, an incredibly brassy lady who had a gutsy, hoarse voice, was very flamboyant. She was responsible for the productions at La Salle College and she wanted me in a production of *South Pacific* she was preparing for the La Salle Music Theatre Company.

La Salle's artistic director Dan Rodden didn't think I was right for the role of Bloody Mary and found me too tall for the ingenue Liat. (I've never played an ingenue in my life!) Jean choreographed an up-tempo dance especially for me, during which I wore the funniest costume of coconut shells and feathers.

After *South Pacific,* the next show was *Music in the Air*, a Bavarian musical—blond wigs, braids, and so forth. Heidi, I wasn't. I became the prop person because I couldn't participate in the production. I learned to take advantage of every opportunity that was offered. I couldn't dance. Fine. What else do you have for me to do? Props. I learned something else about the theater. The situation was advantageous for me. It would have seemed that a door shut in my face, but instead, a door opened. I learned a great deal about the intricacies of preparing a stage for a performance.

I learned how to push an eight-foot grand piano onstage, sometimes by myself. I learned where certain glasses had to go for a scene, how to set up the tableware and make sure one of the props was breakable, how to put the dagger where it was supposed to be. One night I forgot a glass. When one of the actors reached down to make a toast, it wasn't there and he toasted the air.

The more you learn about the entire realm of theater, the better you can enrich your knowledge of dance. You learn everything from the inside out. Alvin's early company had no backstage help—there was no such person as a dresser to help you with your costume. You wore it, washed it, ironed it, hung it, folded it, and then packed it away—until the next performance. When I joined the company, Elmer "Skeets" Ball was our first wardrobe supervisor.

In the daytime I was sometimes left in charge of the box office. One afternoon I was called to help out backstage. I raced backstage and ran into Dan, who asked me what was going on. His jaw dropped when he realized I had just left forty thousand dollars' worth of tickets in the ticket booth, with the door wide open. For me, there was something so totally unrealistic about the theater. It was real, but it was unreal. The tickets were just pieces of paper. Money never entered my mind. Hah!

With all my training my focus was on the performance. When I left the box office to help out onstage, it didn't occur to me that that was just as important. Stage came first.

The tickets were there. Nobody took anything. He got over it.

*   *   *

After three semesters at Fisk, I transferred to the Philadelphia Dance Academy, where I studied with James Jamieson, Nadia Chilkovsky, and Yuri Gottschalk. Nadia was the director. The goal of the curriculum was a teaching degree. I was more geared to performance, though that wasn't perfectly clear to me. It was clear when I was at Fisk that I wanted to dance more, but it wasn't clear that I wanted to perform for the rest of my life.

James Jamieson, one of my favorite instructors, taught ballet. He was full of life, had an extraordinary smile and a lean, taut body. He had danced on Broadway in *Oklahoma!* and *Brigadoon*, in the Littlefield Opera Ballet, and was champion Scottish dancer in the United States, Canada, Australia, and England. Occasionally, he'd show up in his kilt to demonstrate. He was superb. You always had to be so light in order to execute the complicated steps. His was a dynamic personality that said "I'm here" in a most generous way. I considered him to be a brilliant, exciting teacher. In ballet and in any dance technique class, you're basically doing the same thing over and over. (It's like scales on a piano; you've got to learn your scales.) You need someone to encourage you, not just to practice but to take delight in doing so. As soon as you came into Mr. Jamieson's studio, you instantly assumed the correct position because of the example he set. He was very colorful in his language, in the way he would "read" you or compliment you when you were doing something properly. He was excited about giving corrections and telling you whether you were doing things right or wrong.

Yuri Gottschalk was another incredible teacher. He was Latvian, and very handsome, a very masculine dancer who possessed both sensuality and strength. Everybody had a crush on Yuri. He taught me how to jump with the Russian preparation. There was nothing delicate about it. Yuri took advantage of my natural elevation and heightened it. That meant that I could execute movement that was the sole territory of male dancers, then. I learned double sauts de basque and double tours. Men have tight hips and less rotation, allowing for greater spring in the jump. I thank my daddy for his hips!

Yuri took us to New York to attend Bill Griffith's class at American Ballet Theatre. I was so nervous in that class that I didn't get one

A Bill King portrait. *Photograph by Bill King*

combination right, which was odd for me, because I had always been a quick study. I remember things quickly and do them efficiently, but in this particular class I couldn't get anything. If Mr. Griffith disliked you, there were cuts that accompanied his comments. There were people who took his class and absolutely adored him. If he liked you he would compliment you and encourage you. I found him difficult to work with. Yuri was upset with me because I was his pride and joy, and his star pupil had failed miserably. I knew that he had been in a great deal of pain watching me suffer. On the bus back to Philadelphia, he said, "What were you doing? What was the problem, Judi?" I had been overwhelmed by the situation, and he knew it.

In addition to dance, I studied kinesiology, where I learned the relationship of muscles and bones to movement. I also studied dance history and Labanotation—structured dance notation—with Jeri Packman. It's very hard for me to sit still. I have to be moving, unless I'm exhausted. Labanotation was another language, and was very difficult for me to learn. It's written vertically. We detailed every movement down to the last fingertip at the blackboard. I saw a dance broken down into its parts. I wasn't interested in *how* it worked—my interest was in doing it. Anything that got in the way of moving was secondary. I think Labanotation is wonderful for archival purposes and eventually the Ailey company is going to have *Revelations* and *Blues Suite* scored. At that time, however, it stopped my movement.

In addition to my studies at the Philadelphia Dance Academy, I learned Horton technique from Joan Kerr. I was nineteen and I had never experienced Horton technique, which was not included in the Academy's general modern technique class. That class contained a little Graham, a little Wigman, etc.

Miss Kerr's tiny, street-level studio could accommodate only four rows of people, three abreast. It must have been part of her apartment. The windows were covered with curtains; the room was dim. With her wild salt-and-pepper hair, Joan appeared very Bohemian. She had huge gray-green eyes that looked like agates. She was a terribly intense woman, and when she began class the room filled with an air of excitement. You came to attention. It was the start of a very special exchange and Joan demanded our best. There was that kind of devotion. As someone who didn't quite know what I was doing at first, I was riveted by her presence and I knew I had something to learn from her—an *entire* technique.

The technique developed by Lester Horton is very specific, very linear, and very powerful. What I found in Horton was a real challenge. I might have the longest thighbone in history, Magic Johnson aside. My legs are long; I have a thirty-six-inch inseam. When I do a deep plié in parallel position, my center of gravity is so far behind me that I have to lean forward. It's a matter of balance; when I lean forward I'm fine. Getting on and off the floor smoothly and quickly is very hard for me.

The Horton technique was made on a man's body, and I think that contributes to its angularity. You take everything straight up and straight over. In the position called flatback, the torso is parallel to the floor and the arms remain at the sides of the body. The body is bent at the hips to a right angle, lifting the abdominals. It's very square, although there are some rounded corners. It's definitely a technique where you have to develop a strong middle, otherwise you'll wrench your legs, or twist your hip joints, or throw your back out. You have to be strong all over your body to do Horton. You develop that by doing the studies, which include primitive squats, lateral stretches, release swings, torso swings, and deep lunges.

I went to my first performance of the Alvin Ailey American Dance Theater with classmates from the Academy. It was the first time I saw Mr. Ailey dance. Nobody danced like Alvin. He moved like quicksilver. He moved like a cat. I went backstage and I saw one of my favorite Ailey dancers, Minnie Marshall. Minnie became my inspiration when I first saw her dance the pas de deux "Fix Me, Jesus" from *Revelations*. I was inspired. Her whole deportment was so stately, and she was so beautiful, and she could *dance*. My image of *Revelations* was, of course, the first section, "I Been 'Buked," with its staccato port de bras, but it was Minnie in "Fix Me" that made the most indelible mark. I looked at Minnie onstage and thought to myself, "I can do that." I went backstage after the performance and saw this goddess who commanded the stage folding costumes and putting them away. I thought, "Wait a minute, you're not supposed to be doing that." I never met Minnie; she left the company before I joined.

The Alvin Ailey dancers made a tremendous impression on all of us. For the next two weeks our improvisation classes at the Philadelphia Dance Academy consisted of everybody imitating the staccato port de bras from the end of "I Been 'Buked."

One night Agnes de Mille came to the Academy at eight o'clock to teach a master class. I was exhausted. It was the last thing in the world that I wanted to do, not because of Agnes de Mille, but because I was taking five classes a day. I didn't want to think about an evening class, but some of my friends convinced me to go.

Miss de Mille's class was not so much about technique, it was more about focus, and I was good at focusing. She talked a lot, and as everyone does to this day, we listened to every word that came out of her mouth. She's such a profound speaker, just as rambunctious, articulate, and full of life today as she was then. I remember Agnes being very descriptive. We didn't move that much. We were told to warm up ahead of time. Agnes gave us simple exercises where we had to walk across the floor. She wanted us to feel that our walk had a purpose and that we were walking toward or away from something. She gave us images so that a walk became more than putting one foot in front of the other. It was not the full-out dance class I had expected. I found it a bizarre class because I was so used to nonstop motion. We were doing very simple things, triplets, little jumps, and walks.

After class ended, she said, "Thank you very much." Miss de Mille said to me, "Come here." She asked me if I'd be available to come to New York to be in a new ballet she was choreographing for American Ballet Theatre. I said yes, but did not flip out. I knew Agnes de Mille and her history and I knew Ballet Theatre and their history. I had pictures of the dancers all over my bedroom wall.

Agnes de Mille and I attend the American Arts Alliance. © *Emily Medvec, 1989*

AGNES DE MILLE

I saw Judi in this class I was giving, a so-called master class, which means it's no good. Those master classes are ridiculous. It means a master gives an ordinary class. If you're very bright you'll benefit by it and do advanced work. And if you're not very bright it's absolutely useless. A real master class would be with stars talking about essential points of either performance or interpretation or structure or something, the basics, but for masters. But it means someone rather good and known teaching the class. So, I taught a class and there were just the ordinary students, some good, some bad, with this one astonishing girl.

After a while I began talking only to her and all the other students just sat down and listened. And it was all right. They saw me talking, I don't know how much they benefited, but they saw me talking to a really responsive body and a really responsive mind and we talked quite seriously. I remember Judi as an outstanding talent and I got her name and address and so forth and then, later that year, I did The Four Marys. *I phoned Judi and said, "Could you come to New York?" And knowing that I could not pay her very much she said "Yes." She'd make it.*

CHAPTER 4

American Ballet Theatre was celebrating its twenty-fifth anniversary during the 1964–65 season. It began as an outgrowth of Mikhail Mordkin's dance company, under the direction of Lucia Chase and Oliver Smith, and premiered at New York's City Center on January 11, 1940. Agnes de Mille, whose ballet *Black Ritual* (or *Obeah*) had been performed that first season, had choreographed *The Four Marys* and revised her 1944 ballet *Tally-Ho* (renamed *The Frail Quarry*) for the anniversary. Jerome Robbins had choreographed *Les Noces*, to music by Igor Stravinsky.

As Miss de Mille explained it, *The Four Marys* is the story of a young woman, her suitor, and her four servants, all named Mary: Mary Seaton, Mary Beaton, Mary Carmichael, and Mary Hamilton. The mistress's suitor falls in love with Mary Hamilton, the loveliest of the maids, and their subsequent affair produces an illegitimate child. When the child is born, she drowns it and is hanged for murder, while her lover walks away free. "At first there were four Marys, tonight there are but three . . ."

Carmen de Lavallade danced Mary Hamilton, the maid who had to die. To this day, as soon as you've got an interracial affair, somebody's *got* to die. It never works on screen. There's always a negative sense when people of different cultures get together. Judith Lerner and Paul Sutherland danced the leads. Judith spent a lot of time looking over her shoulder and Paul spent a lot of time wrapped up around Carmen. Cleo Quitman, Glory van Scott, and I were the three other Marys. In the photograph of the ballet, the first of my long association with Jack Mitchell, I look like a very naive twenty-two-year-old.

The Four Marys, which was rehearsed at the end of 1964 and had its premiere in March 1965, had about six performances in New York and a few in Chicago. During rehearsals I had the opportunity to study with Fernand Nault, Leon Danielian, who was a guest artist at the Philadelphia cotillions, and William Dollar, all fantastic ballet teachers. William Dollar taught in a wheelchair. Originally from St. Louis, he had studied dance with Michel Fokine, Mikhail Mordkin, and George Balanchine, in whose 1954 *Nutcracker* he created the role of Herr Drosselmeyer. Of his ballets, my favorite is *Le Combat* (The Duel), originally commissioned by Roland Petit for his Ballets de Paris. Lupe Serrano danced *Le Combat* with Ballet Theatre. Miss Serrano was one of my favorite dancers from that era because she exquisitely balanced femininity and strength. She was a small woman, but what a powerhouse!

I took some classes with Fernand Nault's former ballet teacher, Madame Valentina Pereyaslavec. Like Madame Swoboda, she looked like a Russian woman from central casting. She was very friendly and had the highest reputation as a teacher. She used to begin class with "Eeee, one . . . eee, two" for the counting and the phrasing of a combination. She would talk out the combination, the piano would give the introduction, and she'd begin, "Eee . . . one." She stretched out that "eee" forever. Her verbiage was very exaggerated.

OVERLEAF

The Four Marys: Judith Lerner, Paul Sutherland, Cleo Quitman, myself, Glory van Scott, Carmen de Lavallade. *Photograph © Jack Mitchell*

Carmen de Lavallade and her husband, Geoffrey Holder, took me under their wing. I was, and still am, in awe of Carmen de Lavallade. She was always on a pedestal. I had watched her on the shows John Butler choreographed for television, "Lamp Unto My Feet," "Look Up and Live," "The Bell Telephone Hour," and "Omnibus." Carmen created a strong impression in John Butler's choreography for Gian Carlo Menotti's opera *Amahl and the Night Visitors*—that was my first, vivid memory of what dance should be like. From Carmen I learned that it takes time to grow into a role, as opposed to how it is today, which is to "get it down" quickly.

Born in New Orleans and raised in Southern California, Carmen studied with Lester Horton in Los Angeles and was instrumental in bringing a friend she had known from junior high school, a good gymnast named Alvin Ailey, to dance classes. Carmen had been lead soloist with Horton's company and made her New York debut with the group on March 28, 1953. Herbert Ross brought Carmen and Alvin to New York to be in the Broadway show *House of Flowers*. She danced in *Aida* in 1955 at the Metropolitan Opera during the 1955–56 season. In 1962 she and Alvin had formed the de Lavallade–Ailey company and made a fifteen-week tour of Asia on behalf of the State Department's International Exchange Program. The multitalented Carmen had also danced in the companies of Donald McKayle, Geoffrey Holder, and John Butler, where she created a lasting imprint in *Carmina Burana*.

She and Geoffrey were performing in Paris with Josephine Baker when Carmen returned to New York to work with American Ballet Theatre. Geoffrey stayed with his dance company in Paris, whose members included Gene Hill Sagan, who choreographed for Philadanco, and Clive Thompson, one of my favorite dancing partners. Geoffrey, a native of Trinidad, appeared in *House of Flowers* as Baron Samedi, and appeared with the Metropolitan Opera Ballet in the mid-1950s. For his beautiful paintings, Geoffrey received a Guggenheim Fellowship in 1957. He's a true Renaissance man.

Carmen, in addition to guesting in *The Four Marys*, danced the role of the Wife in *The Frail Quarry*. Carmen facilitated my meeting the stars of American Ballet Theatre because when she'd have lunch

A study of Geoffrey and Alvin by Kimati Dinizulu's father. *Author's personal collection*

with her friends Johnny Kriza, Royes Fernandez, and Scott Douglas, the principal dancers, I stuck to her like glue! I think my colleagues at American Ballet Theatre realized how naive I was. I remember them fondly because they were very kind to me. Robert Christopher, a member of the corps de ballet, was so sweet; later he became a ballet teacher at the Ailey school. John Kriza and Danish ballerina Toni Lander were divine. Royes Fernandez was suave, handsome, and dark—a true *danseur noble*. One night at a twenty-fifth Anniversary party, I met the English dancer and choreographer Anton Dolin, for whom Bronislava Nijinska had created the ballet *Le Train Bleu* in 1924 when he was dancing with Diaghilev's Ballets Russes. The Markova-Dolin Ballet, the company he had formed with Alicia Markova in 1935, helped to earn him international fame. At the ABT party, he was witty, caring, and absolutely charming. Maurice Hines, whom I hadn't known back then, was at the party and recently told me that it looked as if I were holding court, sitting in a large upholstered chair. I was actually just resting my legs.

We took *The Four Marys* to the Chicago Opera House by a chartered Pan Am Clipper, with its four propellers—my first plane trip. When we came back to New York I was out of work. I didn't know what I was going to do. I knew that I was not going to leave New York and return to Philadelphia. I called my parents frequently to tell them, "I'm here. I'm fine." To me, there's really no wrong situation. I did what I had to do and it was a challenge to be the best I could be. I was in competition with only myself, or I would have liked to believe that. At that time, as in my days in Philadelphia, the kind of situations that outwardly appear to be negative were really catalysts in propelling me forward.

Martha Johnson, American Ballet Theatre's rehearsal pianist, got me a job selling tickets and dispatching boats for the log flume ride at the Texas Pavilion at the World's Fair, where her daughters Winnie and Lisa worked. We pushed buttons and helped people into little boats. Sometimes, we turned the water level up and added a little splash. It was fun. For the last day of the fair, the staff put soap in the water and it bubbled all over the place. Martha, too, was working at the fair, playing the piano for a show called *To Broadway With Love*.

I frequently went to Martha's house on the Upper West Side for dinner. Once, I walked in and jazz musician Horace Silver was playing the piano. Martha's husband, Dr. Howard Eugene Johnson, lovingly known as "Stretch," was a social activist. I met basketball star Lew Alcindor at Martha's house before he became Kareem Abdul-Jabbar. He was very shy and extreeeeemely tall. I adored Martha and she adored me. There was a warmth to her household that reminded me of home. She protected me, just like Carmen de Lavallade and Geoffrey Holder, with whom I was living on West Eighty-eighth Street, when their son Leo was just a child.

When my job at the World's Fair ended, I was without work *again*. I was twenty-two. I didn't have a job, but I didn't panic. Martha had an idea. A colleague of hers from *The Four Marys* told her that Donald

McKayle was holding auditions for a Harry Belafonte television special. Martha got in touch with me and off I went. Choreographer Donald McKayle danced in the companies of Martha Graham, Jean Erdman, Anna Sokolow, and Merce Cunningham. His 1959 ballet *Rainbow 'Round My Shoulder*, with Mary Hinkson, is still a classic, and part of the Ailey repertory.

I went to the audition but I wasn't very good. In fact, I was dreadful. I hadn't danced the entire summer and I was in very bad shape. When I arrived in the studio some of the other dancers were dressed in fishnet tights, stiletto heels, wigs, and eyelashes long enough to cause a breeze when they blinked. Some of the dancers I met were Ailey dancers on hiatus because Alvin had to stop the company when there was no work. I showed up in my leotards, pink tights, and little ballet shoes. I was standing there doing a structured class and felt totally out of context. I didn't see anybody else standing with one hand on the barre doing grand pliés and port de bras, going into their tendus and dégagés, ronds de jambe and adagios.

Paula Kelly, Donald McKayle's assistant, demonstrated the combination. She had a special way of moving that said "divine." I went "Oh my God." I couldn't get one step. Everybody around me was getting the movement and I felt as if I had two left feet. I was overwhelmed. I hadn't done "catch steps," those transitions that are not glissade or run-run, but which require a background in jazz or in tap. They demand a different change of weight than classical dance, and though I knew what position was called for, I didn't know *how* to get to it.

Donald McKayle was so sweet and gentle that he kept me until the last "Thank you very much." The choreographer calls out the names and says, "These people stay. Everyone else, thank you very much." He kept me until the fourth cut when he was down to the dancers that he needed. If I had been auditioning myself, I would have eliminated myself immediately; I was that bad.

But in dance, as in life, everything comes full circle. It's so nice to remember that Mr. McKayle was kind to me then because it gave me so much pleasure in 1991 to honor him and present a full evening of his works for the Ailey company. Donny's night consisted of *Games*,

I love this photograph of Alvin. *Photograph © Jack Mitchell*

Angelitos Negros, Rainbow 'Round My Shoulder, and *District Storyville*. It was just a jewel of an evening.

However, I left that audition in tears. On the way out I passed a friend of Mr. McKayle's on the stairs, whom I barely saw because I was so upset. I had been given every opportunity to learn a new combination of steps, but couldn't. I was very sad and walked outside to call my mother from a pay phone on the street and told her that I did not make the audition but wished to stay in New York because I felt that there was something that I had to do here. I wasn't quite sure what that was. I couldn't hide the disappointment in my voice.

Three days later, still out of work, the man I'd passed on my way out of the audition called me and asked me to join his company. His name was Alvin Ailey. Without hesitation, I said yes and danced with his company for the next fifteen years.

That was an early lesson in being open and being prepared and well studied. It's a lesson for young people I present when I'm asked to lecture. I didn't know what was going to happen next, but I had a great deal of faith in the fact that I believe that my life is guided and that I had studied. I had learned a certain amount and tried to absorb as much as I could about life and about dance, theater and the arts, because those were my interests.

A lot of young people I meet do not know what they want to do with the rest of their lives, while it's getting later and they're under pressure to make a decision. It's for them not to worry, but to be well prepared, open, and educated. Learn as much as you can about everything. It's hard to tell young people to be patient, but that's what they need to be.

CHAPTER 5

"Backstage, *House of Flowers* . . ."

That's how we used to answer the phone at Alvin's apartment when I lived there briefly after I joined the company. I didn't know what I was talking about because not only had I not seen *House of Flowers*, the Harold Arlen–Truman Capote musical, but I hadn't seen *any* Broadway musical.

It was a long, dark, book-filled apartment off Central Park West. I sat on the couch that doubled as my bed and watched as Alvin tried to get bookings, and tried to figure out how much he was going to pay people, stuffing each envelope with a couple of dollars. In those days, Alvin did everything. I'd sit quietly and watch. That was my first experience with my boss. I watched him work so hard and worry so much about how he was going to hold it together back then.

When I think of Alvin Ailey I think of rivers, the clarity and strength of water, carrying with it the memory of its source as it pushes forward. I think of winding rivers, of water brimming with life. Alvin

Ailey, Jr., was born in Rogers, Texas, into hard times, on January 5, 1931. His mother picked cotton with him tied to her waist. When he was ill and no doctor would come to the house, she carried him for miles to the doctor who would care for Black people. They left Texas and moved to Southern California when his mother got a job with the aerospace industry. He started dancing when he was about eighteen years old, in those years between high school and college. A natural athlete, he played all kinds of sports as well as gymnastics. A superb linguist, he went to San Francisco to study languages, before returning home to Los Angeles. He began his studies with Lester Horton in 1949 and worked with him until Lester's death in 1953. He became artistic director and choreographer of the Lester Horton Dancers in 1954, making his first choreography for that company. After appearing in the film *Carmen Jones*, Herbert Ross brought Alvin and Carmen de Lavallade to New York, also in 1954, to star in the Broadway show *House of Flowers*.

Alvin used to talk about Lester Horton's sense of theater, his sense of structure, and how he wanted a multicultural company. In his brief life, Mr. Horton created over forty works. "Lester trained us as performers," Carmen de Lavallade told me, "he trained you as somebody backstage, so that you knew something about the space, the lighting, the stage area. You knew your relationship to your audience, you knew your relationship to what you were doing backstage. Your decorum backstage was part of your training."

Lester Horton was born in Indianapolis and studied ballet with Adolph Bolm. He became enamored of midwestern America and Native American Indians and was especially influenced by a performance by the Denishawn dancers in 1922. In 1928 he moved to California and began his work at the Little Theatre of the Verdugos; in 1948 he opened his Dance Theatre in Los Angeles. One of his most famous ballets was *Totem Incantation*. He studied with Japanese dancer and dance director Michio Ito for two years, immersing himself in Eastern culture. "That influence," James Truitte said, "is identifiable in Salome's entrance in the choreo-drama that Lester choreographed called *Face of Violence*, his *Salome*." Carmen de Lavallade made her debut as Salome in 1950.

In addition to Carmen and Alvin, Lester's notable pupils included Janet Collins, Joyce Trisler, and James Truitte. Mr. Truitte began his dance studies with Archie Savage, a principal dancer with Katherine Dunham's company. After appearing in the road company of *Carmen Jones*, he told Janet Collins that he really wanted to study more. She said, "It's too late for classical ballet. Why don't you go to Lester Horton?" Jimmy Truitte refers to Bella Lewitzky, his first Horton teacher, as "the master of it all. Technically, a brilliant dancer." Mr. Horton always said, "If Bella can't do it, it cannot be done." Bella Lewitzky had been his principal dancer until she and Horton parted company in 1950.

When the dancers were very tired, Mr. Horton would break the tension by exaggerating the theatrical gestures of dance pioneer Ruth St. Denis, who, along with her husband, Ted Shawn, translated Eastern philosophy, mysticism, and religion into serious dance. But Mr. Horton would say, "Now let me give you my rendition of Miss Ruth hanging out the wash . . ."

Alvin created his first choreography at the Lester Horton Dance Theatre, *According to St. Francis* and *Mourning Morning*, which he based on Tennessee Williams's *A Streetcar Named Desire*. "He worked hard. He made an imprint," Jimmy continues. "Alvin had a brilliant mind. He was always thinking, always choreographing, reading, and doing explorations. And he had outlines of so many ballets he wanted to do but never got around to do."

I see that now in Alvin's early journals from the early 1950s. He began a notebook of dance technique with a quote from Martha Graham: "Technique is the craft which underlies the creativity." The notebooks show the range, diversity, and depth of Alvin's art—his interest not only in dance, but in music, costume, décor, and theater. The notebooks are filled with poems and ideas on music—"analyze Horton use of Oriental and ethnic instruments—showwise and soundwise"—and sketches for costumes. You can see what a rich time it was in Alvin's life, when it seemed he was beginning to transfer his inner feelings to the stage.

"Each artist," he wrote here, in his early twenties, "must create his own unity according to his own experience and belief . . . Let own creativity be guide, avoid too much influence from any one individual."

Ideas poured out of Alvin and luckily he kept a written record. "Poems of Lorca," he wrote down years before he choreographed *Feast of Ashes*, based on Lorca's *The House of Bernarda Alba*. "Tennessee Williams—short stories as choreo motivators"—perhaps additional inspiration for *Mourning Morning*. "Death," he wrote, "is the folded hand."

One of the most interesting pages he titled *"Moses and the River Jordan*," and he wrote: "Scenes at the river—the focal point of beginning and ending—to be represented by a cloth design manipulated by two figures with poles." It seems that Alvin had been planning *Revelations* for many years, the "baptismal at the river."

"I have the feeling," Alvin wrote in a 1970 journal, "that I am going to be Lester Horton's most famous offspring. I would be very proud of that."

In New York Alvin studied contemporary dance with Martha Graham, Hanya Holm, and Charles Weidman; ballet with Karel Shook, and composition with Doris Humphrey. He studied acting with Stella Adler and Milton Katselas, and he appeared as leading dancer in Harry Belafonte's *Sing, Man, Sing*, in the Phoenix Theatre's production of *The Carefree Tree*, and in the Lena Horne Broadway musical *Jamaica*, choreographed by Jack Cole, one of Alvin's favorites. Everybody adored Jack Cole. As an actor, Alvin appeared Off Broadway in *Call Me by My Rightful Name* (with Robert Duvall and Joan Hackett) and *Two by Saroyan*. Late in 1962 Alvin made his Broadway acting debut as Claudia McNeil's son Alvin in *Tiger, Tiger, Burning Bright*.

The first performance of the Ailey company was at the 92nd Street YM-YWHA, where Alvin shared the program with Ernest Parham. Mr. Parham was one of my teachers in Philadelphia. For the first concert on March 30, 1958, Alvin's dancers included Minnie Marshall, Don Martin, Jimmy Truitte, Carmen de Lavallade, and Nat

Horne. Alvin used many dancers from the cast of *Jamaica*. Each dancer got five dollars for the performance.

Revelations premiered January 31, 1960, at the Y. The success of that concert was unprecedented; they received a standing ovation. Dr. Kolodney, the director of the Y, announced that the program would be repeated the following Sunday. The ballet would change, metamorphose, over the years as the company evolved and grew. Over thirty years later, it's still a classic. After the first performance of *Revelations*, John Martin, writing in the New York *Times*, called the ballet "an infinitely moving hymn to God, and perhaps more, man." Walter Terry wrote that *Revelations* was "marvelously imaginative and deeply stirring."

Most of the dancers held other jobs during the day; there were few calls for African-American dancers in those days. Everyone rehearsed at night, sometimes starting at midnight. Costume fittings at Normand Maxon's house at two o'clock in the morning, then back up the next morning to their day job. Minnie Marshall taught physical education; Thelma Hill held three jobs. Many of the dancers were in Broadway shows, performing until 11 P.M.

There were sections in the original *Revelations* that are not done now, including "Weeping Mary," a solo for singer Nancy Redi, and a trio called " 'Round About the Mountain," which was replaced by "Didn't My Lord Deliver Daniel." The last section, "Rocka My Soul in the Bosom of Abraham," was originally called "Elijah Rock."

Mickey Bord, the archivist at the Alvin Ailey American Dance Center, met Alvin when he came to New York in the late 1950s when he started teaching at the Broadway Congregational Church at Fifty-sixth Street. It no longer exists. He then taught at Michael's Studio, on Eighth Avenue, for three dollars a class, before teaching at the Clark Center on Fifty-first Street and Eighth Avenue.

Mickey remembers going to the thrift shops on the Upper East Side to buy the old Irish lace curtains that Alvin used for *Blues Suite*. At an Army & Navy Supply Store on Fourteenth Street, she bought the black-and-white-striped pants for the same work. She would dye the costumes in her kitchen sink—blue, red, hot pink, and lavender.

For the men's mesh shirts in *Revelations* they'd go down to the South Street Seaport to get fishing nets. They had to untie the knots, retie them, then dye them brown for " 'Buked" and white for "Wading in the Water." Mickey would wash, sew, and dye costumes; she even steamed the Beni Montresor costume I wore for *Icarus*. The umbrella for *Revelations* came from Uncle Sam's umbrella shop on Fourteenth, the baptismal water is china silk. The stools for *Revelations* were purchased at a piano stool factory in Coney Island.

This was the beginning of the station wagon days, fitting all the dancers and costumes and stools into a car and touring to play colleges, small towns, and Jacob's Pillow. The dancers included Minnie Marshall, Barbara Austin, Merle Derby and her sister Joan, Jimmy Truitte, and Nat Horne. Some of them stayed at the "Here You Are Inn" in the Berkshires, which no longer exists.

Alvin had what he referred to as "blood memories," deep remembrances of his childhood in Texas, spirituals and gospel music, ragtime, folk songs and work songs. When Alvin first began, the company did only Alvin's work; later, he asked other choreographers to contribute their ballets to the repertory. The company became a repository for modern dance and for the African-American experience.

When I first walked into the studio to work with the Alvin Ailey American Dance Theater, I said, "Hello, Mr. Ailey." Then Alvin gave me the right, the privilege, to call him by his first name. Alvin made everybody feel comfortable; he certainly made me feel at ease, just by his presence. He was a big man with a beautiful face and incredibly expressive eyes. I loved his hair. His bigger-than-life presence made a statement in itself.

He didn't have to say anything. At times, our dialogue contained no words. Sometimes he looked very gruff, his brow would be very concentrated and intense. And then he'd laugh. It would start low and end up very, very high and go back down again. It was a wonderful, contagious laugh. The laughter would spread. Sometimes I think his laughter was out of pain. There were so many times we'd be stuck in situations with bad floors and bad transportation, and costumes not working and money not coming in—the whole bit. I can remember him laugh under duress, while he tossed papers up in the air and said, "Let's go on. Next."

I saw Alvin so frustrated because he knew how things should be—but weren't—for the "gods and goddesses," as he called us all the time. The stages should be perfect, the theaters exquisite. We should have full orchestras. There was frustration in not being able to have these or having to watch his dancers perform on bad floors, even rugs. But Alvin knew how to use his anger . . . and ours.

Alvin could be troubled and full of angst like everybody else. In the years we worked together, I don't remember rage manifesting itself in anything negative. He told us, "However you're feeling, one way or the other, please use it advantageously when you get out onstage." Whatever your condition is, use it positively, because that's part of your humanity.

"I can tell if you woke up on the wrong side of the bed," he'd say. If he could, it meant that we, as dancers, hadn't turned around that negative energy into a positive release.

My relationship with Alvin was based on total awe of his accomplishments as a director, choreographer, and human being. Alvin could be as loving as he could be insulting. He could come backstage after you thought that you had given the performance of your life and cut you down with three sharp words: "What was that?" It was devastating. And then I'd be offended. For about a minute. Or, as my agent Paul Szilard reminds me, for more like a month.

There were no gray areas in my reactions to Alvin. I was either absolutely ecstatic or wanted to tell him to leave me alone and get out of my life, though of course I'd never say that to him. I'd internalize those emotions. I tried to use those feelings onstage and not against any person. But being human, I'm sure I failed in that area many times.

The first time I walked into a rehearsal at Clark Center, Bill Louther was teaching Alvin's *Hermit Songs*, with its Samuel Barber score, to Robert Powell, a beautiful dancer. He was a truly gentle soul with a child's vulnerability. I saw Bill marking the movement and my eyes went to him immediately. I said, "Oh my God, who's this?" He looked exquisite. He could move a finger and the earth would shake. You see that and you know the dancer is in that person. I stood there transfixed.

Dudley Williams, a graduate of Juilliard and a member of Martha Graham's company, was one of the first people I remember from that early rehearsal. I remember his balance, his litheness, and his billowy port de bras, as if he had helium under his arms. Alvin celebrated his unique artistry in the solo "A Song for You" from his ballet *Love Songs*.

When I joined the company the dancers were "marking" in rehearsals and I thought they were doing it full out. When you "mark" movement you underdo it to save your energy for the performance; you indicate it. You do a single turn when it's really supposed to be three. You do a single tour when it's supposed to be a double tour en l'air, or you don't go up in the air but indicate a jump by using your arms, indicate a turn by using your fingers or spinning your wrists. You might do all the arms, the port de bras, and walk through the choreography, rhythmically.

Today, if the dancers in the company are tired I might tell them to mark the movement: "Make sure you do your arms and make sure you're where you're supposed to be when you're supposed to be there." The Ailey company tours more than any other company in the world, so I let the dancers mark, even though they usually rehearse full out.

When Jerome Robbins came to visit us at a performance in Princeton in the spring of 1993, he came to the rehearsal to see how the dancers worked. When I told the dancers that he was coming, they wouldn't mark anything. The dancers gave a rehearsal that was a performance. Once again, I marveled at the strength of the Ailey dancers.

There are many branches on the family tree of African-American dance. Katherine Dunham has always been on a pedestal and I thank her very much for doing what she did so I could do what I'm doing; so we all could do what we're doing. She influenced so many Afro-American choreographers, empowered so many of us. In 1940 she and her dancers took New York by storm with her revue *Tropics and Le Jazz Hot* at the Windsor Theatre. Miss Dunham and her dancers appeared in *Cabin in the Sky*, the Broadway show staged by George Balanchine, shortly after. I remember seeing Miss Dunham in the Lena Horne movie musical *Stormy Weather*, with her dancers Janet Collins, Lenwood Morris, Syvilla Fort, Lavinia Williams, Tommy Gomez, Lucille Ellis, and the one and only Talley Beatty.

When I first joined the Ailey, the dancers were rehearsing Talley Beatty's movement in his ballet *Congo Tango Palace*. Talley would say "Let's do it" in his own inimitable way and the rehearsal would begin. When I first got onstage to do *Congo Tango Palace*, my first entrance was backward. Two girls came from stage left and two came from stage right; I came from stage left. The movement is very taut; the music is Miles Davis's *Sketches of Spain*. You do three steps backward, then fouetté and come three steps into the girls that are coming into you. You pirouette, turn, stop, then reverse it, pull into a contraction.

By the time I turned around for the third step, there was a whirlwind happening around me. I saw the intensity in the women's eyes, not to mention that of the men who were downstage. When dancers are truly focused there is an intensity in their whole demeanor. You can see it in their eyes. It's riveting. It has an edge. I turned around and I thought I was in trouble, but I wasn't. The intensity of the dancers picked me up. I didn't know that I was going to need that kind of energy. The women were going 250 miles an hour and during rehearsal I was giving 100 percent of my effort. That night onstage I learned that I needed more than 100 percent.

I made my debut in the Ailey company in *Congo Tango Palace*, at Chicago's Harper Theatre Dance Festival, during the 1965–66 season. The ballet originally premiered at New York's 92nd Street Y with dancers who included Georgia Collins, Herman Howell, and Tommy Johnson. We had about two weeks of rehearsal, before the requisite six weeks of one-night stands. One day in rehearsal Talley threw an ashtray across the studio; something or someone had made him angry.

Talley was as volatile as he was creative. He scared me to death, as he did most everybody. He's a perfectionist. Talley is very beautiful and he talks to you right on the edge. He sounds as if he can cross that line and really be angry, and then I've heard Talley when he's just the opposite. He was a star in Europe before there was an Alvin Ailey. He was a premier dancer with his own company. Talley Beatty's *The Black Belt* was inspired by the Watts riots. The last section is done with flashing lights and when we ran across the stage with televisions and sofas, throwing things all over the stage, the audiences were stunned. Talley's pieces are sometimes about street life and how rough and how real it is.

He created some of the most extraordinary dances, which were exhausting to do—*The Road of the Phoebe Snow, The Stack-Up*, and *Come and Get the Beauty of It Hot*, of which *Congo Tango Palace* is a segment. Many of Talley's ballets are wonderful urban statements, full of very recognizable street movement, plus ballet, Dunham, and Graham. You've got to be up, down, sideways, and backward. If you haven't studied at least four techniques you will never get through one of his ballets. They are probably some of the hardest pieces I have ever danced. It's just amazing what you have to call on your body to do. You go from a cabriole into contraction into a double pirouette into a penché arabesque that you finish with another contraction. At that point, your face is on your ankle. Talley's movement is fast and both expansive and tight.

When I joined the company Talley put me into the "drag" trio in his ballet *Toccata*, changing a normally male trio into two males and one female . . . me. Once again my jump came into play because there were double tours en l'air to the left, one of my fortes. I was very happy to be in that ballet because of my jump. I could keep up with my partners, Morton Winston, Dudley Williams, and later George Faison. Talley is one of the forerunners of the contemporary jazz dance idiom. He's a wonderful choreographer, but don't get on his bad side.

When as artistic director of the Alvin Ailey American Dance Theater I decided to honor Talley a few years ago, we showed a film of him in which he danced "Mourner's Bench," an excerpt from his ballet *Southern Landscape*, filmed at Jacob's Pillow. I was stunned at how sinuous, sensuous, and passionate a dancer he was, because by the time I met him, he was older and would demonstrate some of his moves, but not that much. But that film! I wish I could have seen him dance then.

When we returned to New York I danced in two of Alvin's signature works, in *Blues Suite*'s "House of the Rising Sun" and in *Revelations*' "Fix Me, Jesus," "The Day Is Past and Gone," and "Rocka My Soul." I loved doing *Blues Suite* because I played the wallflower, the girl that none of the guys wanted. I put everything into that role and then, a few years later, Alvin took me out. I became Mother Earth, Goddess, Queen. He never put me back in the hilarious comedy parts again, even though I continued to do that role straight through 1969. I think Alvin had in mind for me a certain look, a certain bearing, a certain regalness that was the opposite of the comic wallflower.

It's a wonder I still have tendons on the outside of my ankles because I used to walk and turn my ankles constantly. It was my interpretation of the role. I knew how far I should go with a character as far as ad libs were concerned, and as far as staying within the framework that Alvin's genius had created in the first place. I used to walk in and trip and turn my ankles and have a ball distorting all the movement, but in context with the dance. It's what I tell the dancers all the time now. You've got to make the funniness *within* the shape of the movement. It's very important because Alvin knew what he was doing when he choreographed it, so you don't want to add anything. It's such a fine line; it defines what an artist is, and if somebody goes over the edge, it looks ridiculous and makes no historical sense. There are choices of integrity that you instinctively have in you or that somebody has taught you, or that you do not have at all.

I missed the comedic role. I missed the physicality of the role. *Blues Suite* is funny and sad at the same time in its depiction of people trying to get out of a situation they're trapped in. They're still celebratory, they still go on with their lives, but there is an underlying sadness. It's a thread that runs through many of Alvin's ballets.

Hope Clarke, recently nominated for a Tony Award for her chore-

ography for *Jelly's Last Jam*, wasn't dancing with the company by the time I joined, but when Alvin called, she came to rehearsals to help. She's such a marvelously out-there, in-your-face personality— positively. Alvin used to tell the story of doing "Backwater Blues" with Hope. Jimmy Truitte was making a crossover backstage for the next section when he heard Alvin going, "Ouch, ooh . . ." because there's a part in the dance where Hope hits Alvin with her shawl. The joke was that Hope used to beat Alvin up for whatever he'd done to her in rehearsal, giving it right back to him in "Backwater Blues"—all in good fun.

At the time I joined the company Alvin had Anna Sokolow's ballet *Rooms* in the repertory. *Rooms* had its premiere at the 92nd Street Y on February 24, 1955, with a symphonic jazz score by Kenyon Hopkins. Donald McKayle was one of the original dancers in the ballet, more than ten years before Alvin brought it into the rep. It is danced by four men and four women. *Rooms* was very different for me. I danced in the section called "The Letter," which involved my sitting in a chair and miming the reading of letters from a long-lost lover. I held my hands up in front of my face as if I were holding actual letters between two people whose dreams had failed. James Truitte moved like a boxer who tried to punch his way out of his psychological confinement.

It was like nothing I'd ever danced before. I was reminded of *Rooms* recently, after our 1992 season, when a friend came backstage and told me how brave I was for putting Jawole Willa Jo Zollar's *Shelter* in the repertory. That's when I realized that he didn't understand the history of the company. Alvin wanted to show the range of the company's facility, of their expertise in being able to dance many different techniques and styles. That's how John Butler's *Carmina Burana*, how Bill T. Jones's *How to Walk an Elephant*, how Elisa Monte's *Pigs and Fishes* and *Treading*, entered the repertory. Now

The comic wallflower in *Blues Suite*. *Author's personal collection*

With Dudley Williams in *Blues Suite*, 1967. *Author's personal collection*

Garth Fagan will be working with the company for our thirty-fifth anniversary.

Dance at the Gym by Donald Byrd is a recent addition to the repertory. We call it one of our hottest ballets, filled with street movement, classical ballet, and speed. The Alvin Ailey American Dance Theater is still adding works to its repertory that reflect the modern dance history of the company and the African-American experience. Alvin had done several works that are as reflective as *Shelter*—including those about South Africa, *Masekela Langage* and *Survivors*, with its depiction of Nelson and Winnie Mandela. The death of Dr. Martin Luther King, Jr., inspired his ballet *Three Black Kings*.

Change is important because it helps you grow. That's why change is significant—it makes you more open. If you expect everything to happen in a certain way, it's restrictive. The Ailey company is unique in being a repertory company, adding new works and working with different choreographers. The challenge is the diversity of the repertory. The advantage of the tradition of the Ailey company is that it speaks to the past, the present, and the future. That's been the nature of the company since its inception. The company's vision has always been to follow different paths, always adding new repertory, but always paying homage to *Revelations*, *Blues Suite*, *Cry*, *Masekela Langage*, and our other classic works.

Alvin put Ted Shawn's *Kinetic Molpai* in the repertory. It was historical—and hysterical. The hysteria came in *Kinetic Molpai* because there is so much jumping in the piece. John Parks, Kelvin Rotardier, Clive Thompson, and the rest of the men in the company were "killing" themselves dancing it. We had no floor to travel with, and still don't, so the men were dancing up and down on every texture of floor imaginable, including cement. But the men were beautiful. There's nothing like a dance with all men onstage! Historically, it was an important ballet to do. There's a living history to be celebrated.

We did six weeks of one-night stands on our bus tours. Alvin would teach us a half-dozen dances in two weeks and we'd perform at the tiny Clark Center and, beginning in 1971, at City Center. Whenever we're on tour now and we get into spaces that are extremely small, either Dudley Williams or I will say, "My God, it's larger than Clark Center ever was." We were always called upon, when we were on our "last legs," to participate in the filming of the ballets, as well. After we had given our last bit of energy to the performances, our exasperated reaction to Alvin would be "Are you *kidding*?" Today, these films, recorded by the Library for the Performing Arts at Lincoln Center, are invaluable tools. We still film for the library for archival purposes.

At the beginning of the Ailey company there was no time to have class consistently on the road because of tight scheduling, and we would arrive at the theater too close to performance. You'd get off the bus, throw your face on, and go onstage. There was no time for the routine of class until much later.

It was also hard to keep a normal home base in New York. I found an apartment in Greenwich Village with a roommate, through a friend at the World's Fair. Living on Thompson and Bleecker streets, I had the quintessential first New York roommate. She took my money, didn't pay the rent, but got her hair done. When I came home from touring, there were strangers in the studio apartment. I would go on the road and wire the rent money home. When I returned the rent wasn't paid, but her hair looked *fabulous!*

From there I jumped to George Faison's apartment. I also stayed in the Bronx *for a minute* with Morton Winston when I didn't have a place. Folks put me up a lot, or put up with me a lot!

By the mid-1960s the company had become more popular overseas than it was in America. Before our seasons at the Billy Rose Theatre, the ANTA, and City Center, Alvin Ailey had conquered the world. The British drama critic Clive Barnes had helped start the influential magazine *Dance and Dancers* in 1950, and was executive director of *Plays and Players*. He commented recently that before he came to New York in 1965 as dance critic for the New York *Times*, he had "seen more performances of the Ailey company, more performances of the Taylor company, and more performances of the Cunningham company than anyone could have possibly seen in New York."

Whenever we went to Europe in the sixties, people just stared at us in the street. Sometimes I chalked it up to ignorance because I assumed that Africans must have been there. They'd stare and we'd stare back; it was a kind of game. If they'd touch me, I'd touch them back, but graciously, with a smile on my face.

In 1966 I made my first trip to Africa with the company when, at the last minute, we were invited to participate in the First World Festival of Negro Arts in Dakar. We were stranded in Italy. James Truitte, company manager at the time, carefully doled out our wages. Our tour had ended and we waited for word from the State Depart-

In London with Alvin and Kelvin Rotardier. *Author's personal collection*

In Senegal for the First World Festival of Negro Arts, 1966. Back row: Morton Winston, James Truitte, Elmer "Skeets" Ball, Robert Powell, Alvin Ailey, and Kelvin Rotardier. Front row: Miguel Godreau, Loretta Abbott, Takako Asakawa, unidentified man, Consuelo Atlas, and myself. *Author's personal collection*

ment that it was a go. Before we left for Africa, the impresario signed us up for the Piccolo Teatro in Milan. The house was packed for a week and we received enough money to take us to Senegal.

In Dakar, twenty thousand people cheered us after our performance. We danced in a baseball stadium. We had expected a typical stage. However, it was seventy-five feet across, thirty feet longer than the average stage, with no opportunities to exit. You could not get off that stage. You could not go into the wings, bend over, and breathe. You had to stay animated onstage, alive and focused. In those early days with the company we were ten people dancing seven ballets in one night. You never got off that stage, except to change costumes.

In 1966, in Barcelona, the company ran out of money and our tour fell apart. We could no longer stay in our hotel because we could not pay the bill. We were stuck. But we knew that Alvin would take care of us. Stranded with our suitcases, we sat on wooden benches on the colorful main boulevard, Las Ramblas, the street where they sold everything—pottery, flowers, food, jewelry, and monkeys. We stayed there four hours, patiently waiting and hoping that we'd be back in a hotel before the sun went down, and we were.

Not all of us stayed on, especially those with other jobs. Dudley Williams, Takako Asakawa, and Robert Powell returned to Martha Graham's company, Clive Thompson returned to New York to be with his wife, Liz, and their newborn son, Christopher.

Alvin had an association with Rebekah Harkness and we shared billing in Barcelona and Paris for a few weeks. Alvin had begun his work for Mrs. Harkness when he choreographed *Feast of Ashes*, his ballet based on Federico García Lorca's *The House of Bernarda Alba*, for the Joffrey Ballet, under her aegis. With music by Carlos Surinach, *Feast of Ashes* is the story of two Spanish families and the impending wedding that threatens to tear them apart. The ballet had its premiere in 1962, and was one of the works presented on the Joffrey's opening night at the Kirov Theatre, Leningrad (now St. Petersburg), on October 15, 1963. In 1964 Mrs. Harkness formed her own company, with many Joffrey dancers who had been under contract. The Harkness Ballet premiered in Cannes, and Alvin was soon associated with it.

Two years later Mrs. Harkness still helped to support the Alvin Ailey American Dance Theater. We didn't disband; we were on hiatus. The company had been performing since 1958 and this break was seen as an interruption, not an ending. There was always the mentality of continuity. We all trusted Alvin. I was at the age where I thought everything was constant. Fortunately, I've retained that at the ripe old age of fifty. Back then we were literally flying by the seat of our pants and I always had great faith in Alvin. I thought of a saying that we used quite often in my household, "God hasn't brought us this far to leave."

While we were in Barcelona, Alvin took us to some of the most interesting restaurants and flamenco "dives." These out of the way places, in the back alleys and side streets, were where we met some of the most colorful people. We'd have paella and drink wonderful Spanish wine and listen to the local singers and watch the flamenco dancers who came down from the hills into these "holes in the wall," with barely a stage, a couple of chairs, and tables. Alvin was outgoing and easily made friends. It was a wonderful education in the soulfulness of others when I realized that those people who came from rural areas were closer to the truth of spirit than most. Blues, spirituals, and gospel come from rural roots. They're coming from the same central place where honesty in movement originates. There was a savvy to the people from the countryside, and when they came to the city, they didn't lose that. They were without all the distractions that are common in the city. They had to call upon themselves, the way I had to when I was growing up, before we had the distractions of television and our fast-forward society. People read, talked, exchanged stories, used their imaginations, and were creative.

The Harkness Ballet was fortunate to have George Skibine as its artistic director, Donald Saddler as assistant artistic director, and Jeannot Baptiste Cerrone as company manager. Son of Diaghilev dancer Boris Skibine, Russian born George Skibine had been a member of Colonel de Basil's Ballet Russe, Ballet Theatre, the Markova-Dolin group, and the Grand Ballet du Marquis de Cuevas. He became *premier danseur étoile* of the Paris Opera Ballet, and his wife, ballerina Marjorie Tallchief, whom he married in 1947, became the first American ballerina to hold the position of *première danseuse etoile* at the Opera. He resigned from the Paris Opera as ballet master a few years before joining the newly formed Harkness Ballet in 1964.

I loved to take class with Mr. Skibine. He used to start his classes with tendus, stretching and holding. I interrupted him once, and in all my innocence asked, "Did you forget the pliés?" I had never started a class with tendus, which was his preference. He looked at me and very gently said, "This is the way I do it," and continued class.

Joining the Harkness Ballet as assistant to the artistic director, Donald Saddler brought a wealth of experience from the world of classical ballet and Broadway. Mr. Saddler, a native of California, had studied dance with Carmelita Maracci, Anton Dolin, and Antony Tudor. A member of American Ballet Theatre from 1939 through 1943, he returned to that company after the war. His choreography for the Broadway show *Wonderful Town*, starring Rosalind Russell, won

In Barcelona with James Truitte, Morton Winston, and Rebekah Harkness. *Photograph © Jack Mitchell*

him a Tony Award. He also staged the dances for *To Broadway With Love*, the musical created for the Music Hall of the 1964–65 New York World's Fair. The ballets he choreographed included *Koshare* for Harkness in 1966, and he also worked on *Cinderella*, but that production was never realized.

I adored Jeannot Cerrone, the company manager, who was a truly gentle man. He was the first company manager to win the *Dance Magazine* Award, in 1983. A benevolent spirit, he was a tall and elegant man, with salt-and-pepper gray hair. Born in Monaco, Mr. Cerrone began his career in 1936 as property man for René Blum's Les Ballets de Monte Carlo. Two years later he joined the newly formed Ballet Russe de Monte Carlo, and in 1949 was named director of that company. He would later become assistant director of American Ballet Theatre (1954) and general manager for Jerome Robbins's Ballets: U.S.A.

Mrs. Harkness asked Alvin to choreograph *Macumba*, a carnival ballet for which she wrote the score. James Truitte reminded me that Mrs. Harkness had the costumes for the ballet with her in Barcelona, even before Alvin choreographed it. Mrs. Harkness said, "We could do *Macumba* here." There was one other condition to the arrangement, however. Alvin, grown overweight since he had stopped dancing in 1963, had to dance in the ballet . . . and partner Mrs. Harkness.

This was one of the deepest sacrifices that Alvin could have made in order to keep the company alive. I thought it was very difficult for him to be thrust in this situation. He was director of his company; I don't think he expected to be called upon to dance. To this day, I have a vivid image of the pain Alvin must have been going through in order to save us.

In Barcelona, Mrs. Harkness, Morton Winston, James Truitte, and I took class together, in huge cement rooms that had wooden floors. Margot Fonteyn was in Barcelona because her partner, Attilio Labis, one of the principal dancers of the Paris Opera and a guest of Covent Garden's Royal Ballet, was guesting with Harkness. In Mr. Skibine's class, Miss Fonteyn was very simple, no high legs, no grandiose gestures. She didn't have a high extension. Her movements were very direct and clear. She was what I considered to be a true star— gracious, humble—and her talent was enormous. Having Miss Fonteyn in class was distracting because I wanted to watch *her* and concentrate on what *she* was doing.

During the 1960s, Salvador Dalí created "happenings" around famous people. He was a good friend of Mrs. Harkness's and asked a couple of dancers to step into a plastic dome he had created. Finally, I understood how to be invaluable to the company! Once we were inside, he began to splatter paint all over us. It was *gross*. Had I not washed those practice clothes, I'd have an original Dalí.

When we finished performing at the Gran Teatro del Liceo in Barcelona, we traveled to Paris to dance at the Marais Festival. My roommate was Harkness dancer Lili Cockerille. Lili has pixie good looks, a little nose, and blossoms of freckles. She had come to the Harkness at the suggestion of her teacher at the School of American Ballet—Maria Tallchief. When Lili needed work, and Mr. Balanchine said that it would be at least six months before there was an opening, she joined the Harkness Ballet. With Mr. B none too thrilled with Lili's move, she signed the first contract with Rebekah Harkness. Lili and Balanchine's friendship mended and he granted her his last authorized interview shortly before his death in 1983.

One of Lili's first roles at Harkness was as a whore in Alvin's *Feast of Ashes*. Lili remembers that Alvin used to poke affectionate fun at her while he taught her how to manipulate her fan. He would "work" that fan like nobody else. In Paris, after the ballet was presented, Alvin came backstage and said to Lili, "Yes. You learned."

For the 1966 Marais Festival, at the Hôtel de Rohan near Notre-Dame, Alvin choreographed *El Amor Brujo*, to the music of Manuel de Falla, for guest artist Marjorie Tallchief and Ailey dancer Miguel Godreau. John Butler's *After Eden* was danced by Lone Isaksen and Lawrence Rhodes. Harkness dancer Robert Scevers choreographed his *Saint-Saëns Concerto*. Every prima ballerina of the company was out onstage in the most ornate costumes I had ever seen, with detached bubble tulle sleeves, diamond chokers, diamond earrings, tiaras, gloves, and every bangle you could think of! The choreography was very difficult. They were given extraordinary technical things to do. The prima ballerinas included Panchita de Peri, Elisabeth Carroll, and Brunilda Ruiz, who was very warm and friendly and danced in many of John Butler's ballets. In the Scevers ballet, Panchita had to balance in the center of the stage on one foot, on pointe for approximately thirty-two counts in arabesque. What a feet!

After the premiere Panchita left the stage in tears. Many of the dancers were crying. Let us put it gently that the audience was not too appreciative. They booed as only the French can boo. If they don't like something, they let you know. It reminded me very much of the audience at Harlem's Apollo Theatre.

The Ailey company was next on the program. Morton Winston and I took our places onstage to dance in Louis Johnson's *Lament*. (Morton, affectionately called "Tubby" since he was a husky child, had grown into a svelte and beautiful man.) Even though we heard all the booing from backstage and watched the dancers exit in tears, we were determined that we were going to go onstage and do our best.

Morton Winston, whom we affectionately called "Tubby." *Author's personal collection*

We knew we had to go that extra mile. It was very quiet and warm outdoors. In the second movement of the ballet, in the middle of my variation, I got in an arabesque. Suddenly, a gentle wind came and supported me. I claim God was on my side—the wind was blowing in the right direction and I could not lose my balance. I was in "heaven" because I was on balance for such a long time that I missed the music cues for the next step. Eventually, I caught up. Tubby and I danced and it went well and at the end of the ballet the audience was very appreciative and gave an ovation that was overwhelming. They yelled and screamed and bravoed, as only the French can bravo. We came out and took bow after bow.

In Paris, Lili and I roomed together. We wore miniskirts, which were the rage, and platform shoes. I used to buy wigs at Galeries Lafayette and wear them to rehearsal. I'd take the wig off to rehearse and put it on the coat rack we used for *Blues Suite*. At the end of the day I'd gather my practice clothes and my coat and place the wig back on.

After the Marais Festival, both companies were on layoff. Lili and I stayed six more weeks at a pension, the Hotel Lisbon. Our fifth-floor walk-up room cost six dollars a night. Let's just say it wasn't in the Michelin guide. It was located near "Le Drugstore," where we would go for our American hamburgers. We figured out how to survive in Paris on the little money we had saved. There were certain havens of African-American culture that were thriving in Paris, including Haynes, a soul food restaurant, and a jazz club called The Living Room, where I became reacquainted with Horace Silver.

In Senegal, Alvin had introduced me to friends of his who were making a movie. Alvin had encouraged me to participate in the film. I portrayed an African woman who left Senegal for France. We filmed the first part in Dakar and the second in Paris. They wanted a Black woman to explore the markets of Dakar, then walk the Champs-Élysées and wear fashion-oriented clothes. While a camera was perched on the balcony on Avenue Foch, I stood in the middle of L'Étoile, imitated a traffic cop (in a silver miniskirt and jacket), and was almost arrested because we did not have permission to be there. Later, I learned that the film won a prize at the Cannes Film Festival.

Alvin's friends were very wealthy. Lili and I were whisked around in Gérard's limousine. Gérard was known in all the chi-chi stores so we were treated fantastically. We had carte blanche at restaurants, shops, and couturiers. Only someone as naive as I was could have possibly gotten herself hooked up with these gentlemen. I was twenty-three and five years old at the same time.

While I was working on the film, Lili and fellow Harkness dancer Jacques Cesbron agreed to dance the *Don Quixote* pas de deux at a countryside gala. Lili didn't have too much information on what the gala was for. Only after she had changed into her costume was she told that it was a Communist rally—good thing she chose to wear her red tutu!

Another film I was in won a prize in the San Francisco Film Festival in the early seventies. I danced the third section of *Cry*, on the rooftop of the art museum, at the University of California at Berkeley. It was the afternoon, the sun was shining, it was very warm, and the tar roof was melting. I left footprints on that roof and tar on my heels.

In addition to the prima ballerinas, the Harkness Ballet had some of my favorite male dancers in their company, including Helgi Tomasson, now director of the San Francisco Ballet, and Finis Jhung, a very crisp, very clean dancer who teaches ballet at the Ailey school. Lawrence Rhodes was the consummate dancer. He had such a strange body, which could do anything. The "gift" transcends body type. It's something that I knew inherently, and Larry Rhodes was the manifestation of that. He was the Callas of ballet; he had the drama.

The six-foot five-inch Avind Harum and I danced together only in *Ariadne*, Alvin's ballet based on the myth of Ariadne, the daughter of King Minos of Crete. She fell in love with the warrior Theseus and gave him a sword and thread with which to kill the Minotaur and find his way out of the labyrinth.

Ariadne was Alvin's first ballet on pointe, though I wasn't on pointe, I was on ladder. What could be funnier than studying dance all your life only to end up standing on a ladder? In the myth, Ariadne's mother, Pasiphaë, gives birth to the Minotaur, portrayed by Avind. As the ballet began, I stood on the ladder and wore just the torso of a costume that went from the top of the ten-foot ladder to the floor. It was the proportion that made me look bigger than life. Once again, I could see *everything*. I executed contractions and port de bras to announce my presence. I wasn't ready to give birth just yet! My arms flailed, the skirt opened, and out rolled the Minotaur. The lights dimmed and I got rolled offstage. All that happened in the first few minutes of the ballet. Avind's solo came next. God, could he dance!

At Harkness I studied with many of their master teachers: George Skibine, Ramón Segarra, who later became ballet master of the Ailey company, and Patricia Wilde, who is now the director of the Pittsburgh Ballet and for whom I'm choreographing a ballet for her 1994–95 season. Born in Canada and dancing professionally at the age of fourteen, Patricia Wilde was one of the most prominent ballet dancers of her day. Before joining Harkness in 1965, she was with the Ballet Russe de Monte Carlo, dancing in the same company with Alicia Markova and Alexandra Danilova. Later, she was a ballerina with the New York City Ballet, her unique style celebrated in such Balanchine works as *Square Dance* and *Stars and Stripes.*

By the time I met Miss Wilde she had stopped performing and was devoting her time to teaching. When she taught class, she danced full out. She enabled me to bring absolute control to my body through a combination of strength and stamina. I felt that she went out of her way to pay attention to me as a dancer. If you're in a very large ballet class, you have to angle yourself to accommodate other dancers at the barre. When you extend your legs, you have to turn in or turn out. For grands battements you turn outward on the diagonal en avant. For arabesque battements you have to turn into the barre, or else you'd kick the person standing next to you.

Pat Wilde made sure that everyone was corrected and coached. She didn't have to do that. When you're in a company there is a regimentation to daily class. The dancers know the vocabulary and it's up to the teacher to bring life to the class through challenging combinations. In her enthusiasm she reminded me very much of Fernand Nault and Leon Danielian of American Ballet Theatre. There was an excitement when you came into that class, a feeling that you wanted to do your best. Pat could demonstrate combinations center floor, unsupported, while we held on to the ballet barre. In demonstrating, her balance was unwavering. She could do things center floor that many dancers had difficulty with at the barre. She could demonstrate and talk at the same time and change her arms and look around over her shoulder while she stood on perfect balance. She could do everything.

She would demonstrate so that you could emulate the exercise precisely.

I looked forward to Pat Wilde's classes because I did not have a full rehearsal schedule at Harkness. In most ballets, I was not in the first cast, except in *Cain*, a work that was never performed, choreographed by Vicente Nebrada, presently director of the Ballet Internacional de Caracas. I was in the third or fourth cast for a ballet John Butler was doing. But I really didn't know John then and he didn't know how I danced. That would all change in a few years when Alvin brought his work into the Ailey repertory. Of John's ballets in the Harkness rep, *Sebastian* with Larry Rhodes was my favorite.

Ramón Segarra taught class in the evenings. At seventeen years old, he had been one of the guest artists at the Philadelphia cotillions I'd danced in. I hadn't known him then, but he was exquisite, a true *danseur noble*. I had the energy and the time for his classes, which were very difficult. The center floor adagio was interminable. Halfway through the adagio I couldn't feel my legs. I felt as if I couldn't support myself. Everybody fell apart in the adagio but you fought to keep it together. It was a strength builder, strength of character, mind, and body.

Elisabeth Carroll was one of the Harkness dancers who had incredible feet. I used to think, naively, that a dancer had to have feet like Pavlova's to satisfy what I wanted to see in a dancer in pointe shoes. Feet come in all different shapes and sizes and arches, but it's important that the line on the shoe be at least straight when you're up on pointe. If you get that high arch bulging, it's wonderful, and if you're slightly bowlegged, it's "fresh." Elisabeth Carroll had to be a strong technician because Brian Macdonald gave her such difficult steps to do in *Canto Indio*. Her feet were not Pavlova feet, but they were strong and *worked* feet. *Worked* means a dancer has paid attention to every aspect of his or her body, from the tips of their fingers to the tops of their heads to their toenails. Nothing is left out. In an immature dancer you will see, for instance, in a port de bras, that the arm carriage is correct but the hand loses its context in relationship to the arm. It becomes an appendage—there's no energy coming out of it. In an exquisitely *worked* dancer, where the entire body has been plied, you will see sparks fly—the stage is virtually bursting with energy. The stage becomes hot.

In the Harkness House for Ballet Arts, on East Seventy-fifth Street, just off Fifth Avenue, Mrs. Harkness had created a palace, very much in the tradition of the Paris Opera House, with its ornate studios. The heavy glass doors were encased in wrought iron. You walked into the foyer and to the left was the "Chalice of Life," a butterfly urn, behind glass, that rotated while the sapphires and diamond butterflies opened and closed. The urn, designed by Salvador Dalí, was to be Mrs. Harkness's final resting place. Next to this imposing display was an elevator decorated with multicolored paintings of dancers. A grand marble staircase led up to the gilt-trimmed first-floor studio, lit with chandeliers.

It was so unlike the "sweat rooms" that I connected with dance, those sparse studios that contained no more than a wooden floor, mirror, and barre. Dancers get used to working in some pretty rough places. I think Mrs. Harkness went overboard in trying to create a "civilized" space for dancers. When I walked into the Harkness studio, I entered a stage set, an ornate scene. At first I found it distracting, but then I realized that I was still sweating and huffing and puffing and it mattered little where I was.

I prefer to work in the simplest of spaces. Of course, I'll take the chandeliers on the outside! I would love to walk into a studio that had no accoutrements except barres, mirrors, white walls, high ceilings, and a sprung floor. It would be very much like a blank canvas where the dancer became both paintbrush and painting.

One night after leaving Harkness House, Alvin confided in Lili Cockerille about how difficult it was to work for Mrs. Harkness, but it kept the company alive. Lili, Stan (her husband), and I lived in the same apartment building in Manhattan, and of course, Alvin was very caring of whom I knew. And Alvin loved them so much. It was all impromptu. We'd get together in each other's apartments to eat, talk, and listen to music. Alvin was totally relaxed with them, and Alvin was not one to be totally relaxed. Lili is now the dance critic for the Tulsa (Oklahoma) *Tribune* and writes for *Dance Magazine*.

Mrs. Harkness was very shy and very caring—the complete oppo-

Alvin and I in London. *From the collection of Lili Cockerille Livingston*

site of her reputation. With me, she was very pleasant, always benevolent, a touch eccentric. We didn't exchange stories, but she would express her concern for me. She didn't like to stand in front of the dancers and talk. When we performed at Kiel Auditorium in her hometown of St. Louis, one ballerina, Sarah Thomas, collapsed during the rehearsal and died shortly thereafter at the hospital. I wasn't there, but when I arrived a few minutes later everyone looked stunned. Mr. Cerrone and Mrs. Harkness stood in front of the studio to reassure the dancers with their presence, but it was Mr. Cerrone who spoke while Mrs. Harkness stood by his side.

I slipped and cracked my ankle during a rehearsal of *Macumba* in Kiel Auditorium. My foot came out from under me and I sat with it twisted beneath me. It wasn't the last time I would injure myself this way. I returned to New York, and Alvin sent me to his doctor, who diagnosed the fracture as a broken ankle. More important, Alvin told me that he was about to resume the company.

Morton Winston stayed with Harkness. Harkness really didn't know what to do with me. *I* didn't really know what to do with me. What are you going to do with a five-foot-ten-inch female dancer, in any company? I can't imagine somebody coming up to me and saying, "You're Black. We can't use you." That's part of the problem of racism in the first place—people can deny it because you can't put your finger on it. But a five-foot-ten woman would have difficulty fitting into any company.

Looking back now at my time with Harkness, I realize that I really missed the family feeling of the Ailey company, and I missed the repertory. I wanted very much for that to continue. I couldn't wait to return to Alvin. But at the first rehearsal back, I was glad to have had the Harkness experience under my belt because it strengthened me both physically and mentally.

CHAPTER 6

In 1967 the State Department sent us on a tour of Africa where we danced in nine countries in two and a half months. It was a revelation to experience many African cultures firsthand. We arrived in Addis Ababa, Ethiopia, which is approximately eight thousand feet in elevation. When we danced there, we had to have oxygen tanks in both wings. We flew down to Madagascar, and after we performed in Tanzania, Uganda, and Kenya, we then traversed the continent to Congo, Ivory Coast, Ghana, and Senegal. In several countries, upon our arrival, the religious leaders would give libations and bless Alvin. In Ghana we were welcomed with a choreographed greeting where the celebrants danced right up to the plane. We were welcomed warmly by what we did for a living—dance.

While still on the tarmac we would look out the windows and see dancers in colorful traditional dress and drummers surrounding the officiating elder. As we carried our luggage and souvenirs toward the arrival gate, a mask under one arm, a basket balanced in the other, we were escorted by the Ghanian dancers.

In Kenya we were invited by President Jomo Kenyatta, leader of the independence movement, to dance at his residence. He could not attend our performance in downtown Nairobi. We danced on a makeshift wooden stage, three inches off the grass, and *on the bias*. It was 110 degrees. We'd had many stages put together for us at the last minute, so this was not at all unusual. The platform sloped a few degrees down stage left. We danced excerpts from *Revelations*, and had no time to change costumes for *Blues Suite*. The women danced in their "Wading" white skirts, and the men in their *Revelations* pants.

President Kenyatta loved us. He was a stately man with a mighty leonine head, who walked with a cane. Alvin sat on the ground near President Kenyatta and beamed angelically during the performance. He was proud of us, and we felt privileged to have presented our African-American culture and our way of movement as a gift for President Kenyatta. We were brought over to meet him after the performance. He sat in a marvelous, ornate chair. I had the chance to look into his eyes. There were several lifetimes in those eyes, which had lived through so much pain and finally triumph. I was over-whelmed to dance in his presence.

I had a strong yearning for African identity. Every marketplace I would visit on tour, people would come up to me and start speaking in the native language. I'd give them a puzzled look, then smile. I wanted to find "my" African nation. Instead, everywhere I went I was over-whelmed by the differences between the people.

A rumor started that President Kenyatta wanted to keep me, which was a complete distortion of the truth. When I was at his residence, he told me there was a woman who worked for him who could have been my sister. She had dark gums, dark lips, small eyes, and the same kind of nose. I was very excited about meeting her so that I could look into her eyes and be given the one clue I had been seeking.

The following afternoon a group of us went with all the other tourists to the Nairobi game reserve, expecting to see lions. My camera was loaded! Instead, the lions slept during those hours and we caught only an occasional glimpse of a paw sticking out of the high grass. There was still such incredible beauty, as when our path was crossed by a herd of zebras, or when swift-footed ostriches fanned out their wing and tail plumes.

The next morning at 4:00 A.M., Alvin and a smaller group of us went back to the reserve to see those lions in action. The females were out hunting, but when we saw two, about five hundred feet in the distance, we got out of our Land Rover to watch. While we were outside the vehicle, our guide pointed out a cheetah in fairly close proximity. But when we got back in the Land Rover, the motor failed. After a couple of false starts, the motor kicked in and we were on our way.

When we went to Congo, the mercenaries were being brought through and there were all sorts of little riots going on in the downtown area. We found ourselves in the middle of a war. James Truitte and George Faison were detained for several hours in Zaire because they were foreigners. In Zaire, Alvin and I saw movement that would eventually become the last steps in *Cry*. One night we were in a club where the walls were covered with black and white monkey fur. We were listening to music and enjoying ourselves when we noticed that there were young women in the club performing indigenous dances. They were from the bush. It was pure movement and it translated into the last crossover of movement in *Cry*. When the young women in the club started doing that step, Alvin and I just looked at each other. It was fabulous. Next thing I know it's 1971 and it turned up in *Cry*. Alvin and I remembered it.

In Zaire we performed in Kinshasa. The Minister of Culture brought several different groups from the bush who had never been onstage before. The performance was in exchange for our performances. When they danced their traditional dances, George Faison and I jumped up excitedly as we both remembered the movement from an old Deborah Kerr–Stewart Granger movie, *King Solomon's Mines*. One of the inspirations for the way I move is the Royal Watusi dancer from the film's last five minutes, whose presence, grace, and strength overwhelmed me as a young person. I could not believe the artistry that was in his body. I called it "blood movement." Dr. Pearl

Primus lived with those very same people who were in the movie, and she studied their dances.

It took from 1956, when I first saw the film, to 1967 to see the Ntore dancers do the same dance. The music was authentic and it hit me right in the heart as soon as the musicians started playing that special rhythm. They had intermarried with the Masai from Burundi, who do the wonderful dance with raffia headdresses. After they intermarried, they weren't six feet seven or even seven feet. They were five three or five four, very short people who did the same exact dance. They were absolutely glorious.

We performed in Dar es Salaam. We played Accra, the capital of Ghana. From there we flew to perform in Kumasi. That's when I had my first fear of flying . . . as much as I loved planes. We were in a "Friendship" plane. I'm here to tell the tale—it was very friendly, a good plane. We got caught in a violent thunderstorm. That was the first time I saw Alvin look frightened. We looked at him, the way one looks to a leader, for a reassuring look. *He didn't look like that.* The seat belts broke. We dropped hundreds of feet and moments later were pushed back up by air drafts. It felt as if we had hit a mountain. We hadn't, but we couldn't see out the windows. The sky was dark gray, broken by streaks of lightning. I tried to be calm and explain what was going on to the other dancers about turbulence and aerodynamics. "Don't worry," I said, "the plane's just going up a little, down a little. The spoilers are doing this or that." I didn't know *what* I was talking about. A little bit of knowledge is a dangerous thing. Because the planes were small and heavily booked, the company had had to separate and take two flights. James Truitte landed a half hour later with the other dancers. They'd had a perfect flight and looked at us as if we were nuts. We were just so happy to get down safely. The pilot kissed the ground.

I was nearly electrocuted in West Africa during a lecture-demonstration. Alvin was in front of the curtain, addressing the audience. I was listening intently to Alvin; when he spoke, I was spellbound not just by his words, but by the meaning behind them. It seemed effortless, unpretentious, and unplanned. Alvin was a brilliant speaker as well as a brilliant choreographer. He understood people and theater. He had my focus. The stage was tiny and I put my hand on what I thought was a wall. It was actually a lighting tower. *Never* put your hand on a lighting tower. I couldn't pull my hand off. Alvin was out in front of the curtain talking about how wonderful it was to dance.

George Faison saw me from across the stage. There was an arch over me from one lighting unit to the next, like in a Frankenstein movie. I felt like Elsa Lanchester. George yelled, "Cut the power," and Nicola (Nick) Cernovitch, who did all of our lighting, did. I became unstuck from the pole and George helped me to my feet. Alvin was still speaking. A few minutes later the curtain opened and I danced in Talley Beatty's *Taccota*. Needless to say, I was energized for that performance.

A dancer has to adapt to different stages, which can be either horrendous or spectacular. We never knew what condition a theater would be in until we arrived. In the late 1960s we danced in *Schauspiel* houses, the smaller theaters in Germany, places not accustomed to dance. The stages were covered with canvas or burlap. We'd perform *The Road of the Phoebe Snow*, where in one of the pas de deux the girl has to get dragged across the floor in a split and she'd pick up splinters in some very strange places, a lot of floor burns, a lot of open wounds.

We had to protect ourselves but we also had to give the best performance possible because not only were we representing ourselves as dancers and Alvin as a visionary, but we were unofficial ambassadors of the United States. We had to constantly keep in mind that despite the difficulties of the theater we were representing something much bigger than ourselves. I think that all of us had that in mind and we could adapt accordingly, depending on the circumstances.

It was difficult for Alvin to make the decision to perform at some of these venues, I'm sure, but there was always a reason. There were certain choices that Alvin had to make, that sometimes we questioned, but we trusted his reasons for doing what he did. We did not go blindly into what we were doing; we trusted Alvin. That trust was developed instantly, as soon as I saw the company dance, as soon as I saw his movable vision, what was in his heart and what was in his head.

We were after a goal. Our incentive was to keep the company alive and get the company recognized. We knew that Alvin Ailey had something special to contribute to the world, and as his dancers we were purveyors of that message. That was our motivator. We were after exchanging what was felt so deeply within, the spectrum of emotion from joy to sorrow and every emotion in between, onstage. Humanity brought us together, no matter where we were in the world, no matter who we were dancing for. That message was always very clear.

The very worst circumstance was when we danced at a German beer hall during Oktoberfest—beer, sawdust, oompah bands, and us. You could see the anger rise in Alvin's face. If you said you went into "flatback," it meant that you were angry. Jimmy Truitte went into "flatback" and said, "No way." Sparks were flying. If I had understood what it was to be an artistic director, I would have been more sympathetic to what Alvin was going through. We needed the job for the money, to tide us over till the next real theater to dance in. The producer said, "Just do this," and Alvin said, "Yes." He knew all the ramifications and that we were all going to "jump down on him." He knew we'd all be angry with him but he was willing to be the sacrificial lamb to get us to the next stage. He could see further than we could see. He also had more information than we had. That was the visionary in him. He could see straight through to our November 1992 appearance at the Paris Opera House, raked stage and all. He knew that someday we would be there, even if he wasn't there physically. He could see that far.

Because we didn't travel with a floor, we danced on floors that were used for everything—grand pianos had been dragged across them, orchestras had set up their chairs and stands on them, all kinds of sets had been built on them. Some of the stages were covered with canvas, nailed down. By the time you did your first couple of turns, the canvas would loosen. After two weeks of these floors, I got water on the knee. I'd turn my knee, but my foot would stay with the canvas.

Today, we still don't have a portable floor. We travel now with a marley floor, which covers the existing floor of the theater. Instead of having to dance with splinters going up your feet, now you can dance and knock your back out of whack because the wooden floor beneath the marley has no air pocket in it and it's sitting on top of cement, which is the way most old buildings were constructed.

I've been in so many hotel rooms that my mind goes into automatic the moment I arrive: where to step down, where the bathroom is, where the chairs are. The whole layout of the room gets into my mind immediately. It's the same as when we arrived for a performance and barely had time to become familiar with the stage. It would have been a privilege to have arrived early, because I remember those one-night stands when there was no time to get onstage before the curtain went up. But we'd have done anything for Alvin and he for us.

I remember once when Jimmy Truitte fell off the stage in Caesarea, a Roman ruin in Israel. We were opening the program with *Blues Suite*, the lights had dimmed, and I heard a crash. James hurt himself and I had to do "Fix Me, Jesus" with Kelvin Rotardier. "Fix Me" was really difficult to adjust to. It looks so simple. If the proportions of the bodies are off, it's difficult to adjust. One dancer has to fit into the other like a glove. Everyone has a different length torso, different length arms, different length legs, a different center of gravity. If you've had the same partner for a long time and then you have to switch, you have to adjust.

We danced in Israel six days after the Six-Day War. I remember being in Teheran, driving around in bulletproof cars while the Shah was still in power. In Lebanon we stayed in Beirut for the night and then moved closer to Baalbek to play the Roman amphitheater. It was a festival space. We participated in the last successful festival there before the political scene made it impossible for us to return. Alvin rechoreographed entrances for ballets to take advantage of the unique layout. The stage was raised, a platform that jutted out from magnificent towering columns. We entered from crumbling steps from behind ancient structures.

For rehearsal, in the afternoon, there were soldiers with rifles who were supposed to protect us. They surrounded the elevated stage, with their guns pointed in every direction possible. It was a bit unnerving to rehearse with rifles and bayonets a few feet away from us. It wasn't the most comfortable situation. At night, in our hotel, the power went out, and then we heard, from way off in the distance, a steady mechanical sound. The next morning we learned that what we heard was the sound of Syrian tanks rolling through town.

In Egypt we danced in an open-air theater, in Giza, near the Sphinx. The mosquitoes had it in for us. They said, "Here come the Alvin Ailey dancers . . . attack!" When we checked into the hotel they sold bug repellent at the desk. We thought it was a strange thing to sell, until we sat out in the sun and started slapping ourselves to death. We couldn't lie still for a minute, but would get up, go to the counter, and buy the repellent. We'd spray it on, but it still didn't work.

The theater was built close to the pyramids and the Sphinx. A stage had been set up for us in the middle of the desert. Before we had a chance to perform, condensation came through the stage and through the floor. By the time of the performance you could slide from one side of the stage to the other. We mopped up as much as we could.

The curtain went up. On the program we were scheduled to dance *Blues Suite, Cry, Rainbow 'Round My Shoulder*, and *Revelations*. We got through *Blues Suite*. I didn't have to dance in *Blues Suite* because I was on next in *Cry*. In the third section of *Cry* I started to slide, when what I really needed to get through the dance was traction. I began to notice that I was moving my skirt a lot, but my feet weren't moving a whole lot. (I was exaggerating the movement of the skirt to distract from what my feet were doing because there was no traction.) When the ballet ended, I took my bow and left the stage. Donna Wood was doing the lead in *Rainbow 'Round My Shoulder*, which begins with the entrance of the men on the chain gang from upstage left. I was backstage—or behind a curtain is more like it. I heard the music "I've Got a Rainbow," and then a tremendous thud. The music continued and then I heard another thud. The men were hitting the floor like flies. I looked at Alvin. He didn't say anything, but I could see he was tense. When Donna did her solo, she didn't hit the floor, but it was the lowest arabesque she'd ever done, the smallest movements she'd done in her life. You could see your face in the floor it was so wet.

The next day the performance was canceled and we were moved into a theater in Cairo that hadn't been opened in forty years. There was dust on the floor up to our knees. Poking out of the dust were wooden splinters, shafts of the floor that broke and cracked. The stage was swept and vacuumed and we did our best—in shoes.

Later, I went to the Egyptian Museum of Antiquities in Cairo. There were so many exhibits crammed together and many of the artifacts were not identified; or if they were identified, it was in Egyptian. I was fascinated by a collection of Nubian sculptures with their marvelous features—high bone structure, full lips, and broad noses. Most of the mummies were still there, but Tutankhamen was out of the country. Like us, Tut was on tour.

The Swedish Broadcasting Company commissioned an Ailey television ballet, *Riedaiglia*, which subsequently won the Grand Prix Italia in Ravenna as the best musical television show of 1967.

I fell in love with a Swedish man named Orjan, and we lived together for a while in Gamla Stan, the old section in Stockholm. The architecture was elegant, but there were no toilets. There were potties on the top steps that were changed in the morning. I wanted to settle down and have babies. I knew that that wasn't going to work because every time I returned, I knew that he had a new girlfriend. He wasn't what you'd call the understanding type, but he was good-looking. When the Ailey company returned to New York after its European tour, I returned to Orjan.

When I was alone with Orjan, it was a whole different ball game than when I was with the company. I felt a slight lack of identity. It's very different going places when you have a company with you, when you're in front of audiences and people recognize you.

One snowy Christmas, I walked the streets in search of collard greens, which many of the shops used in their windows for holiday displays. I walked until I found an out-of-the-way market that sold some fresh enough to eat. Diane Gray Cullert, a friend from the Philadelphia Dance Academy who moved to Sweden, Herman Howell, Talley Beatty, and I were the only African-Americans practicing *that* particular cuisine.

I lived on and off in Stockholm for six months. I came back at the end of that time and Orjan was speaking with a British accent. I then found out he was dating a British girl. So there went that, but it was fun while it lasted.

During my beginning years of touring with the Ailey company, the contemporary music scene was different. In Europe, we'd bring popular music *and* the current dances with us. The rhythm and blues charts weren't overseas yet. There were no George Michaelses or Elton Johns imitating the soulful sounds of African-Americans. The scene wasn't funky yet.

We would go to the discotheques in Paris or Milan after the performance and practically put on another performance because we were so "hyped." We'd offer the DJs our music: Marvin Gaye, Otis Redding, Stevie Wonder, and Sly and the Family Stone. The other people in the club, although they loved what we were doing, didn't know *what* to make of us. They couldn't imitate it. They looked at each other, as if to say, *who are these children?* People became just as interested in these impromptu performances as they were our performances in the theater. Dudley Williams, Morton Winston, George Faison, and I used to *turn those places out!* We danced all hours of the night, slept till noon, woke for rehearsal, performed, ate dinner, and did it all over again. That is, unless we had an embassy party or an official function to attend. More often than not, Alvin stayed behind when we went out after the performance. It wasn't his *thing* to go out with us to dance.

CHAPTER 7

Alvin could be very gentle. In rehearsal, he would not grab a dancer's leg and move it abruptly to where he wanted it. Instead, he'd say, "Can you get it a little higher?"—and offer a subtle touch. He'd do it graciously and jokingly, and in the meantime your leg would be going higher and higher. "Get the arabesque up. Give me some line," he'd add in the most cajoling way. But if he wasn't getting what he wanted from a dancer, he'd move on to the next person who needed his information.

He didn't have to tell me too much. I come from the generation of dancers with a minimum number of images. For instance, in *Masekela Langage*: You're a frustrated woman. You're hot, you're tired. This is South Africa. You can't get out. IMAGE. *Masekela Langage* has a tautness to it, from beginning to end. It's like a knot being tightened and tightened, then having water put on it to make it even tighter. This correlated with the Judith Jamison who was on the road in 1969, who

In *Masekela Langage*. *Author's personal collection*

had gotten on thousands of buses and had been on some of the worst stages in the world, who had torn her legs up so badly that they bled. Everybody went through that. Alvin used whatever was pent up inside us.

We went onstage no matter what. There were only ten of us; there was no such thing as a cover—an understudy. And afterward we had to get back on the bus with the props stuffed around us—the stools and the yellow fans from "Rocka My Soul"; the umbrella, poles, and yards of fabric from "Wading in the Water"—and all the costumes.

Sometimes we'd arrive in a town and they'd act as if they weren't expecting us, because there was no publicity. If there was a poster, it showed the company as it had been five or ten years before. Once, when we were in a European city (that shall remain nameless), the presenter decided that he had a specific image of what the Ailey company was. They shot photographs of some glamorous Black models, photos that had nothing to do with us, and those became the souvenir program. We have misconceptions about what the Ailey company is about, even today. All African-Americans do not dance the same way—we cannot be categorized. Many people want to "ghettoize" their conception of us. Alvin hated to be pegged—he loved defining himself for the purpose of showing diversity and variety.

All those frustrations rolled into one. At the time, I was angry, hot, and couldn't get out of the situation. Alvin knew how to use all of that, and we, as professionals, knew how to use it as well. It worked. Therefore, you got a work like Alvin's *Masekela Langage*, which he based on the South African experience. Alvin had never been to South Africa, but he'd read about it and knew that those people were suffering the same way people were suffering in the United States during the 1960s. He could explore that experience, as well as the experiences of his dancers.

That was the first character solo Alvin made for me, a very, very personal solo. It took about thirty minutes to choreograph at Connecticut College, in a room the size of a closet. Masekela, in a way, is my favorite role. Masekela is many people doing a slow, continuous burn, until the situation boils up and then recedes—temporarily. The people in *Masekela Langage* survive, but you still feel they're trapped, literally, because they end the ballet as confined as they begin it. It's a continuing mounting of tension and then a release. It's an incredible solo.

Masekela is also a reflection of the frustrations you have as an African-American living in the United States. We're still here, after all the turmoil we've had to endure. Even though it's about South Africa, and was choreographed before South Africa became a headline, it became universal in that it could apply to anybody's frustration, to anybody's feeling of being stifled. Alvin was so good at that. He understood that and was able to transfer that into movement.

When Alvin made this work he trusted that I could carry the emotional weight. It became a stepping stone to *Cry*, which followed two years later, where I was onstage by myself carrying *all* the emotional weight.

We had faith in Alvin and believed in his purpose. He believed his dancers had to keep going, no matter what, when he choreographed. He didn't have time to go back and try to perfect what was not coming to him, or to perfect the dancer. You had to keep going because Alvin had to finish the ballet, and you had to finish learning it. Then you could back up once the entire framework was complete, and if you had time, you could edit or add. But there was never any time. It became a matter of trust. He trusted us, as professionals, that we could get things to work. He trusted in our abilities and we trusted in his. And there were times Alvin would even say, if we were getting completely uptight, "It's *just* a dance."

When I worked with Alvin in the studio and something wasn't going right after a certain amount of time, we'd move on to the next section of the dance, because we had to get the piece done. There was no time to backtrack. Maybe five days after the fact, what wasn't working would all of a sudden fall into place because you hadn't been trying to fix it. As you're working you don't stop and say, "That worked." Or maybe you do, or Alvin or any other choreographer will say, "I like that. That's nice."

You can also come to the conclusion that you've had a breakthrough during a rehearsal. What happens sometimes when you think you've done your best is that a choreographer like Alvin will tell you the truth about your performance and say, "What was that?"

Alvin choreographed every year. We'd go on the road for six weeks of one-night stands, then come back for two weeks. He'd choreograph four ballets, then we'd play Hunter College, then go back out on the road again. It was ludicrous, but that was the ritual. We had to be fast and respond with a quick mind and a quick muscle memory. He would put the music on or not put music on; he'd start moving and you had to follow. Not only that, he depended on you to make the new dance your own.

That's where the illusion comes in, that's when the vulnerability comes in, that's when your passion has to lock in. You've got to dig inside for your own passion. That's why I speak to dancers today about vulnerability, how wonderful it is that you're in a marvelously controlled space on the stage. In life, all our techniques are not the same, and people have a tendency to shut down; therefore, their brilliance, the light that is in all of us, dims. But as a human being, the onus is on you—it's your homework with yourself. "This above all: to thine own self be true." Alvin would give me the space to do that homework because he could see what the possibilities were and take advantage of them. I'm very musical. We all have our own inner rhythms and our own musicality. Alvin's rhythm and musicality were very much on the same wavelength as mine, so that he wouldn't have to count phrases when he choreographed. Some people are on the back of the beat, some people are in the middle, and some are at the front. God forbid they should all be in the middle. It's very boring to watch.

We didn't count back then, as many dancers can attest. Instead, there was "phrasing." We phrased everything and prayed that each time we did something in rehearsal it would come out the same way in performance. In rehearsal, in the creation of a work, there was a constant playing around with how you could execute a movement within a certain musical phrase. Onstage it was already phrased.

When Alvin first choreographed *Streams*, he sent me home with the music by Miloslav Kabeláč and said, "Would you count this, please?" I was shocked. *What do you mean, would I count this?* Of course, I'd never have said that to Alvin. I'd just "throw him a look." At home, I put the music on. What I heard in the counting were very long phrases going up to "twenty-seven and," "fifty-two and." You don't count that way, but that's the way I heard it. The phrase finished at fifty-two. It didn't finish at thirty-two. It didn't finish at sixteen. For me, musically, it finished at fifty-two. So, Alvin created the ballet using these counts.

Alvin always used to say about me, "I like the way she moves so much because each movement is justified." There was no wasted movement. There was always a beginning, a middle, and an end. It came from somewhere and it went somewhere else. It's important for dancers to understand what happens in between the steps. The transitions are just as important as the arrival at the next picture. They are the glue that holds the dance together. Alvin called it "rubato." I call it connective tissue.

The dancers of my generation were not as technically proficient as the dancers of today. I also think that audiences did not demand that of us. They didn't demand fifteen pirouettes; they didn't demand triple cabriloes. I think one of the major changes happened when the Russians arrived in the 1950s. All of a sudden you saw a woman getting thrown from one side of the stage to the other, or Galina Ulanova bent back in attitude with her rib cage extended. Everything became exaggerated and very big. Plisetskaya kicked the back of her head in attitude. All of this initiated a shift that took place when Rudolf Nureyev arrived in 1961.

There was nothing he could not do. Rudi was abandoned in his movement; he threw caution to the wind. In ballet, it was the first time I had seen somebody eat up the stage. He broke through a wall. But it led to a certain competition. It became one-upmanship. If one dancer did six pirouettes, then another dancer did twelve, then another dancer had to do fifteen. That's when some of the dance world started stressing technical prowess for its own sake and forgot about the kind of expressiveness Rudi had when he moved. He was pliant and so manly onstage. His technique enabled him to be as free as he was in his roles.

You need a good dance foundation from which to work. The foundation for the Ailey company is Horton technique, ballet, Dunham, Graham, and jazz. Alvin had always said "dance is dance" and that if you could do one technique, then you should be able to do others. You ought to be able to go back and forth, to transverse, to combine. We began being more technical around the time we started having classes more regularly. That was the result of fewer one-night stands and better-structured tours. On the road we started having more time to study on a consistent level. Alvin brought in Ramón Segarra and Ali Pourfarrokh to teach ballet class. Whenever we started having more ballet classes, there was a certain resistance from members of the company. Today, we have a balance among ballet, modern dance, and jazz.

CHAPTER 8

The spirituals sing of woe triumphantly, knowing well that all rivers will be crossed and the Promised Land is just beyond the stream. The spirituals ask no pity—for their words ride on the strongest of melodies, the melody of faith. That is why there is joy in their singing, peace in their music, and strength in their soul.

—Langston Hughes,
especially for the Alvin Ailey dancers, August 1964

Revelations is a suite of spirituals in three sections. For me, the first section, "Pilgrim of Sorrow," which includes "I Been 'Buked and I Been Scorned," is about deliverance, about hope, about truth. It's about people who have been abused and it's about faith. It's very difficult to convey the sense of weight expressed in this section. You should feel like the burden of the world is on your shoulders. "There Is Trouble All Over This World," "Ain't Gonna Lay My Religion Down"—that's all hope and faith. Alvin called "Fix Me, Jesus" a spiritual aspiration.

The second section is called "Take Me to the Water," which Alvin based on his own childhood memories from Texas, when one was baptized outside the church by a lake, all dressed in white, a memory he theatricalized. The third section, "Move, Members, Move," concerns the energy and spirituality of the Black church. The dancers carry large yellow fans and wear Sunday-go-to-church straw hats. All these things were part of Alvin's blood memories. It's a very intense and very personal work, but universal in its message, which is why it can still bring the house down, performance after performance.

We usually close a program with *Revelations*. It affects each member of the audience and it affects each dancer in a way that is uplifting. You're able to give full expression to it. It's inspired choreography in the truest sense. It's kind of a baptism for the dancer, too, who only after his or her first *Revelations* truly feels like a member of the Alvin Ailey American Dance Theater.

When I first joined the company, I walked into a rehearsal of *Revelations* as the company was practicing the staccato port de bras from "I Been 'Buked." When I first saw the company in 1963 I had said, "Oh, I can do that!" Guess what? *You* try it sometime. The dancers made the movement look easy. It's not. It takes unbelievable coordination. It takes passion, commitment, dedication, and love to know that every step you do should be infused with 100 percent of yourself.

Alvin taught me how to be generous with movement, that there is no step that is not useful to your growth, that there is no *feeling* that is not useful to your growth. He also taught me how to keep a sense of humor. There is a spirit within *Revelations* that keeps it fresh every time. At the end of "Rocka My Soul" the audience is indeed moved, taken to another place in their lives, someplace lasting that's touched their hearts and minds and changed their perspective.

Part of my enjoyment of dancing *Revelations* was the profound contribution of Brother John Sellers, a protégé of Mahalia Jackson's. He sang in his yellow robe and skullcap. It was the kind of singing I had heard as a child in Mother Bethel—unaccompanied singing. Brother John became part of the fabric of the ballet when he sang "Rocka My Soul," "Wading in the Water," and "The Day Is Past and Gone." It changed the whole feeling of *Revelations*.

Consuelo Atlas did a wonderful "Fix Me, Jesus." That's when I got "bumped" from the role. Connie had an incredibly flexible back. That is when "Fix Me, Jesus" changed. Connie could arch all the way back

In *Revelations.* *Photograph © Jack Mitchell*

In "Fix Me, Jesus" from *Revelations* with Jimmy Truitte. *Author's personal collection*

so that the top of her head almost touched the floor. The original "Fix Me, Jesus" had a T position, a Horton-technique position, without any arch in it. That's the way I used to do it, and that's the way Minnie Marshall used to do it, on whom the movement was made. When Connie came along, she had a truly flexible back. Alvin saw new possibilities. What she did was absolutely valid. She took the movement to its conclusion. I wish I'd been able to bend back that far. When Alvin saw her do that I was immediately shifted into another role. He asked Lucinda Ransom to teach me the umbrella role in "Wading in the Water."

At the time, I was upset, but not at Connie. I felt that I'd been demoted, that I was taking a step down. I just felt that after two and a half years, he just didn't love me in "Fix Me." Alvin never explained, but that's where faith came in. I got mad but I had faith that he knew what he was doing. Lo and behold, I went out there with that umbrella but I was so mad I didn't know *what* to do. So I smiled and then I ended up smiling for the next thousand performances.

Two of my closest friends, Consuelo Atlas and Ernest Pagnano. *Photograph © Jack Mitchell*

That's knowing how to use your emotions, be they detrimental or positive, in a constructive way, even if you've got to force it. You've got to start somewhere. I learned then that there are no minor roles. They are all major roles and it's what the dancer does that makes it major.

At the Palais des Papes in Avignon, during a photo call, I slipped and fell on some water that was on the stage in the courtyard. I was running around with the umbrella, doing my first entrance in "Wading in the Water." I turned the bend and fell flat, but completely relaxed. I got up, continued, and when the baptism began I realized that I couldn't bend over and was having difficulty breathing. I was whisked to the back of the house and a doctor shot my back full of Novocain. (When in doubt, shoot her with Novocain.) That was just in case I had to perform that night. Every time I would take a breath, it would catch. What I had was a back spasm, though I thought there was something more seriously wrong. That was the first and last time that ever happened to me. I guess that's why they shot Novocain in me, to scare me to death so it wouldn't happen again. It rained three days in

Avignon, so we were unable to continue our performances. I was saved.

The "Fix Me" woman is the mother figure who stands in the central position of "I Been 'Buked." However, I stayed in that position even after Alvin took me out of "Fix Me." That's when things started shifting around. The mother and father figures in " 'Buked" are also the couple in "Fix Me," and the central pair of churchgoers in "Rocka My Soul." In addition, the father figure dances the solo "I Want to Be Ready." Even when I was shifted into "Wading," I still retained my motherhood(!) and that central position in the other parts of the dance.

Alvin gave Dudley Williams leeway in "I Want to Be Ready," while staying true to the choreography. The coccyx balance study, one of the basics of Horton technique, is what you learn in the classroom; it takes an artist to make it look like a dance. That's what Dudley does, and what Jimmy Truitte, who originated the movement, did. Jimmy turned what was essentially a coccyx balance study into a moving dance. It was his sheer artistry, talent, and divineness that made it what it is today. "I Want to Be Ready" is about simplicity and focus. You've got to be able to sit in the middle of the stage and do a coccyx balance and have the audience feel that you are growing out of the floor.

John Parks, now a professor at the University of South Florida in Tampa, always reminded me of a bald eagle—regal, elegant, soaring, and commanding attention with the "wingspan" of a 747. He had a marvelous small head set on top of broad shoulders tapering down to a small waist. (Leonard Meek is very much like him.) He was very reassuring, a wonderful partner with a beautiful speaking voice and a glorious sense of humor. A sensual man, onstage and off. It was also wonderful dancing behind John when he did "Wading in the Water" with Mari Kajiwara. He gave her advice on their projection when they danced because they had me behind them. "Just do your thing," he told her. He was trying to encourage her to become completely rooted in her role and not to worry about who was behind or in front of her. It's something they had to think about. As Alvin used to say, "If you just do the step, you'll be fine." Do the step and have confidence in that step. *Revelations* is a classic; just do the steps and you'll be fine.

*   *   *

Revelations is universally understood. It's been done all over the world for the past thirty-three years. I think that because Alvin understood the humanity in all of us—because he understood that everyone has sorrows, joys, pain, and laughter—*Revelations* is just a reflection of the journey we all take in life, which has its ups and downs—and, hopefully like the ballet, ends rather triumphantly. Like many of Alvin's works, it's a ballet about people who survive. I think we all like to see ourselves as survivors, with much hope and many tomorrows. I believe that's what Alvin was trying to say when he created *Revelations*. It's universal and it's accessible. That's why it's been around for such a long time. Other than that, people just *love* it. And we love doing it.

CHAPTER 9

ALVIN AILEY'S JOURNAL

Monday, September 21, 1970
Today at 5 P.M. the company gathered at the YWCA—at Clark
Center at 51st St. and 8th Avenue, our former home—a place that
stirs up many memories relevant to the company's beginnings—to go
to Russia. It had been a hectic day—a frantic day full of last minute
shopping—a borrowed bag from Brother John—a dash to the bank to
get not enough traveler's checks—a day full of tension and anxiety for
all of us—a day that had telephone calls to Washington & London—
a day where all things relevant to this adventure had to be tied up,
brought together and made into the neat package which would be
opened on Thursday night in the Russian city of Zaporozhye. Russia!
In 1970 at last after its having been mentioned first as a possibility for
the company in 1962 when we had danced before the assembled
Bolshoi ballet in the rain in the Delacorte Theatre in Central Park.
Many miles of travel, many hours of rehearsals, many faces no longer

with the company have met us in former years at the YWCA. In 1962
we had rehearsed here and then taken buses to the airport for
Southeast Asia. In 1963 we had met Ben Jones here at the YWCA,
gotten in his station wagon (along with the costumes & scenery—our
stools, ladders, fans for Revelations *and* Blues*). Then we were 6.*
How in 1970 we are 16 dancers and 8 technicians with 4,000 pounds
of cargo. (16,000 I learn later.) The years have really gone—we have
traveled so much, seen so much, heard much applause, danced before
thousands of people in many, many tours at home and abroad and
here we are again—but this time en route to the Soviet Union—
fearful, anxious (now we have some married dancers whose spouses
were not that anxious for them to leave (Leland from North Carolina,
Alfonso who I later learn was just today married, Linda married only
a few months and very happy with her bright young musician
husband). Lovers at the bus. We have changed. They have changed.
Today the group around the bus to see us off seemed very young, very
long haired—even militant looking in the way young blacks look
now. Harvey Cohen who was seeing Renee off. Harvey whom I had
asked to join the company again after having refused him at first—
and who had said no I think out of . . . pride. George Faison . . .
Charlie Rheinhart & Meg Gordean who were there to collect changes
in the programming for our upcoming Broadway season at the ANTA
in January. Ramón Segarra (with a new haircut). Nino Golanti.
Brother John. Judy. Miguel. Dudley. Kelvin. Beautiful faithful
Kelvin—the longest standing member of the company. A real friend.
A devoted dancer. Kelvin who had met at this YWCA so many times
before. My age but still dancing beautifully. Thin, elegant, calm, a
rock in a sometimes troubled sea (or should I say always troubled
sea?). Dudley who complains so much . . . but he too in his way a
rock—a pillar of the company—but he too had almost always been
there, or had been there since 1964. Ghosts survive around departing
from the YWCA. Minnie Marshall—beautiful, black, tall—now
gone. In the same year as Langston. Thelma Hill (grown too fat to be
lifted). James Truitte (a long story) but gone since 1967. How many
more!—A who's who of the black dance. Ghosts. Bill Louther.
Loretta Abbott, Hope Clarke, Joan Peters, Lucinda Ransom, Joyce

Trisler (two of whose works we now carry with us). Lester Wilson, Glenn Brooks, Julius Fields, Michael Peters, Connie Greco, Don Martin, Ella Thompson and Charles Moore.

In 1970 we went to Russia for the first time and we played the city of Donetsk, which hadn't been open to outsiders for fifteen years. It was a closed city; nobody could come to visit it from either Russia or the Ukraine. Not only had the residents not seen Black people in person before, but they hadn't seen other Russians. We were literally the first outsiders allowed in for fifteen years. We were a real attraction, to say the least. We understood why they stared at us.

In New York we had to run through the ballets we were planning to perform in the Soviet Union in front of members of the State Department so that they could pick "appropriate works." They would not let us take *Monument for a Dead Soldier*, the solo Geoffrey Holder choreographed for me, because a military jacket was used as a prop.

In Moscow I met the poet Yevgeny Yevtushenko, author of "Babi Yar," who wasn't very friendly until he was introduced to Connie Atlas, whom he wanted to meet. I was anxious to visit the Pushkin Museum because Pushkin was descended from an African. At the museum I saw one of the world's largest collections of Impressionist art, especially Gauguin. The museum, however, was in disarray. Some of the paintings were unframed, some on the floor, others hung in direct sunlight. That's when I realized that in American museums the art is well cared for.

I saw the great gate of Kiev, which is about as high as my elbow, with a plaque on it. I stood there with the strains of Mussorgsky's "Pictures at an Exhibition" running through my head, trying to imagine what it was about the gate that inspired such profound music.

One Russian woman, a fan of Hector Mercado's, followed him wherever he went. She was like a groupie, but the Russians were not allowed to talk to foreigners. One day she appeared on our train and was promptly arrested.

Halfway through the tour, we ran out of food. Rice and potatoes started appearing for breakfast. Cold kasha and weak tea for lunch. I remember that all of us lost a lot of weight. Trying to get a decent meal, I said that I could eat only fish. They got me a piece of fish. It was an old fish, but it was a fish, and that's what I ate when we returned to the hotel from the theater at night. The food would be laid out at a certain hour, and due to Russian bureaucracy, that hour was constant, no matter what time the performance finished. If the audience applauded for half an hour, the hotel didn't care. The rules had to be obeyed. When we arrived, even the *marozhenoe,* the ice cream, was on the table and had melted.

It was the *blues.* It was what the blues were about. You think we didn't know how to dance *Blues Suite* after all the things we went through? It was as if we were being treated like a bunch of cattle. Alvin was very upset about that. Within the company, there were little explosions of personality at being treated like third-class citizens. Alvin took the brunt of it all.

We were invited to watch a class at the Bolshoi School. You could watch how the children went through a metamorphosis. They would enter the school at ten years old, young, eager, and in position. When they got to be teenagers you could see that the boys wanted to be outside playing games. The boys were good, one or two were sensational. By the time the girls were teenagers, they were starting to get their curves; they were "perched." About half a dozen were fabulous. All were extraordinarily placed. You could watch them go from the eagerness of the ten-year-olds into the restlessness of teenagers. That growth, which we were privileged to witness briefly, was fascinating to observe.

American dancers never used to wear as many layers as they do today, leg warmers, sweaters, and scarves. When I began to dance, we wore our tights and leotards and shoes. When we took class in a Russian studio, the space was cold and unheated and we saw the necessity for all the added-on clothes. The raked floors were wooden, but worn from years of dancing. There was no resin: instead, there was water in a bucket, which you'd sprinkle on the floor in order to create traction.

We danced so many ballets in one evening. A typical program we took to Russia was *Toccata*, *Journey*, Joyce Trisler's *Dance for Six*, *The Prodigal Prince*, and *Revelations*. We also danced Lucas Hoving's *Icarus* and Pauline Koner's *Poème*. Pauline, one of the original dancers in the José Limón Dance Company, was the first Emelia (called His Friend's Wife) in *The Moor's Pavane*. We also danced *Masekela Langage*.

Our performances at Moscow's Variety Theatre were followed with at least twenty minutes of applause. Nobody believes you these days when you tell them that people applauded for that long, but they did. If you hadn't seen anything like the Ailey company before, then it was a revelation. "The reception after our Moscow closing was indeed historical," Alvin noted in his journal, "the ovation lasted for at least fifteen minutes of rhythmical clapping." Grateful members of the audience would wait for us at the stage door, then sometimes follow us down the street yelling "Vodka," the only word we'd all understand, to show their appreciation.

The dancers were given white flowers, and Alvin a box of chocolates by a man who had been waiting outside the stage door every night. "He was mad for Judith Jamison," Alvin wrote. "As I got in the bus I gave him a picture of *Prodigal Prince* and a portrait of Judi. He was overjoyed. Judi came from the back of the bus in her maxi coat and signed the photo. He, with fanatic and fantastic eyes, then kissed Judi on both cheeks."

When Alvin returned from Russia he told Lili Cockerille, "Incredible dancers and horrible choreographers, because the choreographers are not hungry." The dancers, too, had contracts that lasted forever. We saw dancers who were stuck, obviously bored, who didn't want to be where they were, but were obligated to fulfill their contracts. It was boring onstage.

You have to be desperate, as though you were catching your breath. Dance has to be that way to you. But dance cannot be a truncated, parochial experience. It has to incorporate the world and world situations, encompass everything and everyone, from the rich to the homeless. You want to eat life, so you have to be famished all the time, not physically, but in wanting to know and in wanting to absorb and in exploring and stepping out over the edge, sometimes by yourself.

Today, as artistic director, I know some of the pressure Alvin was under. In 1990 we returned to Russia on the twentieth anniversary of our first performance there. Now, even though there had been major political changes, we were going through many of the same troubles that the company experienced the first time around. A State Department official warned us that there was racism in Moscow, but luckily, our trip was uneventful that way. There was still a shortage of food, except at the end of the tour when we were in Tbilisi, Georgia, where we had great food at a party given in our honor. The ending of the 1990 tour was very much like the beginning of the 1970 tour. When we arrived that first time, the borscht was thick, with a healthy dollop of sour cream on top. By the time the tour finished, the borscht was like water, topped with sour cream the size of a dime.

The one Black ballerina in the Bolshoi in the 1960s invited us to her house for dinner. We had a wonderful evening looking at her old photographs.

The individuals that we met were warm, friendly, outgoing people who wanted to help us. But the infrastructure that was taking us from town to town was atrocious. I had fifteen dancers with food poisoning by the time we left.

To this day, the Russian people still want our blue jeans and our records. We gave away jeans and sweatshirts with school insignias and the Alvin Ailey insignia. Of course, we were sold out every night because tickets were purchased far in advance. I ran into the same people who had seen us twenty years before.

I had interviews in Moscow explaining to reporters that the dancers have to study ballet and many different modern techniques, including Horton and Graham. By the time the article came out, it said the Ailey company was based on classical ballet, the root of dance. Somebody once wrote that ballet is the only dance, that everything else is secondary and derivative. If that's true, what happened before ballet? Did the first man or woman who got up to dance do a tendu, did he or she turn out in first position? Or did they take the rooted, grounded stance of eternal strength?

When we were leaving Georgia in 1990, the government sent the wrong kind of plane for us. We were due at the American festival in Lyons, France. My dancers and my crew had to load the plane themselves. There was no actual cargo hold for the crates that contained our wardrobe. We had to unpack all the costumes and place them in the rear of the plane, loosely, with whatever luggage we could fit.

When we were at least five hours late, the captain of the plane got up, walked straight past Calvin Hunt, who was our production manager then, to Masazumi Chaya, associate artistic director, who was one of the few non-Black people on the plane. He asked Chaya, "How much does your cargo weigh?" We had no idea how much the cargo weighed because it had been unloaded, and half of it was still on the tarmac. Meanwhile, E. J. Corrigan, master carpenter, had to wait by himself for a second plane to take the balance of our cargo. He found himself in the company of soldiers, who patrolled the airport with their very visible weapons.

Finally, we took off, but the angle of our ascent was really flat, as if we were in a prop plane and not a jet. It felt as if the plane was slinging a bit as we were cruising down the runway. We had images of the cargo slushing around in the back. We were nervous until we arrived in Budapest, an interim stop. Donald Washington, company manager, called the office and poor Bill Hammond, former executive director, "caught it." When Donald finished talking, Chaya got on the phone, and when Chaya finished, I took the line. Poor Bill, he had to listen to the three of us scream at him.

From Budapest we flew to Lyons, keeping our fingers crossed that all our cargo would find its way. When we landed, we were told that the luggage handlers had gone home for the day. Here we go again. My men, dancers and crew, had to unload the plane. And they were exhausted from having danced for two weeks, having very little food, and being sick. At one o'clock in the morning I sat on the tarmac of the Lyons airport and watched these gorgeous creatures, these beautiful dancers, unload the plane. The images just didn't go together.

In Lyons, the cuisine capital of France, we had to wait until the next day to get some food. Half of us couldn't eat because we were sick, half of us had doctors' appointments, but we knew that down the block from the hotel was something not readily available in Russia— *sole meunière et haricots verts et pommes de terre et beaucoup de vin.*

The saving grace of both trips to Russia was the audiences. We could speak only a little bit of Russian and they could speak only a little English. But it didn't matter. When we danced, no translator was needed.

CHAPTER 10

At the end of the dance the curtain fell. I heard applause. The curtain was raised and I heard applause, screaming, bravos, followed by a long ovation. I had heard that before, not just for my solos, but for the entire company. Alvin came backstage. I'll never forget what he said that night. He said my performance was wonderful. A few seconds later he looked right at me and said, "What do I do next?" He was exasperated. "What do I do *now*?"

He was absolutely right. What was he going to do for me after *Cry*?

Alvin choreographed *Cry* in eight days as a birthday present for his mother, Mrs. Lula Cooper. As usual, we had just come off a tour and had one day to recover. I met Alvin at our Fifty-ninth Street studio to

In *Cry*, as photographed by Max Waldman. © *Max Waldman Archives, Westport, CT USA*

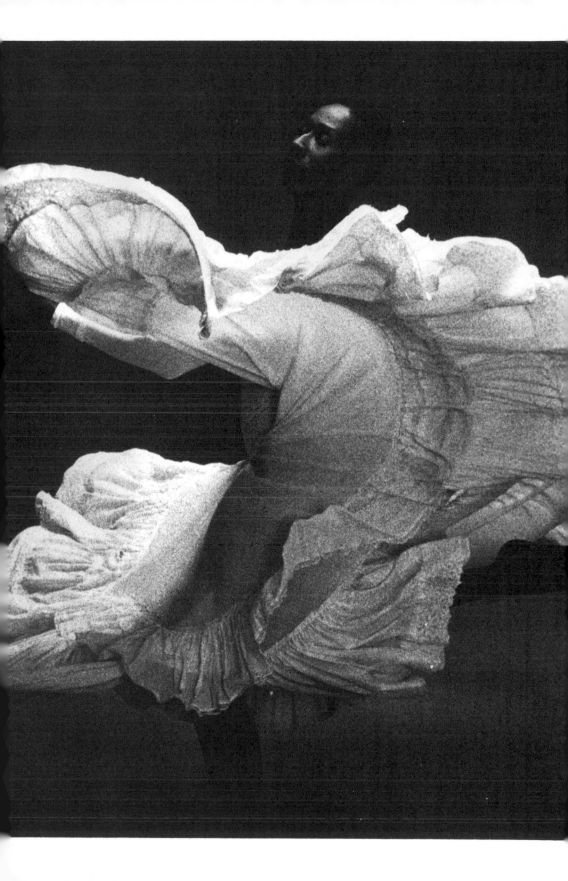

begin our work. Almost immediately, there was a special feeling in the room—it's what happens with any choreographer who thinks of the studio as a holy place. When people ask me what *Cry* is about I always say that it's about dancing for sixteen minutes, nonstop, as if you're running around the block full speed. It starts out with the weight of the world. The shawl you're holding is representative of a woman scrubbing a floor, of a mantle around your head, of a stole around your shoulder, a burden lovingly carried. Of a protective blanket spread beneath the floor. The cloth carries the weight of many experiences.

Exactly where the woman is going through the ballet's three sections was never explained to me by Alvin. In my interpretation, she represented those women before her who came from the hardships of slavery, through the pain of losing loved ones, through overcoming extraordinary depressions and tribulations. Coming out of a world of pain and trouble, she has found her way—and triumphed.

In the first section she celebrates her beauty, but in the meantime she's out there scrubbing floors. She celebrates life by acting as if she's smoothing a blanket for a baby she's been cradling. She walks across the stage defiantly as if to say, "Look at me. I'm a gorgeous being. I have something to say. I'm *here.*" Her tone of voice is of one who presents herself and displays the burdens she carries as well as the blessings.

In the second section she's really wracked with the devastations of what's going on in this world. Here Alvin used Laura Nyro's song "Been on a Train," which speaks of the catastrophe of drugs—how, instead of eating life, you let life eat away at you.

The third and last section is very celebratory, matching the music—the Voices of East Harlem's "Right On, Be Free." In the end, she acknowledges what's going on in the world, but decides to press on. She is going to keep her "eyes on the prize" despite the odds. She is full of pride and elegance, and represents the strength of women who have endured since the beginning of time—the head is held high. It's steeped in tradition and love. If you look at grandmothers, mothers, and daughters, you'll see that. You can see the strength in their faces, the pain that they've been through, and the wisdom that they have. I think Alvin was trying to convey that through movement.

Alvin, however, had difficulty finding music for the first section, but finally decided on a piece by Alice Coltrane. When I first heard it, I felt that the music was all over the place. I did not know Alice Coltrane; I knew John Coltrane and the shapes that he used musically. Her music was very foreign to me. I didn't know what to expect and I had to phrase the first section.

Until the night of the premiere, we hadn't done the ballet from beginning to end. We ran out of time in the tech rehearsal. If you run out of time and the crew goes to dinner, that's it. My first experience of going from start to finish was at the premiere, May 4, 1971. It was quite an experience. Sixteen minutes later, my lungs were on one side of the stage and my heart on the other. The audience went wild, as they still do, no matter who dances. That's what I love about *Cry*. The dance has passed from dancer to dancer to dancer, from generation to generation. *Cry* is about the dance *and* the dancer, but the dance holds up by itself.

People always ask me, "What were you thinking while you danced *Cry*?" Just before it begins, I could be thinking of anything: My brain might be processing whatever happened to me during the day or two years ago or a hundred years ago in another life. My thoughts could be as mundane as whether I took the garbage out or paid the phone bill. All these thoughts happen in milliseconds. Anything and everything that is part of my life is going through my head when I'm dancing. But once the curtain goes up, you recognize the fact that the stage is a very sacred place. It's like a vacuum. You only hear and you only see and feel what is happening at the moment in your creative work. Usually, in the pause before *Cry*, the electricians have to change the lighting gels. I used to sit on the floor with the shawl on the floor in front of me. Some days I spoke, while on other days I was completely quiet. After I danced it for twenty-six times in a row, I thought, "How am I going to get through this?" I did not have an understudy. I was dying for somebody else to do it.

After the premiere of *Cry*, Alvin called me at four the next morning, and I knew something was afoot. He read Clive Barnes's review from the New York *Times*. The review was like one big bouquet. My name was in headlines. Here's an excerpt:

THE DANCE: JUDITH JAMISON'S TRIUMPH

For years it has been obvious that Judith Jamison is no ordinary dancer. She looks like an African goddess and her long body has an unexpected gracefulness to it, but it moves in a manner almost more elemental than human. Her face is fantastic.

It is a long Modigliani face, like a black sculpture. It is a tragic face, a mask of sorrow. It is a face born to cry the blues, but when she smiles it is with an innocent radiance, a joyfulness that is simple and lovely. And she dances with an articulated beauty, serene, together and womanly. She holds herself a little aloof from the audience, but she is reserved rather than shy. She never tries consciously to please an audience. She is wonderfully proud, from the poise of her head set perfectly on a long, strong neck, to the lightly sculptured muscles of her long legs.

So for years it has been obvious that Judith Jamison was no ordinary dancer. Now Alvin Ailey has given his African queen a solo that wonderfully demonstrates what she is and where she is. It was given the world premiere at the New York City Center last night, and it was a sensation. Rarely have a choreographer and dancer been in such accord.

The solo, which lasts some 15 minutes and must be one of the longest solos ever choreographed, is called "Cry." Ailey has dedicated it: "For all black women everywhere—especially our mothers." You can see why, for here crystallized is the story of the black woman in America told with an elliptic and cryptic poetry and a passionate economy of feeling.

Thank you, Clive Barnes!

I hadn't thought after the first performance that anything spectacular had happened, other than that I made it through the dance. I hadn't even known about Alvin's dedication. If I had been told that I was to represent every Black woman in the world, I would have dropped the cloth and left the stage *immediately*. My focus was on getting through the dance, in one piece. Dudley Williams saw me from the front of the house. He told me that during the end of the last section he didn't know if I was going to be able to get from one side of the stage to the other. 'Round about the second section, I couldn't feel my legs. By the third section, I was so far inside of the movement that nothing else was going on. I couldn't hear anything but the music, and what was going on in my mind. You could see but you couldn't see. You could feel but you couldn't feel. There were many contradictions.

It was different every time—impossible to categorize. Sometimes I didn't think I was going to make it through the first section. Sometimes I'd thought I'd done a magnificent job and Alvin would come backstage and say, rather flatly, "It was OK." It was always unpredictable how I would feel it, section by section. The first time, however, it was called getting from the beginning to the end without having done that before, so everything was a surprise. I didn't know I wasn't going to be able to feel my legs at the end of the second section. The third part of *Cry* begins in second position, standing, with the torso bent over, to the strains of "Right On, Be Free." Alvin probably told the sound technician to "jam it." I heard that intense beat and was into the final section.

He already knew then, because of the ovation and what he had seen, that something out of the ordinary had happened. But I had another *Cry* to do the next night. On that night, I was scared to death because I knew how hard it had been getting through the premiere. I was scared because I'd "lost my legs" at the end of the second section. What was I going to do?

That's when a dancer learns something called pacing. But you don't learn it immediately. You have to do it over and over and over again in performance to learn how to pace yourself. There *is* such a thing as pacing in *Cry*. But after you see someone do *Cry*, if you're backstage when she finishes, she's flat-out on the floor gasping for breath. But when the curtain goes up for the bow, you pull your nerves together quickly as if you haven't been in a collapsed state—winded, sweating, tired—two seconds before.

I would collapse after *Cry*, then pick myself up off the floor because the audience was screaming. I'd get up and take that bow and forget about being tired. When the curtain went down, the exhaustion hit me again. There were times when I'd bow, the curtain would come down and I'd be halfway down the hallway toward the dressing room, and I'd have to come back. By that time, if I didn't have *Revelations* to do, I'd have my makeup half off. I used to wear false lashes and I'd have danced the lashes off. The glue wouldn't hold because I'd sweat so much. There are pictures of me doing the headrolls, with water coming straight off of me. When I danced, I sweat so much the costume would stick to me. Sometimes my feet and knees would split open and there'd be blood on my costume and the stage.

Even though the first part is gentle, your energy is so keyed and pointed to convey that kind of stillness, it takes as much energy to do that as it takes to do the last section. There, you're allowed to vent the energy that you've internalized in the first two sections. You've got to go all over the place. It's emotionally draining and physically exhausting.

Sometimes when I danced *Cry*, the turban wouldn't wrap properly around my head and it would drape over one eye. Alvin would come backstage and laughingly say, "Blinded yourself tonight." I hear now what Alvin told the women who subsequently danced *Cry*: "Alvin told me that this should be a weight, a heaviness." I look at the dancers with surprise because Alvin never told me that, because it was created on me and I brought the weight with it, whatever the imagery was supposed to be.

I don't fully get what people saw in me doing it. In a way, I think that's what kept my feet on the ground. I think the knowledge might have destroyed my approach to *Cry* if I had understood what people told me.

Alvin and I were like two limbs of a tree, growing and climbing together. He brought his Alvin to *Cry* and I brought my Judi to *Cry*

The way the turban looked when I stood still! *Photograph © Jack Mitchell*

and we grew separately, yet together—there was so much overlap. I don't think that you can create anything unless that happens. I was Alvin's muse. It's a difficult relationship to describe because it was so evident to us.

For the premiere, Alvin ordered a new costume—it was a dress. I'm wide, broad-shouldered, and I have no waist. I have an imaginary waistline which is up around my ears. I felt awful once I saw the dress and worse when I put it on. I knew that it wasn't right. I looked like a walking box. In the afternoon, I came out onstage for the technical rehearsal in this costume. There were invited guests and photographers in the audience. Suddenly, I heard loud groans coming from the house. It was Alvin. In the time between the tech rehearsal and the evening performance, the costume designer had to run out and buy a white leotard, scoop the neck out, scoop the back out, and, because my arms are so long, add a few inches of material to the sleeves.

I wore my "Wading in the Water" skirt. Because it was so old and had been washed so many times, the skirt used to shift on my body. Four years of washing cotton had made it extremely sheer and frail. It was supposed to be worn above my hipbone. The only thing holding the dress up was my rear end. When I got into the skirt, a half hour before the performance, the zipper broke and I had to be sewn into the skirt. If I had to go to the bathroom, I was in trouble.

The seventh woman I taught *Cry* to was former Ailey dancer Deborah Chase. Her second movement was so beautifully fragile, but just before she had to perform it, she became slightly ill—her stomach churned. She was mature enough to use her emotions when she danced, but just before she had to do it, it was gut-wrenching.

There is also the image of me dancing *Cry*—in books, in photographs at the Ailey offices—and a history that goes with it. I try and get dancers over that hump, over the initial fear of doing a dance that has several indelible stamps upon it, so in rehearsal I'll seldom demonstrate a step. I try to pull out their information, to see what their bodies can do. Basically, I just teach the steps. There are tricks I will teach on how to get through certain sections, but whatever I tell them, they know they're going to be flat out on the floor at the end. Nor do I want to give them too many nuances, because those were developed while I danced. Donna Wood, too, created her own subtleties. I don't want a repeat of myself, which I think would be boring, and impossible, in the Ailey company, where there is a wellspring of uniqueness waiting to be tapped.

A recent rehearsal consisted of Debbie Manning, who danced *Cry*, giving steps while I waited until the end of the run-through to speak. "You should be on this angle. Give me more of your torso. You really have to lean over for the lateral." What I offer is very subtle. I don't want to mess with what I know is already wonderful and I know is going to be better with the least amount of interference.

Alvin was that way with me. He let me find my way. He was there as a guide but he let me find my way. It's important, because what you're dealing with is so precious—somebody's inner light. You can snuff it out. It's very exciting to see someone grow right before your very eyes onstage. The dancer can discover a new approach to movement, usually by accident. That growth is a blessing to me. It's why I stay where I am, why I love doing what I'm doing—to see sparks ignite and become a part of the vocabulary that's been building in the body since the dancer took his or her first step.

I added nuances to *Cry* that Alvin liked and left in the ballet. Therefore, they get passed on to each woman who learns it, even if I'm not the teacher. In the second section, during the pause between "I saw a man" and "take a needle full of hard drug," I looked to my side, rather than down. Alvin liked the change and said, "Leave it in."

If I had finished on a phrase too soon, I would bring my arms in slightly and then stretch them out. That was not choreographed. I had put it in because I had arrived too soon. It was the most natural thing in the world for me to do without changing the shape of what Alvin wanted.

It's the tiny details I did naturally that Alvin would take advantage of, and incorporate into the ballet. The steps are all his. I did not choreograph *Cry*. It was not a collaboration. Alvin gave me the steps and I did them in my own way.

Everyone who's ever danced *Cry* helps teach it. If I'm not around, I call on Donna Wood. It took her a couple of years but she really grabbed hold of the part. She grew into it. That's what should happen to me when I see any dance that I've done: you should be able to stun me with what you're doing with dance.

Alvin used to ask my advice on casting *Cry*. He'd say, "What do you think of this person?" because he really didn't want anybody else to do it. Period. A lot of people don't know it, but *Cry* was made on two people. Consuelo Atlas and me. Connie was in the room at the same time I was learning *Cry*, as an understudy. She had only a couple of opportunities to dance *Cry* because the box office began to get calls asking if I was performing. Alvin wanted only one person doing it. She was a "cover."

Initially, there were supposed to be only a few performances but Alvin had to add more because people started going up to the box office and asking if I was dancing *Cry*. After the seventh or eighth performance in a row I woke up and my neck had become immobile. I went to Dr. Bachrach's apartment at 11 A.M. and he shot Novocain into my neck. A few hours later I went out onstage for the matinee. That first performance was great because I couldn't feel anything. By the second performance, though nobody could tell, I was in excruciating pain.

I don't remember the words my grandmother said to me after seeing *Cry* in Philadelphia. I kept seeing, in my mind, flashes of her in the audience. She hadn't seen me dance since I was eight years old, and I wanted to give the performance of my life. I remember feeling and thinking that the dance was like a transfer of spirit from my grandmother to my mother to me. Things were a lot worse when my grandmother was growing up, and she overcame so many hardships.

Cry was about a much older woman than the twenty-eight-year-old Judith Jamison who danced it. Alvin was talking about a much older, mature woman. He was talking about our mothers. My sense of journey was just beginning. I hadn't come that far. I was dancing a woman who had contributed much more. I believe that Alvin thought I had the wherewithal as a dancer to convey that, even in my innocence.

It's very hard for me to watch myself dance *Cry* on video because I don't know what I really looked like doing it. I was working so hard and it looks so easy. Video, like television, steals energy. That's what I think is so interesting about choreographers and directors who are trying to make dance work on television, rather than just flat on. However, in trying to make it come alive, they're in control of where your eye would naturally go if you were seeing it in a theater. They're in control of what you're seeing.

Everything's moving in *Cry*. I brought the full-bodied woman on the stage, nouveau as opposed to deco—Alvin liked well-rounded women with all the curves. I was the antithesis of the small-boned, demure dancer with a classically feminine shape. Rarely do you hear about full-bodied dancers. When people talk about the unusualness of my physique, they usually talk about my height.

Some of the best photographers captured *Cry*. Max Waldman was an amazing photographer. I thought it was very odd how he worked. He had photographed many dancers, including Baryshnikov, Makarova, Cynthia Gregory, and Ulysses Dove. His dance photographs are among the most acclaimed. His studio was rather small and I was thinking to myself about different poses, but Max didn't want me to pose, he wanted me to dance. His camera had motors mounted on each side and he would shoot in rapid succession while I kept moving. Max was a very warm and open person, and I felt very comfortable dancing in his studio. I cherish those photographs. Even though each is a still moment, Max was able to capture the flow.

The only shots that I had seen that grainy before were taken when we were at the Palais des Sports in Paris. Many photographers used camera lenses that were the size of bazookas. Because they were so far away, and because of the lighting, the prints came out grainy. Two days later, for a couple of francs, the photographs were lined up outside the rounded entrance of the Palais des Sports. I'd arrive at the theater, and there I was, in beautiful, huge, blown-up poster-size photographs. I ended up buying them because they were so fabulous and so cheap. I gave one to James Baldwin, who came to see us in Paris. Baldwin, a true man of letters, left an immeasurable imprint on literature and African-American culture. I couldn't get over the odd beauty of his face, his expressive eyes, filled with dignity and humility. I was very pleased to be in his presence and I *loved* that Alvin knew him. Alvin introduced us and I signed the photograph for him. Alvin said he kept it above the mantelpiece in his home in the south of France.

CHAPTER 11

I felt the naiveté of a child in my dancing. I cherished that feeling. I had what I call a knowledgeable naiveté, and it worked for me. When I went out onstage, there was *motor memory* already there. I remember not wanting to know how all my muscles and bones worked together. I didn't want to "break it down." I can go into places totally cold and have things happen that wouldn't happen for anybody else.

Today, if a pirouette goes off balance, a dancer will most likely know the muscles involved. To me, you fell off the pirouette. It's as simple as that. So, my knowledge of the body, even though I studied kinesiology and anatomy, does not interfere with my naiveté and my approach to movement. Of course, this can be terrible sometimes if you need to correct a movement and you want to know what your placement is. What I depended on, as a dancer, was my teacher's eye.

Everything is linked. Movement comes from the center of your body. Spiritually, it comes from the light that is inside. It's supposed to emanate from the very core of your being. If your core is in your kneecap, then have it radiate out from there. You have to think of your body as one instrument from the top of the head to the bottom of your feet. I find that when I'm teaching, I'm constantly telling the dancer that the arm comes from a much deeper point than is anatomically defined on the body. It starts way back there. You want the feeling that it's coming from your "light."

When you get onstage it is an arena, and that arena is a reflection of what is going on in life. Whether you're performing a ballet that is abstract or a dance that has a story to tell, the audience should have a mirror held up before them. I think it is important for a dancer to understand that he or she is that reflection. How can you be that reflection if you know nothing about yourself, if you've explored nothing about yourself, if you haven't tapped into your innermost feelings?

I remember always the need to know myself because if I avoid knowing who I am deep inside then I can't express what I have to say through the talent that I have. I can't say what I need to say as a human being. Dance has its own vocabulary. When you put your foot down in a certain way, everyone knows what it means. You put your foot down in another way and the audience receives the message. You jump and the meaning is clear. You must be clear to me who you are, be generous in the process and try to share what you know about yourself so that you become a recognizable reflection.

I thought that Miguel Godreau was the most incredible dancer I had ever seen. He was short, compact, and very unique-looking. His face looked like a mask. His technique was flawless, he could turn on a dime, and he had incredible musculature. Miguel was a real "creature." And I was absolutely in love with that "creature." Born in Ponce, Puerto Rico, Miguel attended New York's High School of Performing Arts. He joined the Ailey company in 1967, and four years later Miguel and I were married in Oslo, by the justice of the peace in a town hall, in a very quick ceremony. We didn't even have rings. We returned to New York and lived on the Upper West Side and then in

the Chelsea section. But the marriage didn't work and ended nine months later. It was just the wrong time for us. We were flying two different directions, literally and spiritually.

I've always fallen in love with people who are extraordinarily gifted. It had little to do with what was going on inside of them. As a dancer, the first thing I'm dealing with is a physical image. I've been dealing with physical images since I was six years old and I've been dealing with people who have physical attributes that are beyond the realm. You can grab me with your talent in a minute because you have revealed who you really are and sometimes that can be blinding, because sometimes that has nothing to do with what you're putting out when you're not putting out your truth. And that's when I get into trouble.

I thought that Miguel was as extraordinary as any imported dancer. He could do anything. People remember Miguel for "Sinner Man" from *Revelations*. Once he did all three variations from "Sinner Man," the way Alvin used to do, and now Desmond Richardson has the capability of doing them as well. It was absolutely amazing to see.

Miguel and I danced together in Geoffrey Holder's *The Prodigal Prince*. Geoffrey incorporated us into the making of the music for the ballet. We went into a studio and Geoffrey sang and whispered and whistled and blew into a microphone. I slapped on a bass and somebody hit on a drum. Geoffrey made us feel regal whenever we worked with him, that we really were kings and queens.

Geoffrey had presented an earlier version of *The Prodigal Prince* at a concert at the 92nd Street Y, before I joined the Ailey, with Hal Pearson as the Haitian painter Hector Hippolyte, Charlie Blackwell as John the Baptist, and Merle Derby as Erzulie. In the folklore, Erzulie was his inspiration and John the Baptist guided Hippolyte's arm as he painted with a feather. For the Ailey company, Geoffrey chose Miguel to portray Hippolyte, because of what Geoffrey referred to as Miguel's "aristocratic, matador defiant look." Geoffrey dressed him

Miguel Godreau in "Sinner Man" from *Revelations*. *Author's personal collection*

in red. Jimmy Truitte, about to retire from Ailey, was St. John the Baptist. I was Erzulie, as Geoffrey described her to me, "The goddess of love, in Haitian lore, akin to the Virgin Mary in Catholicism." Geoffrey designed the costumes and dressed me in blue, with a crown of white tube roses, twenty-four inches tall, balanced on my head.

I wore myself out dancing next to Miguel. He's five feet five, I'm five feet ten. He moved so much faster than I did, I had to push twice as hard. Anybody tall does, because your movement is going to look lethargic, at the back of the beat, unless you *push*. I never thought of myself as a legato dancer, as an adagio, slow-moving, dancer, though that's obviously what I was.

When the cast changed, John Parks did John the Baptist and George Faison, who was much taller than Miguel, danced Hector Hippolyte. One always makes slight adjustments; you accommodate your partner.

In Lucas Hoving's *Icarus*, John Parks was Daedalus; Miguel, his son, Icarus; and I was the sun. My challenge was the Beni Montresor dress. It had a train that was so long, that on some of the smaller stages it would remain in the wings. I had to turn so that the skirt would wrap around my ankles. Undoing it was difficult, too. I had to keep an expression of no expression. This, while the other dancers backstage would tease me by cracking up in the wings. It was hard to keep a straight face.

The sun basically goes from center stage, ravels, unravels, and then leaves. It took an awful lot of focus to get from one side of the stage to the other and keep that look of an all-seeing sun. It was a wonderful lesson in stillness, which is very hard for dancers to do. There is a fear of not moving. If you're a dancer you want to move, and you think standing still is not moving, but it is. It's a being that you have to assume, so that you're growing as you're standing. You're literally growing. You should leave the stage about a foot higher than when you arrived.

With Miguel Godreau in *The Prodigal Prince*. *Photograph © Jack Mitchell*

Lucas Hoving, former member of the José Limón company, was incredible to work with, as was Chase Robinson, the original Icarus, who taught Dudley Williams, Miguel Godreau, and George Faison the role.

George Faison is tall, about six feet two, *wiry*, very fast with a good jump. He and I always used to do *Toccata* together, as did John Parks and I, which is from Talley Beatty's *Come and Get the Beauty of It Hot*. It's one of the sections I first learned when I came into the company. George Faison was the first person who said to Alvin that although he loved what Alvin was saying choreographically, he wanted to say something else. Alvin said to him, "Well, if you do, then go ahead and do it." He did and started his own company, the George Faison Universal Dance Experience, which lasted about fifteen years. One of the pieces he made for his own company was *Suite Otis* in 1971. Alvin went to see it, and invited George back to put it on the Ailey company. I've always said, "God bless Alvin," because he was generous that way. And God bless George, because George said that he had another voice that needed to be heard, so he went out on his own and did it. I think that's very important. Once he found that voice, Alvin invited him back to put that voice on his company so that George would get the kind of exposure that he would never have gotten anywhere else.

That's the advantage of this company. You put a work on the Alvin Ailey American Dance Theater and you know it will go around the world, you know more people will see it than with any other company, ever, because we tour more than any other company.

Sara Yarborough is a woman with a quixotic personality. Sara was born in Brooklyn, the daughter of dance pioneer Lavinia Williams, who moved her family to Port-au-Prince, Haiti, in order to teach dance education on the island. Lavinia signed a one-year contract with the Haitian public school system and stayed for forty-four years. After

OVERLEAF

In Lucas Hoving's *Icarus*. *Photograph* © *Jack Mitchell*

a year of teaching in the public school system, Lavinia began to teach privately as well, the school located in the same house as the school. Lavinia had made a name for herself with the Katherine Dunham company in the late 1930s and early 1940s. Lavinia, Talley Beatty, Walter Nicks, and Syvilla Fort were all a part of Miss Dunham's company.

Sara was dancing at the age of one. When she was eleven years old, Lavinia, Sara, and Sara's sister came to New York for the summer because Lavinia had the opportunity to teach Haitian folk classes at the Harkness School of Ballet. That summer, her mother enrolled Sara at George Balanchine's School of American Ballet. After the summer program, Sara was offered a full scholarship to attend the school. They were unprepared, it wasn't the right time, and the three of them went back to Haiti. One year later, the offer was repeated and Sara returned to New York to spend the next four years at the School of American Ballet. A Ford Foundation scholarship paid for most of her expenses.

At the time, she was living at the Barbizon Hotel for Women on Lexington Avenue, at the age of twelve. She and Gelsey Kirkland spent four years together in the school. After her fourth year, in 1967, she took a ballet class at the extension school of the Harkness School of Ballet with Benjamin Harkarvy, who became the artistic director of the Harkness Ballet. Sara joined the Harkness Ballet in the fall of 1967, becoming one of the youngest members of the company. Today Sara says, "Benjamin Harkarvy gave me my upper body."

Alvin came the following year to set *Feast of Ashes* on the Harkness company. Brunilda Ruiz was the principal dancer who had the lead role. Sara was in the corps, one of the three street girls. Two years later when Harkness folded up and disbanded, Sara joined the Ailey. The first dance she learned was "Rocka My Soul" in *Revelations*.

Sara learned *The Lark Ascending* with me, the ballet where Alvin tried to give me something new after *Cry*. He wanted to create something completely different for me so that it would not be compared to *Cry*. That was very, very difficult but the advantage in that situation was that he had Sara. In Sara, I saw a delicate look that Alvin wanted.

The way she approached classical ballet was wonderful. When she would do an assemblé and pull it down to a fifth position, it was clean, neat, and beautiful. I did the premiere. Sara was the second cast but the role fit her like a glove, so eventually Sara ended up doing it the most. She was beautiful for Alvin's balletic vision.

I was uncomfortable doing *The Lark Ascending*. I know that Alvin wanted to give me something completely different to do, and there I was in chiffon. I went to Alvin and asked him if I could *not* do it—something I had never done before.

But I was uncomfortable because of *me*, not because of Sara. I could not be the ingenue. When I came onstage you knew I looked like half a battleship. I don't look like a cruiser. Roles are not possessed. Dancers are important but dances don't live unless they're performed. If you don't do it the way the choreographer wants you to do it, the dance isn't going to last. The *dance* needs to continue. If you have in your mind that you do not possess a role, then you don't go through any symptoms of withdrawal when you stop doing it.

I thought Sara was lovely in *The Lark Ascending*. I did it for a season and that was that. There were no parts problems with Sara. We had some personality difficulties but it did not affect what was going on onstage; we were both professionals. I loved doing *Carmina Burana* with her because she always pushed me by being as good as she was. I respected her as a dancer and that would make me dance even harder. Sara had a great extension. To this day, people will come up to me and say, "My God, you used to raise your legs so high." Actually I didn't. Sara had her legs up. Sara was a beautiful dancer. She didn't have the same kind of weight I had in movement. But it didn't matter. When she got onstage, there was an energy level that was palpable.

During Sara's eleven years with the Ailey, she left a few times to guest with other companies, and then returned to Alvin. She took a three-year leave of absence to be with the Joffrey Ballet. For the bicentennial, Gerald Arpino created a duet for Sara and Kevin McKenzie, now artistic director of American Ballet Theatre. She also took a leave of absence to work with Arthur Mitchell and the Dance Theatre of Harlem, who began his company shortly after the death of

Dr. Martin Luther King, Jr. I was so pleased in 1991 when Sara asked me for a letter of recommendation to the dance department at Spelman College, where she now teaches.

In 1972 I was honored with the *Dance Magazine* Award. I brought my parents and grandmother Annie May Brown to New York for the luncheon. One of my proudest moments was seeing Alvin take her by the hand. That was a wonderful time for me, especially in that infamous dress—a black dress that was up to my neck in the front and cut extremely low in the back.

Katherine Dunham presented me with the award and read the citation. When Alvin asked to speak, his words, some of them given here, were so special: "I'd like to say something about Judith, who is an extraordinary person in American dance, in the history of dance. Judith is a lady who came in 1965 to my company. A tall, gangly girl with no hair. I always thought she was beautiful . . . Judith has developed, she has grown; she's a beautiful, extraordinary person. She must say something about the virtues of early training in our dancers. She was trained very young, and we must do something in our country about training all our dancers from an early age . . .

"We must learn, however, to love one another. We must learn to appreciate; we must learn to live; we must learn to give. I salute Judith's grandmother and mother and father. I am only a messenger for the human message; I am only a messenger for what is real, for what is beautiful in mankind. And I think that Judith is a fine representative of that. I thank you all for giving her this wonderful tribute."

Three years later Alvin himself received the award. He certainly deserved the award way before that, before I got mine, certainly. On the day of the ceremony, I went with Lili Cockerille and her husband, Stan Livingston, to Alvin's apartment in Hell's Kitchen to help him get ready. He was to receive the prestigious award along with Arthur Mitchell and Cynthia Gregory.

I'd never seen him so nervous. He tended to wear his insides on the outside. Alvin was always very generous and for the most part unassuming. Once, when we were in Brazil, people were very rude and he became *very assuming* and told them "where they could go." In Brazil we encountered the kind of problem dark-skinned people have all the time, like getting a cab. It happens everywhere, except in Africa.

Alvin was on a mountaintop by himself. I don't think most of us appreciate sometimes how unique we are and how much we're given. We don't pat ourselves on the back for fear of blowing ourselves out of proportion. Alvin was not full of himself; the fullness he did have he gave to others. He was always that way. He never thought it was enough. He never thought he was doing enough or giving enough. In fact, it was just the opposite. He was always giving too much, but he never recognized it.

"Frightened" was not part of the vocabulary of how Alvin felt. I'm sure he was frightened in other situations, but I knew Alvin as a performer, as an entertainer, as the choreographer, with complete command of his craft.

CHAPTER 12

John Butler's first concert was two weeks before Alvin's, at the 92nd Street Y. John told me that after the performance he sat in the hallway near the Kaufmann Concert Hall and let Alvin cry in his lap. They both said, "We're never going through this torment again . . ." But they did and John Butler became instrumental in my life. I loved John's striking appearance and bushy eyebrows. He always looked serious and he spoke quietly and beautifully, his words accurate and precise. His manner reminded me of my favorite pastor at Mother Bethel, Reverend Stewart.

John choreographed *According to Eve* for the Ailey in 1972. When John gave directions, he whispered. There was always a tranquillity in the room that enabled his soft words to be audible. John demonstrated some of his movement and always infused his choreographic gestures with significance. To have watched John bring his hand to his heart was to have watched an artist in command of his craft. The detail was exquisite. Any other choreographer would have needed a series of complicated steps to create the same message.

John worked in simplicity, in purity, and in beauty. He rarely got angry. If he got frustrated, I could tell because he'd knit those brows. His approach to movement was different from that of other choreographers, who might have thrown temper tantrums and "read your beads" if you missed a step. Not John. He worked in a meticulous, pointed way. His works reminded me of the understated ballets of Antony Tudor. John was very specific on characterizations, as opposed to Alvin, who gave less information. Alvin gave me the freedom to add my own nuances; John had already choreographed every last gesture.

In *According to Eve*, I was the first woman on earth, reacting to the slaying of my son Abel by my son Cain. Masazumi Chaya and Michiko Oka danced those roles. Chaya, born in Fukuoka, Japan, joined the Ailey in 1972, after performing with the Richard Englund Repertory Company. He's now my associate artistic director. Chaya spoke little English, but Oka spoke none, so Chaya translated John's words for him. "Did they understand?" John would ask me, and I would ask Chaya, and he would ask Oka. If John's information was verbal, it would be given and returned in a circle—John, Judi, Chaya, and then Oka. If the information was physical, and movement was being demonstrated, we were all able to follow John's instruction. Most of the information was given for Chaya and Oka's difficult pas de deux. John had them in a lot of cantilevered positions. If either of them moved, even an inch the wrong way, the entire structure collapsed.

With *Carmina Burana*, John choreographed an epic ballet, with a haunting score by Carl Orff. It's absolutely exquisite. I loved doing *Carmina Burana*. I always felt very much like the soft woman when I was partnered by Clive Thompson, because most of the parts I got were for strong figures. I was the biggest woman in the company, and I wasn't partnered that much. In *Carmina Burana*, we fit together perfectly. Big as I am, Clive always made me feel light as a feather. That helped physically but also created a wonderful rapport when I felt that reassurance by just looking at my partner.

At Avignon, we performed *Carmina Burana* at the fourteenth-century Palais des Papes, whose open-air courtyard theater is one of

With John Butler, rehearsing *Facets*. *Photograph © Jack Mitchell*

my favorites. One evening, the lights flickered and went out in the middle of the ballet. I had to restart one of the hardest solos that I'd ever done. There were three Horton-like T position balances that I had to execute. I danced Carmen de Lavallade's part in *Carmina Burana*, which is the ballet I first saw Carmen dance live, in 1966, at City Center. I had watched her on television and danced with her in *The Four Marys*, but for *Carmina*, I watched her from the audience. Nobody could dance *Carmina Burana* like Carmen de Lavallade. I had that image in my mind as I danced. It was very hard for me to get my own image. Once I got over that initial hump, I was fine, but that's how strong spirit can be—that's what touches me about dancers. It's what I tell dancers today: "Imitate first, then blow my mind." That was a lesson I learned over the years as a performer.

John came back a few years later and put *Portrait of Billie* on the company. I was uncomfortable in the role of jazz great Billie Holiday. I

gave *Billie* everything I had, but I wasn't vulnerable-enough-looking. I think Billie Holiday must have been quite a strong woman, but fragile inside. It was one role that I really wanted to do. As soon as this monumental woman stood on stage it looked as if I was going to beat up my partner, Kelvin Rotardier. I did not feel soft or vulnerable in *Portrait of Billie*. *Billie* was originally danced by Carmen and John Butler for his young company. Thirty years later, with John in the audience, it was incredible to see Carmen, partnered by Ulysses Dove, dance *Billie* at the 1992 Jacob's Pillow gala. Her artistry only improved with age.

My relationship with John continued when Alvin asked him to create a solo for me—*and what a solo!* He choreographed *Facets* for me in 1976, using music by Bessie Smith, Dinah Washington, Lena Horne, Ethel Waters, and my "homey" Patti LaBelle, to illustrate five facets of one woman . . . or every woman. I had taken John to see Patti, at one of LaBelle's last performances. He had never seen a concert quite like that before. Consequently, the last woman of *Facets* was developed into a LaBelle-like character.

I had to dress onstage. It's hard enough to get into a costume quickly offstage. If you can imagine having to make costume changes onstage, out of a trunk! The costumes had hooks and snaps. For Patti's segment, the last in the ballet, I put on an outrageous fire-engine-red sequined jacket. At the end of this section, I opened the trunk suddenly and manipulated the dress in such a way that it formed a train behind me.

The audience went wild. I pranced off the stage like a peacock. I imagined John and Alvin looked at each other and said, "The girl is out to lunch."

I came back to the center of the stage and took my normal bow. The audience was screaming. The curtain went down, and when it went back up, I raised one hand over my head in my best *Vogue* magazine imitation. The audience went nuts. Every bow went into a different pose. People loved Patti LaBelle and loved the idea that I

In *Facets*. *Photograph © Jack Mitchell*

had transformed myself into these various women. It was a colorful piece and ended with a lot of flair. It was fun to do—particularly the bows.

Alvin didn't have to teach me how to bow. Bowing is the most personal statement an artist can make. For me, bows are supposed to be individual. It's *you* in your purest sense. The bows should be who you are, not some altered state, unless designated by the choreographer. Bows say to me: thank you very much for appreciating what I love to do. In all humility, I bow to you, in all graciousness and in all grandeur.

I could watch Alicia Alonso or Maya Plisetskaya or Carmen de Lavallade bow forever. After they gave everything during a performance, they gave even more. The more generous the bow, the richer the experience is of having seen that person dance.

John Butler choreographed *Commitment* as a birthday tribute to Leonard Bernstein, and I danced that solo to music from Mr. Bernstein's *Mass*. John loves yards and yards of fabric, and for *Commitment* I danced in three different capes—black, white, and red—to signify the vows of a religious commitment.

It was familiar music for me because when Leonard Bernstein's *Mass* was the inaugural event at the John F. Kennedy Center for the Performing Arts in the fall of 1971, Alvin choreographed the dances. Over one hundred people performed on that stage, including two marching bands, twenty soloists, a boys' choir, and an adult choir. Interspersed in all that activity, we danced.

Everybody respected Mr. Bernstein. He was an ebullient character . . . and he had a great head of hair! His flamboyance and personality were wonderful. I remember him vividly from one of our more intense rehearsals. Alvin was working nonstop, and had acquired a choreographic flow, when all of a sudden Mr. Bernstein walked in and stopped everything. He said, loud enough for everybody to hear, "I just wrote this fabulous piece of music," and then proceeded to play. We dancers stood around the piano, sweating and catching our breath, as Mr. Bernstein played with all the histrionics of a unique composer and musician. He said, in effect, "Isn't this wonderful?" That was part of his nature, and that's what made him get up on a podium and conduct as if he were the top part of a tornado. I adored Mr. Bernstein, wet kisses and all. He inscribed a sheet of music from *De Profundis*, one of the sections in which I danced.

I was the lead acolyte in the dance and entered in a pink cape (my grandmother always said that was my best color!), cloche, and robe. I tore out half of my hairline trying to keep the hood on with combs and bobby pins. In one section of prayer, Mr. Bernstein wanted the whole stage to be still. But Alvin gave us instructions on the night of the premiere—*to move!* We were all lying down, then slowly doing easy port de bras, gradually allowing our movement to get bigger and bigger. There was nothing anybody could do, and I don't know if words were exchanged between Mr. Bernstein and Mr. Ailey, but the movement became a part of all our subsequent performances.

At the premiere, a nun stood up in the audience and yelled, "This is sacrilege!" It added to the electricity of the performance.

After the Kennedy Center, we took the *Mass* to Philadelphia and then to the Metropolitan Opera House in New York. The set was too big for the Academy of Music and had to be cut down. The cast changed a bit, but Alan Titus was still the lead. I loved his voice.

I met Tom Ellis during the *Mass*. He was a wonderful singer with a lion's mane of hair. He became a dear friend and was a lifesaver when I was having some personal problems. He came along at the right moment in my life and supported me and held me up and made me feel very special. At his apartment on Canal Street and Broadway, he and his folk-rock group would give parties and perform. Friends would drop by and sing, have something to eat, and, in general, enjoy themselves. It was a great atmosphere. Tom is a respected, fine artist who now lives in California.

It was difficult for Alvin to find partners for me who were my height; however, I was the easiest person to lift. The men always used to tell me that . . . unless I had gained weight. I know how to be lifted because I had studied partnering and I had a huge jump.

With Clive Thompson. *Photograph © Jack Mitchell*

I was blessed with some of the most gifted partners, beginning with my first, Jimmy Truitte. For two years, we danced "Fix Me, Jesus" together and bowed with each other at the end of *Revelations*. In Talley Beatty's *The Black Belt*, Kelvin Rotardier turned me overhead and then caught me by my arm and leg and continued to turn with me. During one performance, he slipped. We were on a gymnasium floor. I was wearing "Mary Jane" jazz shoes, and as he was turning, Kelvin's feet came out from under him; my head cracked on the floor, and you could hear it in the last row of the bleachers. The audience seemed to gasp at once. Alvin came running back. They wanted to take me to the hospital, but I said, "No. I'll be fine." I was stunned, but I was OK. They thought I had a concussion, but who knows what I had, because I didn't go to the hospital.

Hector Mercado partnered me in Brian Macdonald's *Time Out of Mind*, a work I had admired since my days in the Harkness Ballet. Hector was, at the time, one of the strongest dancers in the company. He was also the matinee idol, very muscular, a real hunk. The ballet was very physical. The men had to throw the women over their heads and catch them. The music was ritualistic. I love Brian Macdonald's work. He's now in Canada. He did another work, *Canto Indio*, with Elisabeth Carroll and Helgi Tomasson, who is presently director of the San Francisco Ballet.

Morton Winston and I were dancing partners on and offstage. He was a beautiful dancer whose career tragically ended when a grievous illness resulted in the amputation of both of his legs. He still came to performances to support the company. I had heard of another former dancer who would come to the theater and say, "We didn't do it that way." You can back up and celebrate what came before, but comparisons don't make any sense. It's a different era. You don't sit there and go, "We didn't do it that way. It's wrong." I always say I hope I never grow up in dance and look back on another generation and look forward to another generation and say what they're doing is not valuable. What they're doing is terribly valid because *they're* doing it and they're doing it their own way. Each generation is different.

Clive Thompson, a native of Jamaica, came to the company with a ten-year background of being in the Martha Graham company. Arriving in New York in January of 1960, he entered the Graham school. Two weeks later he received a scholarship; six months later he made his debut with Martha's company. His Graham debut was on Broadway, and Alvin was in the audience, and they were introduced during intermission. Alvin invited him to see a performance of his company at the 92nd Street Y. Alvin and Carmen danced in *To José Clemente Orozco* and *Roots of the Blues*. *Revelations* followed. As Clive says, "I was swept away." In 1965 he began to dance with the Ailey company; by 1970 he danced exclusively with us.

When he walked into Clark Center, I was wearing a black top and slacks. The first time he saw me, I reminded him of a plate of Alaskan king crab, "with legs here, and legs there with just this little center." Because of my high center of gravity, when Clive went to partner me, he realized that he had to place his hands lower on my body than with other women in the company. Clive was one of my strongest partners. He could throw me over his head, which he literally did. We danced together in "Fix Me, Jesus," and on Clive's first tour with the company in *Come and Get the Beauty of It Hot* and *The Road of the Phoebe Snow*. There were so many unusual lifts.

Clive danced Theseus to my Medusa in Margo Sappington's *Medusa*. *Medusa* did not work for me. Sometimes you "lock" into the choreographer. With Margo, who was a friend, I thought that that would have happened immediately, but it didn't. It was very difficult for me to understand Margo's movement quality. I wore a headpiece as big as a lampshade, stuffed with snakes. I couldn't convince myself that that particular headdress worked for me. It worked for the ballet, however. There were other dancers who did the ballet beautifully and who understood the movement.

I don't like masks or heavy accoutrement unless it moves when I'm dancing. If I have twenty yards of fabric, I love it. I don't like something on me that doesn't have a life of its own, that could say what it has to say even if I stand still. There are masked dancers all over the world. Those masks are indicative of being spirit-filled, once you put them on.

CHAPTER 13

He wore a silk bathrobe, silk stockings attached with garters, silk bedroom shoes, and a silk scarf wrapped around his head. No one could look more elegant in these clothes than Duke Ellington. He passed quickly in my vision as Alvin and I walked down a long corridor of his home. I averted my eyes: I thought we had arrived too early and I wasn't meant to see him dressed like this.

Once I got over that, Alvin introduced me and I shook his hand. I was in such awe of Mr. Ellington that I wasn't in control of my words. Instead, a big grin told him what I was feeling. He sat at his piano and played gently—a tape recorder at his side picking up every golden note. Alvin and Duke Ellington were working out music for *The River*, the ballet Alvin choreographed for American Ballet Theatre's performance at the New York State Theatre in June of 1970. Alvin was in such a panic because he needed the music to continue his work, but Mr. Ellington was completely laid back and very calm. "It will be fine. You'll get it. Don't worry," Mr. Ellington told Alvin.

I assisted Alvin at Ballet Theatre's studio. He had previously worked out some of the movement on Miguel Godreau and me. On me, he set "Lake," the section that would be danced by Cynthia Gregory.

"It would be sensational, darrrrrrrling."

Paul Szilard, my agent, had been trying to get me together with Mikhail Baryshnikov, professionally. Paul, a native of Hungary, studied solfège with Béla Bartók in Budapest, and ballet with Olga Preobrajenska and Madame Rousanne, the teacher of Violette Verdy, in Paris. When his dance career was interrupted by World War II, he became an impresario. As such, he brought Dancers of Bali to the United States, toured in the Orient with his own ballet company, of which Nora Kaye, Colette Marchand, Sonia Arova, and Milorad Miskovitch were the stars (1954). He managed the Far East Australian tours of New York City Ballet (1958) as well as American Ballet Theatre. Paul brought the first Broadway production of *West Side Story* to Japan. He is the exclusive international agent for the Ailey company as well as for Alvin's choreography.

Paul became my agent when I began to be a guest artist after the success of *Cry*. Among many appearances, I danced at the Vienna State Opera and the Munich Opera. I would be involved in galas that involved all the classical pas de deux. It was incredible for me to be up on the stage among all those tutus in my white skirt and with my taped music. Everyone else had live music and more elaborate presentations.

At the invitation of Alicia Alonso, I danced *Cry* at an afternoon performance in Havana, Cuba. I had respected and admired Miss Alonso ever since seeing her with Ballet Russe de Monte Carlo when I was a child. Children from the school performed in the gala that night. I sat about twenty seats away from Fidel Castro in the horseshoe-shaped balcony. I would have liked to have said hello, but I couldn't

In *The Mooche*, part of the *Ailey Celebrates Ellington* series: Enid Britten, Estelle Spurlock, myself, Sarita Allen. *Author's personal collection*

leave my seat to introduce myself. I was a guest and couldn't go "charging" my host.

I remember being at one gala where I met Allegra Kent simply because she was in the wings, in a fourth-position split, with her torso flat on the floor. I almost tripped over her. Melissa Hayden was about to do a variation from George Balanchine's *Stars and Stripes* with Jacques d'Amboise. I'll never forget the promenade in développé à la seconde as it's supported with one arm up. When they turned around and faced upstage, almost halfway around, she winked. Miss Hayden was quite an entertainer and, of course, a powerful dancer. She looked as if she was having a good time. It was refreshing to see her so relaxed, because she was secure in who she was and what she could contribute to that evening.

After *Cry*, the media latched on to me. I did several fashion layouts and a lot of publicity. In 1972 I was appointed to the National Endowment for the Arts under President Richard Nixon; however, I was sworn in by Vice President Nelson Rockefeller. I found out later that both Alvin and I had been recommended, but I received the appointment.

Our task at the NEA was to relegate funding. The council was comprised of appointees from different areas of expertise. Nancy Hanks was the chair and guided us. What a dynamic woman she was! She knew how "to chair." A few times a year we'd receive a thick notebook of synopsized proposals put together by the members of the various panels. We'd vote on each proposal. I served with Gregory Peck, Rudolf Serkin, James Earl Jones, and Rosalind Russell, who was so nice and outgoing, so full of energy, even with the arthritis that knotted her hands. I remember fighting hard for Agnes de Mille's Heritage Dance Theatre. "Agnes came before all of us," I said. "She deserves the grant because she's one of the great ladies of the dance world." I thought she deserved the small grant she had requested. I was able to get her grant approved—my way of acknowledging Agnes's contribution to the dance, and thanking her for what she did for all of us.

Another highlight was the barbecue for the committee members at

With Misha and Alvin doing prepublicity for *Pas de "Duke."* © *Jack Vartoogian*

the LBJ Ranch in Texas. Though my plane was delayed and I arrived late, Mrs. Lyndon Johnson, a gracious hostess, waited for me to arrive before the meal began. It was held in an enormous airplane hangar, down the road from the Johnson residence. Though my appointment to the Endowment was to last for six years, I had to resign after four. I kept missing too many meetings due to my scheduling with the Ailey company. The only other person to resign in the Endowment's history was the divine Duke Ellington.

Paul orchestrated my meeting and dancing with Baryshnikov. Paul wanted me to get to know Misha a bit before we worked together, and would take me over to Misha's place on Park Avenue, where Natalia "Natasha" Makarova would be. Ballet master Jürgen Schneider was there, too. We'd all sit down and shoot the breeze. Misha would tell stories about Russia, about ballets that he liked, ones he didn't like, and who was doing what to whom—dance talk. I also met Alexander Minz, who played Herr Drosselmeyer in *The Nutcracker*. We used to hang out after rehearsals. Misha, who had recently defected, was hungry and wanted to test the waters.

Alvin created *Pas de "Duke"* (a part of *Ailey Celebrates Ellington*) in 1976, for a May premiere at City Center. It almost drove me crazy. My nerves were almost gone, and so were Misha's. The evening of the premiere we sat across the street at the local "greasy spoon." The owner of the restaurant was a wonderful man and we all used to go over there to eat, grease and all. It was convenient. Misha said, "Let's go get something to eat." Misha was very jovial and flip with me, in a positive way. As if we didn't have a world premiere two hours later, with the whole world about to descend on us—the first time Judith Jamison and Mikhail Baryshnikov were dancing together. He ordered eggs and I ordered a hamburger patty. He kind of messed with the eggs and I kind of messed with the burger. We didn't say too much. I was very nervous.

We danced *Pas de "Duke,"* a fifteen-minute pas de deux Alvin choreographed to the music of Duke Ellington: "Such Sweet Thunder," "Sonnet for Caesar," "Sonnet to Hank Cinq," "Clothed

Woman," and "Old Man's Blues." It followed the basic pas de deux structure; we danced together, then solo, solo, and coda.

Because so much of Alvin's movement derived from Horton technique, so many things were to be done on an angle. If he choreographed the torso on the angle, that's the way it had to be danced. If your head was supposed to duck down and kiss your knee when you were in a penché arabesque and a contraction, it was supposed to be done that way.

But people go back to what they know. In performance, they are sometimes "safe." You go with what you know, regardless of the shape the movement is supposed to have. Misha straightened up most of the things Alvin had put on an angle. Alvin choreographed laterals and Misha was unfamiliar with them. He would try them in rehearsal, but by the evening of the performance, his movement was straight up and down. But Misha could cover ground! That has nothing to do with height, but with the largeness of the movement and how he filled space. That's why some dancers can do solos, and some can't. He was remarkable.

Do you know how rare it has been for me to work with people who are taller than I? Finding a partner for me was the hardest task in the world for Alvin. Offstage, Misha is a couple of inches shorter than I. Onstage, he grows. From what I heard people say, we looked fine together—he did not look like a midget and I did not look like a giant. Hopefully, we were both sending out so much light you didn't notice. Any dancer worth his or her salt gets bigger than life when onstage. Even I was getting bigger, but it worked. Rouben Ter-Arutunian designed the scenery and the costumes. Misha and I were both dressed in pantsuits, mine black and his white.

Misha and I danced Pas de "Duke" that summer with American Ballet Theatre at the New York State Theatre, and later in Austria. Gelsey Kirkland, Misha, and I once drove around the Vienna Woods together. Gelsey, as she herself has written, was having problems in those days. But when she and Misha danced onstage together they were magic.

Misha was such a different dancer from Nureyev. Rudi was hot to me, a most passionate dancer. What I remember of Misha is that he was very technical. He could do anything, technically. The requirements were not the same for different generations of dancers. It's not that I thought Misha was technically better than Rudi, it's just that he was required to do more. I believe that if Rudi had come along at the same time he would have been required to do more, and he would have done it. My preference is a combination of both.

Alvin never wanted dancers to be parochial-minded. You have nothing to offer onstage unless you've lived your life. Otherwise, you are like a robot on the stage doing steps. Alvin encouraged us to look at other disciplines, to know people other than dancers, to talk to writers or architects, and to visit museums. He encouraged everyone to experience his or her life.

I tried to get the essence of a characterization directly from the choreographer. I relied on what Alvin told me. He was a walking biographer, dictionary, and encyclopedia. Alvin had started the movement in *The Mooche*, before suggesting that I do a little research on the life of Bessie Smith. Alvin hadn't given me that many roles where I portrayed historical figures. I read a couple of items about her life—most tragically, how she died by the side of the road because a Black person could not be taken to a White hospital. Eventually, I went to a film archive to watch a very old film of hers. It wasn't very good. It wasn't a distillation of her. She played a woman who is done wrong, who leans on a bar and sings the blues. It was so unlike listening to her music, because she was a magnificent singer. This Hollywood vehicle did not bring out the truth about Bessie Smith. It didn't aid in my development of her character in *The Mooche*.

CHAPTER 14

José Limón was breathtaking—the face of heaven. You could see the spirit rise in his face. Two days before the Ailey company opened on Broadway, in 1969, I saw the Limón company for the first time. I saw one of the pieces that would become part of the Ailey repertory, *Missa Brevis*, danced by Mr. Limón.

I had been dancing *Cry* for five years when I was given a breath of fresh air by one of Mr. Limón's dancers, Louis Falco. My career has been a series of highlights, a series of real gifts from Alvin and from other choreographers. Nothing, I thought, would satisfy me as much as *Cry*.

Louis was exquisite, and I always listened carefully to his every word; he had *such* a sexy voice. Louis Falco created his performing ensemble, Louis Falco and Featured Dancers, in 1967, after dancing regularly with the Limón company. In 1968 he premiered his ballet *Huescape*, with Juan Antonio and Jennifer Muller, at Jacob's Pillow. I needed a work to do and Louis choreographed *Caravan*. Michael

Kamen wrote a "rock" treatment of classic Ellington scores, including "Sophisticated Lady," "Satin Doll," "A Train," and the title piece,
"Caravan."

One solo in the beginning of *Caravan* gave me the blues because it
didn't feel organic to me. One step didn't connect to the next. It was
as if all the letters of the alphabet were rearranged into another
language. It was all over the place. It took forever for me to learn
Louis's vocabulary. Once my body learned it I was fine. It was a new
way of moving. Louis and I had a strong rapport. I loved working with
him; he was so beautiful.

I was dancing *Caravan* with Warren Spears when my dog, Emma,
was stolen, December 14, 1976. I was in the middle of the pas de deux
when I started crying all over Warren. It takes a lot of breath to keep
sniffling. I ruined my breathing, reddened my eyes, and my makeup
ran all over the place.

When the Ailey studios were on East Fifty-ninth Street, there was
a pet store across the street. Emma, a two-month-old Great Dane, was
in a cage. When they took her out of the cage for me to pet, she
couldn't stand up on her legs. It was terrible.

Emma was stolen out front of a supermarket on 102th Street and
Broadway. I tied her up as I usually did, went into the store to get some
salmon. When I came back outside, there was no dog. One hundred
forty pounds of dog not there. I was in a panic.

The newspapers ran stories about Emma. A local television station
sent a reporter to my apartment. He walked in and immediately asked,
"Is this a publicity stunt?" I was in a state of shock but went ahead
with the interview in the hopes that it would help me get Emma back.
Two weeks later *Newsweek* ran the story in its "newsmaker's" page,
with a picture of Emma and me.

A few days later the police received a call from a woman who
worked with drug addicts in a food program at the Cathedral of St.
John the Divine. She recalled that two people came in with a gorgeous
Great Dane, claiming they were taking care of it for friends. She didn't
want to break the trust she had built up with these two people, so she

Louis Falco. *Photograph* © *Jack Mitchell*

wouldn't say who they were. So there went my dog, never to be seen again.

As artistic director of the Ailey, I brought Louis Falco's playful ballet *Escargot* into the company, in 1991, not just because I thought it was a delightful piece and I loved the music, but because I knew Louis was ill and I wanted to honor him before he was no longer with us. Once he got to a certain point in the choreography, Louis was comfortable with people coming into the studio to watch the rehearsal. The dancers had a chance to do it one day for our outreach program when we brought students from the outlying boroughs to experience a day at Ailey. They sat around the edges of the studio floor spellbound. They watched as the dancers practically *flailed* themselves, as they took their daring throws and jumps. Louis always had nonstop movement and dancers thrown in every direction possible. The young people were enthralled and the dancers had a captive, mesmerized, first audience.

When Louis came into rehearsal, his assistant demonstrated most of the movement. It dawned on me that Louis was older, and that his body couldn't necessarily do everything that it used to do. Louis had the most incredible technique. Louis was *sprung*. He had a second-position plié that was elastic. He was completely turned out. He was a mover, and he was so gorgeous to watch. A beautiful mouth and eyes and voice . . .

That first day of the rehearsal of *Escargot*, I noticed Louis was thinner. He looked preoccupied. That's when I knew something was wrong. Louis spoke to the dancers about the piece and demonstrated some of the steps. He was very gentle to most of the dancers. He had a problem with one dancer who came to me and said, "Louis is giving me a hard time. He's picking on me." But as artistic director I had to consider the bigger picture, that Louis wasn't well. We dealt with it. I really wanted *Caravan*, but we couldn't afford it. It costs four times as much as it originally had in 1976. One of the last things I got to say to Louis, in December 1992, was, "The dancers just performed *Escargot* and they were wonderful . . ." He died shortly thereafter.

* * *

American-born John Neumeier recently celebrated his twentieth anniversary as artistic director of the Hamburg State Opera Ballet. He began to choreograph when he was a young dancer with John Cranko's Stuttgart Ballet. My first meeting with John, and the first time I saw his company, was for a performance of *Third Symphony by Gustav Mahler* with Zhandra Rodriguez, the ballet he choreographed to Mahler's thrilling music. I've always admired John's ability to tackle difficult scores, not only half a dozen of Mahler's symphonies, but sacred music as well. It was also the first time I saw Kevin Haigen dance. At "half hour," John's assistant, Frau Phitzner, took me to John's backstage office. It was very dark and very mysterious. John seemed to infuse all common gestures with drama. I couldn't wait to see how that translated onstage.

In 1976 I began my work with John on *Josephslegende*, the ballet he choreographed to Richard Strauss's score. Potiphar's Wife, who is not named in the Bible, tries to seduce Joseph, but Potiphar accuses Joseph of trying to seduce his wife. Joseph gets beaten and smitten *and tortured* and finally an angel comes to protect him. He is saved from Potiphar's wrath, becomes blessed of God, and ends up running Potiphar's household.

As the ballet began, Kevin Haigen (Joseph), who had one of the most sculpted bodies I had seen to date, entered rolled in a rug. His dancing was mercurial, and he was "pumped and cut." He had an effervescent personality and it was wonderful to watch him dance as if there were a wellspring inside of him. During this entrance, Franz Wilhelm (Potiphar) and I sat on gold benches, at opposite ends of the stage, angled on the outer edges of the downstage area, diagonally facing upstage. Kevin was doing his variation for our pleasure. It was absolutely breathtaking. Right behind us, in the Vienna State Opera House, was the ballet orchestra. Strauss sometimes reminded me of the music of Disney's Tinker Bell. Strauss puts celesta in his music, a percussive instrument which is very ethereal and makes me think of cherubs.

OVERLEAF

Louis Falco's *Caravan*. © *Jack Vartoogian*

For the first two weeks of rehearsal, Kevin practiced his solo in the afternoon, and in the morning we worked on our pas de deux. Kevin is about five feet seven and he could pick me up over his head and hold me straight up. He was strong as an ox, but in his dancing there was a lyrical quality and lightness. On the Thursday of the second rehearsal week, while working on the pas de deux, a fairly strenuous variation, I jumped, came down, and landed on my ankle. It was Kiel Auditorium all over again! Apparently, I like to sit on my ankles.

I ended up shredding the muscles on the outside of my ankle. The muscle popped. I was lying on my back and my foot was involuntarily twitching from trauma. I was groaning and rolling on the floor in agony—but the beat went on. While Kevin ran around trying to find ice and help, John got up, came over to me and looked concerned, and then returned to his seat. His creative process didn't just stop because I fell on the floor. I loved John's combination of concern and nonconcern, because he had a ballet to finish. And one of his lead dancers was on the floor, in agony.

They took me to the doctor to have my ankle wrapped and put in a cast. They immobilized it. The next day I was going home and it was the first and last time I had to be wheel-chaired through an airport. It was great. It was before the airports had all moving sidewalks. I was wheel-chaired from plane to plane and I loved every minute of it. I was very worried about my ankle because John, Kevin, and I were on a roll, and wouldn't have the opportunity to regain that momentum for three or four months. I also had to retain all the choreography while I threw myself back into the diverse Ailey rep.

When I came back, I saw Dr. William Hamilton, who removed the cast and told me to return to class, to work slowly and carefully, but to do as much as I could. Within two weeks I was dancing with the Ailey company and I didn't miss a beat.

Months later, I returned to Hamburg for the second rehearsal period to finish *Josephslegende*. In between our first two rehearsals, John went to Vienna to teach the State Opera Ballet corps their roles.

With Emma, my favorite dog, enjoying our usual romp in Riverside Park. She thought she was a dancer. *Photograph by Bill King*

This was a huge cast, with four principals. Ray Barra, dancer and ballet master, was John's faithful and meticulous assistant director; he always showed great concern for the dancers. A few weeks before the premiere, we went to Vienna to put all the components of the ballet together, including costumes.

They were exquisite. I went for countless fittings and had two double sets of costumes. It was overkill. The costume was a unitard with jeweled chiffon panels, front and back. One was orange and one was white. The designer was Viennese. He wanted to add gold bikini pants with little jewels on top of my unitard. Instead of me doing my usual, polite "I don't think so," I went "Not in this lifetime." Of course, I incurred his wrath, and when it came time to give out sketches, he gave Kevin a sketch of his costume but he didn't give me one of mine. He didn't speak to me from that point on.

Backstage was fairly elaborate, too. We were in the wings, four legs up, waiting for our entrance. Members of the crew walked back and forth, opening the ventilators, to keep the air clean and moist, which is done mostly for opera singers. It didn't help Kevin too much when there was lint in the rug and he wanted to sneeze when he was unrolled! There was a cue man in the booth prompter's box who turned pages and said "Now" to the extras to get them onstage at the right time. All this was done in German, of course, but I caught the intent of the words. The corps was in the wings in the front, and we principals were in the back, in the dark, and saw all this activity going on around us. The curtain rose; the overture began. Then I got wheeled on behind an unlit scrim. When the music cue came on, and the lights were about to hit, I assumed the position.

The preparation for my entrance had me sitting on a throne, which was on tracks, with two women on either side of me who were my attendants. We used to talk like crazy before we were wheeled on. One girl held a bunch of grapes against her cheek and the other was fanning me. It was quite dramatic. It was illustrative of the kind of fantasies you have about story ballets. In Europe, they can afford to put on elaborate productions: Béjart did that as well.

With Franz Wilhelm as Potiphar in *Josephslegende*. *Author's personal collection*

I was supposed to be queenly and disturbed. My character was bored, didn't want to be there, and couldn't stand being queen. I had a ball doing it. It was fun to act her role, especially when Kevin made his entrance. He bowed to me with his hands extended. It was so melodramatic. John knows how to *work* drama. I looked like a frozen queen, and Kevin was gorgeous. At the end of his variation, I went to touch him, but couldn't, because of Potiphar.

The very first time we did the ballet I was very relaxed. I didn't have time to get nervous. It was a dress rehearsal before the premiere. That was fine. In New York when you have a dress rehearsal, you don the costume and put on a little makeup, you know the photographers are there, and you dance. Now I was sitting in my dressing room in Vienna. I put my full face on. I had three dressers and two hair people, for my two inches of hair! At the State Opera, everyone is there to wait on you hand and foot. *It's called Diva Time!*

I sat in the dressing room, makeup and turban on—actually a *gele*, a Nigerian headdress wrapped from long, colorful material. John liked the way it looked on me, so we kept it. I wrapped and tucked it in, and the costumer sewed it tight so it would stay on. The next thing I knew I heard static coming from the overhead intercom, really heavy static. I didn't know what was wrong with it; besides, it was out of my reach.

I left my dressing room, which was stage left, and went into the hallway. I was about to go out onto the stage when someone grabbed my arm. In that instant, I realized that it was a full house. They sell minimally priced tickets for the dress rehearsal. So we had a full house at eleven-thirty in the morning for what I thought was going to be an unattended performance.

I ran to John and said, a bit frantically, that I hadn't known about this. John was calm and Kevin kind of got a kick out of it. Kevin and I had had dinner the night before, and he had not said a word. My nerves are different at eleven-thirty in the morning than they are at eight at night, when I've had time to prime myself and think about what I'm going to do, and get nervous if I'm going to get nervous. But at eleven-thirty in the morning, there was no time for that.

We were very confident in what we were doing. We knew that the

At John Neumeier's home in Hamburg, October 1991. *Author's personal collection*

ballet was wonderful. I was energized. John spoke to the audience first and reminded them that during a technical rehearsal the performance stops and starts. It's the very same thing I do with the Ailey audience during tech rehearsals at City Center—usually a small, invited group—but the Vienna State Opera was full, from floor to ceiling.

When John finished speaking, we danced and brought the house down. That meant that for the world premiere, the next night, if anything, we'd have to pump ourselves up so as not to get overconfident, since we knew that it was a hit. They just yelled and screamed and bravoed and there were twenty-minute curtain calls, paging, the whole bit. They would not let us off that stage. The reviews came out and they were raves.

It was quite an experience to be in the aura of this particular opera house, which possesses a distinguished reputation and history. I'm in an institution that's thirty-five years old, with its own vibrancy and its own life and its own history and its own roots. It's more exciting for me now, I think, than when I was dancing.

When you walk the halls of the Vienna State Opera as a guest artist, the children that are studying ballet in the school have to stop in their tracks, curtsy, say *"Grüss Gott,"* which means good morning and god bless. And then when you pass they're allowed to continue. I'm talking about twenty girls all dressed in little pink tights, with their pink shoes and their hair up in buns. The first time it happened I was walking in one of my usual getups, tights and a baggy sweater, and I saw them. And as they approached, I thought, "Don't they look cute." Then all of a sudden the whole herd of them just stopped and went, *"Grüss Gott."* I was impressed.

And then I realized that this was the etiquette of the institution. If you were a young person learning your craft, you had great respect for the older, *wiser* performer. Teachers were held in total respect and awe. I was the star dancer from America and I was treated as such.

Karl Musil, a beautiful man, danced the role of the angel. There was such a marvelous duet that he and Kevin did. John could make the most fabulous duets and trios, lyrical, beautiful, and sensuous. Very clean and very clear. You knew, choreographically, the intention. I was very inspired by John and how he moved men onstage together. That created a strong impression, and choreographically came out in my ballet *Forgotten Time*, where I had two men entwined and moving around each other. There was a realization that the two men could partner each other, as opposed to a man partnering a woman. I have many men in the Ailey company, and had in the Jamison Project, who can lift other men over their heads. That's when I found out that a lot of men liked being lifted, though many are still afraid, and will scream or buckle in the air. But once they get used to it, they're fine.

We filmed *Josephslegende* for UNITEL. In the last part of the ballet, I had to run backward. That was the hard part. I started off slowly and then had to pick up speed. I was sweating bullets, running backward on the Vienna State Opera stage, in a circle, maybe four or five circles. In the libretto, it says that Potiphar's Wife strangles herself with her pearls. In the end I had to look distraught, to say the least, and I finished on my knees.

If you take a close look at the UNITEL film, you can see that I'm heavier in the last part than in the beginning sections. That's because they had to refilm the darn thing and I had to practically starve myself because I knew that film had put about ten pounds on me. I spent two weeks preparing for the reshooting.

In those two weeks I was waiting for John Neumeier and Kevin Haigen to arrive. I was stuck in Vienna with an American actor who one evening took me to dinner. He was doing a film at the time. It was the first time I had ever seen a grown man sit in a restaurant and eat a piece of fish with his fingers. Terrible table manners, and not even that good-looking. He then asked me if I wanted to take a sauna with him. I looked at him like "Are you kidding?" And he couldn't get over that. He thought he was the cat's meow. Anyway, I wasn't purring.

I would go out with the UNITEL crew, but I also spent a lot of time alone in my room, reading. I'd eat crackers, cheese, and mustard. That was it. It was ration time. I said to myself, "You are going to look *tight* on this screen."

When we began filming, Kevin had to do his variation eight or nine times. After he had danced perfectly, there was a mechanical problem with the cameras and he had to repeat his variation once again. And that variation is difficult, just plain old hard, and he kept "whipping it off." He finally danced it the way John wanted it—it was absolutely perfect—but the camera didn't capture it. You only dance that way a couple of times in your life. He was in tears and we had to have a little cheer-up talk.

I was concerned, as well, with the lighting. You cannot light a dark brown-skinned person with the same kind of lighting you use with pale faces. The Black person will look featureless because you won't be able to see him or her. We were filming the second section, where I have on a white dress, up against my brown skin. They finally realized that they had to *throw* some light my way.

When it was completed, I joined the Ailey company on tour. Soon after, I received a telegram saying that because of another technical error, they needed me to return to Vienna so that they could reshoot it.

But by this time I had already gained back the ten pounds I had lost to do the film in the first place. I had to go back there and try and "suck it all in" while I was running backward.

We performed the ballet in Vienna, Hamburg, and Munich . . . which was probably the largest stage I've ever danced on, outside of the stadium in Dakar, in 1966. We also performed at the Brooklyn Academy of Music. When I couldn't participate because of scheduling, I suggested to John that Donna Wood was capable of dancing the role beautifully, so she stepped into it. Later I recommended Carmen de Lavallade, but she almost killed me because I had told her it was a "piece of cake," don't worry about it. But she has a bad hip, and when she got over there it was harder than she thought it would be. But she was fabulous.

I always loved it when people showed you how much they liked a performance. Fans would get you at the stage door. Many carried pictures that they would ask you to sign, or they would hand you envelopes that were self-addressed and stamped, so that you could sign them later, then drop them in the mail.

CHAPTER 15

The first time I saw Maurice Béjart and his company was in 1966, when Alvin took a couple of us to a performance in Paris at the Palais des Sports. Alvin knew Maurice. That evening, we entered the Palais des Sports in the dark, so I had no idea of the enormous size of the arena. We came in late, in the middle of Béjart's *Rite of Spring*—the end of the first section, where it looked as if a hundred men were onstage. Michaël Denard was dancing the lead. My mouth just hung open. It was absolutely astonishing to see that many men doing the same step and exiting upstage right. Béjart has such a wonderful talent for getting *fierce* men in his company. I always admired that!

A few years later, Alvin took me to dinner with Béjart. I thought Béjart looked Svengali-like, with his hard green-blue eyes, his very riveting presence and stance—equal parts fire and ice. Very stocky, very intense but likable. He was warm but at the same time had this steely exterior. I was immediately taken with him. He seemed a generous man. He hears a different drummer and goes with the beat.

His works are so filled with fantasy. You don't have to try to imagine what's in his mind: it's all right up there on the stage. Béjart has the gift of translating his dreams into the dance. I always adored his work. They always got my attention. I remember going to Madison Square Garden to see his *Nijinsky, Clown of God,* which was done in the round. He created a huge puppetlike Diaghilev and separated Nijinsky's personality into five components, based on Nijinsky's most famous roles.

I absolutely admired one of his principal dancers, Jorge Donn, a most exquisite and beautiful man. He's passed away now, but his dancing was magical. The men in Béjart's company wore as much makeup as the women. I loved that back then.

Paul Szilard arranged for Béjart to choreograph a work for me, *Le Spectre de la Rose.* That ballet, first choreographed by Michel Fokine for Diaghilev's Ballets Russes in 1911, starred Vaslav Nijinsky and Tamara Karsavina. Two years before, he had created a ballet for ballerina assoluta Maya Plisetskaya. *Le Spectre de la Rose* premiered at the Théâtre Royal de la Monnaie in Brussels, with his Ballet of the 20th Century. We performed it next in Paris at the Palais des Sports and then at the Minskoff Theatre in New York. I danced with Patrice Touron; he got the chance to grand-jeté through the window. The whole theme of the ballet was so "out there." I was in an evening gown and I came in holding my slippers as if I had just come home from your basic dream date. Patrice looked as if he could have been Dracula, with white makeup on his face and a high-collared cape. The premiere went well, but not quite as well as I wanted it to go.

At one point before the premiere, Béjart asked me if I wanted to do *Bolero*, one of his signature works. It had been danced by a woman before, but usually it was danced by a male. It was Donn's piece. I hate to do a work that's already been done by someone else who's currently dancing it, because of the inevitable comparisons. Even though I could have brought my Judith Jamison persona to the role, I immediately felt

Maurice Béjart . . . a special mentor. *Photograph © Jack Mitchell* that Béjart thought the *Spectre* was not going to work, so he needed a cover. I preferred not to do it.

As a choreographer, Béjart did step for step. He would show something and then one of his dancers would demonstrate. For the dancers, his movement was organic; for me, it wasn't. Choreographers are all different and you try to understand how to unlock the combination of what they're trying to give you.

In Paris, Maurice took me to Club Sept, which used to be a famous hangout for movie stars and celebrities, with a disco underneath and a restaurant on top. Sophia Loren was there, right across from us, checking her makeup in the silverware. From a little suede sack Maurice took out a ring, placed it on the table, and started kicking it around. He said, "It's nice, isn't it?" He put it back in the sack and said, "It's for you," and passed it to me. I took it out and in the dark it didn't look like much.

When I finally got the history of the ring I thought it was too valuable to wear and I put it in a safe place. It is a three-hundred-year-old Italian poison ring of braided gold. The slivers of the fleur-de-lis are sapphires and emeralds. The workmanship is exquisite, down to the little men supporting the base. The back of the ring is ceramic.

One day, at the Palais des Sports, Maurice and I watched his company rehearsing *The Firebird*. I'll never forget Maurice telling me that you could always tell the older dancers from the younger ones because their shoulders were "up." As you aged, he said, you developed a strain that caused you to raise them involuntarily.

He also pointed out that you could tell the parts of a dancer's body he or she disliked because of what was worn in rehearsal. Injury also played a part. Béjart's dancers always wore a shawl here, a leg warmer there, something on the elbow, a rag on the calf, a scarf or a sweater. They were all layered with little bits of things to "keep them warm." Now in the Palais des Sports, you had every reason to want to keep warm, but there was something very raggedy chic about what they had on. According to Béjart his dancers were wearing different things around what they wanted to hide.

Sure enough, one dancer didn't like the width that he had across the waist, so he wore a shawl wrapped around his middle. Or somebody's calves were not as big as he wanted them to be, so he wore leg warmers around the calf muscle. Or, if the feet weren't too well articulated, the dancer had on thick leg warmers around the ankle.

In 1982 Maurice Béjart and Léopold Senghor, former President of Senegal, invited me to come and visit and observe Moudre Afrique, Béjart's school in Dakar. In addition to his Moudre in Belgium, Maurice had opened this school, in conjunction with the Senegalese government, as a place where dancers from West Africa—Chad, Nigeria, Ghana—could study.

I flew from New York but was not allowed to fly directly into Dakar because there had been a terrific sandstorm that had just caused a plane crash. I was late, so we went to Abidjan, Ivory Coast. I arrived in Dakar the next day, but the hotel had already given away my room.

They spoke French. I didn't, and no matter whose name I dropped, President Senghor or Maurice Béjart, they weren't impressed. I stood there in a panic with my bags. Then the hustlers started to approach me. I was desperate and asked a young man if he knew of any other hotels. Last time I was there, in 1966, I had stayed with the Ailey company in a hotel that was not exactly four-star.

After a couple of hours of this, the concierge promised me a room for the next day. I still didn't know what I was going to do for the night when in walked Maurice, saying, "Where have you been?" We hugged and I was immediately reassured when I looked into Maurice's extraordinary eyes.

I stayed a week and observed dances from the different regions of Senegal, which had a hundred different dialects of dance. To return the favor, I got up and taught Talley Beatty's *Toccata*. Dou Dou N'daye Rose, the master drummer of Senegal, invited me to his home—a complete village. He had four wives and thirty-two grandchildren. We sat on the covered floor very comfortably. His wives made the meal, and served it in big bowls, which were placed on mats.

The meal was huge chickens surrounded by rice and vegetables. You ate with your right hand, never your left, using the thumb and the first two or three fingers. I didn't know *what* I was doing. First, each person got a finger bowl, which stayed throughout the meal. Then

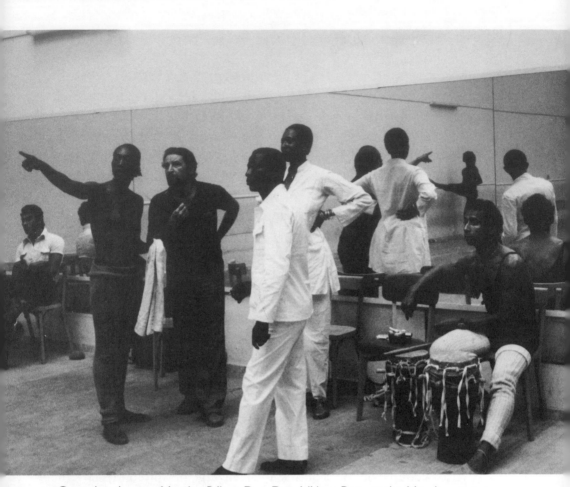

Germaine Agogny, Maurice Béjart, Dou Dou N'daye Rose at the Moudre. *Author's personal collection*

there was a towel for a napkin. You took the meat and you scooped up the rice. It was wonderful, and showed a different kind of grace than is used in the Western world with forks and knives and spoons—that is, if it's done properly. Except I made a mess of it. As far as finger etiquette was concerned, I failed.

Every time I ate some chicken, there was a mess all over my lips, things happening in my lap, and I'd take the towel and try to subtly clean up. No one else had a mess, no grease on the napkin, nothing. Everybody's hands were clean, perfectly free of debris. Nobody touched a towel until the end of the meal. Mine was sticky, with little fingerprints all over the cloth. My hosts appreciated the fact that I didn't know what I was doing. They began to tear the chicken and place it in front of me. At the end, we dipped our fingers in the water.

We drank bright pink-red hibiscus juice, served with sugar. Muslims do not drink alcohol. The evening was very gentle and quiet. The next day I told Dou Dou I wanted to take a drum class. Not a chance!

It was very much like the time I went to Hawaii and wanted to see real hula, not what was danced in the clubs. I was taken to a genuine master hula teacher. She was rather old and large and sat in front of the class. I told her what a pleasure it was for me to be there and that I would like to take at least one class. She looked at me and said, "No."

Of course she said no. I compare it to a dancer adept in ballet entering an advanced Horton class without having any Horton technique. I'd tell that dancer "No." You have to start from scratch. You start from the beginning. You have to act like a baby when you're learning a new technique. Act like you know nothing within that technique, because you don't. At first I was put off by the hula teacher's response, but after I thought about it for a while, I realized she was right. I sat and watched the class, which was phenomenal. The movement looked so difficult.

So back at the Moudre Afrique with Dou Dou N'daye Rose. When I said that I'd like to take class, he said, "Why don't you watch it first."

I went to Gorée Island, which was the last place many slaves were kept before they were packed inhumanely into ships. The Dutch lived there, in sparkling, brightly painted homes. But once you descended to the dungeons, it was hell. As soon as one walked down there, the suffering of the slaves was still palpable. You could feel the pain—its memory was in the air. I imagined it was like Auschwitz. In places where people suffered, there's a residue of spirit you can actually feel.

When I descended, my breath almost halted. Tears came automatically. You don't even have to try to cry, because we've been through it for such a long time, so that it's blood. You don't have to make an effort to remember. It's in your genes.

Across the room, I spotted a peephole no bigger than a quarter, through which you could see the ocean, blue and vast. You could see the last thing the slaves saw, their own land getting smaller and smaller until it was all water, the land literally removed from beneath their feet.

You could cut it with a knife, the air was so thick down there.

I spent the night on Gorée Island, in a house that belonged to a friend of Maurice's, one of the few Black people to own property on Gorée, because it had become very chic, like SoHo, where nobody could afford to live. The house was lovely, surrounded by bougain-villea and trellises filled with flowering vines. We were so close to the ocean that all you had to do was open the door and there it was.

I had my hair braided on Gorée. It takes anywhere from six to eight hours, depending on how simple or how elaborate the braid, and how many people are working on your hair. People ask me how I could sit for so long and I explain that braiding is a very social art. It's not just about your hair. It's a social event, just as it is many times in the West. You meet people, you discover things about them, you carry on a conversation, you have a good time; it's an event. I had *yoss* woven into my hair, which was put in three little buns, with one antique amber bead in each bun.

My return to Dakar was under different circumstances than my first two trips to Senegal in 1966 and 1967. Now, I was under the arm of Maurice Béjart and the former President of the country, which still hadn't gotten me a hotel room when I needed one. Regardless, I loved how rich the indigenous dances were, and the eagerness with which the dancers learned ballet and modern. The variety of hairstyles and dress added to the rich heritage. I revisited movements I was born with, but had been away from for so long. Still, they're ingrained in me or in a child on a corner doing the latest dance. It's there, you can't deny it.

Having my hair braided in Dakar. *Author's personal collection*

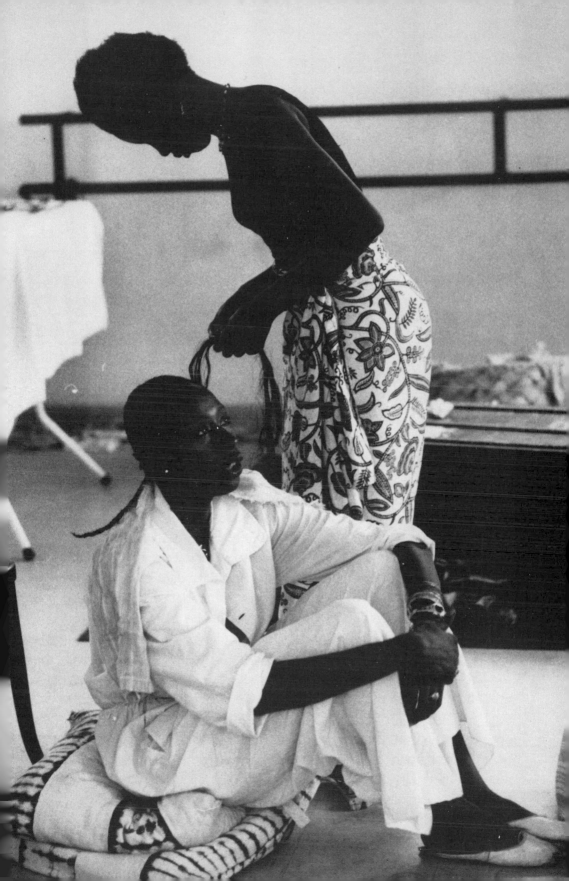

CHAPTER 16

As a dancer I ignored injury whenever I could. Nowadays, most dancers take care of their bodies much better than we did; they are very health-conscious and try to eat correctly. However, when you're on the road with the Ailey company, it's a little difficult because of our touring schedule. In fulfilling our obligation to make dance accessible, we go into cities and into theaters where other dance companies wouldn't. Alvin always believed that dance should be taken to where it was needed the most, unless it was an impossible situation that would have endangered the dancers.

The one time when I thought I knew where my body was in space was when I cracked the ball of my femur. George Faison and I had an accident. We were trying to figure out how to do a lift and then how to get me down. It was a fabulous lift—I acted as if I were lying sideways on a chaise longue. George held me over his head, straight on, and ran. The hard part had been to figure out how to get me down from there. I kept getting down strangely and I guess this bone decided to do what it wanted to do—I broke my leg. We weren't in a company rehearsal. We were just playing around and having a good old time.

As therapy, I had to take floor barre from a marvelous woman named Zena Rommett. I relearned how to work correctly. I did a ballet barre on my back. Then I went to the barre and stood up and everything aligned and adjusted. And then I came to center floor. It required a very correct way of moving and Zena got me back on my feet again. Zena has saved so many dancers from future injury. She only wishes that dancers would come to her sooner so they can be working correctly all the time. Kathy Grant teaches another kind of physical therapy that can emotionally heal dancers. She's quite a mentor. I've had to have her call on dancers to get them out of emotional slumps. A dancer is a spirit manifested in physicality, so that spirit has to be taken care of. Neglect it, and you get a robot.

When I jumped back into the repertory of the Ailey company, however, I had to throw caution to the wind. Instead of stepping out and taking a chance to go further, I found myself stepping into piqué arabesque under myself. It took time . . .

I loved working with Ulysses Dove, though it almost killed me. I had had the accident with George Faison the year before. Dr. Hamilton inserted four steel pins through the crack in the ball of my femur. If I had landed on the leg too hard or incorrectly, the leg would have splintered. Dove knew all that. I favored one side of my body because of it. If my best side was turning right, he'd give me turns to the left. He gave me double tours on the knee—you could hear my knees crack at the back of the theater. When was the last time you saw a woman do a double tour on the knee? He gave me a series of those in his ballet *Inside*. We fought the first day of rehearsal and the second day and the third. I was giving him a hard time. In all exasperation he said, "I'm trying to give you something new."

When he said that, I realized I had been resisting and my body language was saying no. I made a conscious decision to do the steps rather than fight, knowing that I could shatter my leg. Either you think you are going to shatter your leg or you get it completely out of your

Working with the one and only Ulysses Dove on his ballet *Inside*. © *Bill Hilton*

head. I ended up with technically the hardest solo I ever danced. The most difficult solo was *Cry* because it's about dance, not just the technique you need to do it. The transcendence of technique makes it look easy. That's the whole idea. But shortly after *Inside*, I retired.

Inside was the last solo that I ever did with the Ailey company. I admired Dove because even though he knew that I had four steel pins in my left thigh, he presented me with a choreographic challenge. As I've always said, you either do it or you don't. You don't enter a dance studio and say, "I can't do that." If you do, then why are you in the studio in the first place? So, he ignored the fact that I had anything in my hip and said, "Let's do it," which was the right thing to do.

Ulysses Dove has a unique movement vocabulary, visible in its "coolness." It is to the point. You don't miss it. It's riveting when he's at his best . . . *Episodes*, *Vespers*, and *Bad Blood*. It's crystal clear. It's like a drill going through you when you see his works. I admire his being so articulate about his movement, and what he says goes on the stage. What you see is what he just said. He's able to transfer the words into the actual movement. He challenges the dancers.

I made the decision to leave the Ailey company when I got an offer to do Broadway, because I had finished doing my work dancing with the company. I wanted to try something else and Alvin was really exhausted as far as creating works for me. In a way, when you have a dancer that is your muse, you're constantly on the line as to what else you're going to do for them. It was a blessing to work with Alvin and so many other talented choreographers—Talley Beatty, Louis Johnson, John Butler, Louis Falco, John Neumeier, and Ulysses Dove—but I had to make a choice: did I want to continue in the repertory or did I want to experiment and try something else and get out of that marvelous cradle of the Ailey organization? I gave up safety and jumped into Broadway.

Alvin always put his dancers in front of his own needs, but it always hurt like hell when somebody left. Alvin was upset that I went to Broadway. He cared very much that dancers stay in the concert area—especially African-Americans because there were so few of us there. Alvin felt it was important to maintain the tradition of concert dance.

When someone you love leaves, the pain is complicated. There's the initial reaction of anger, but tied in with the anger is your hope that the person leaving does whatever is needed for self-fulfillment. In the meantime, you're left with the feeling of loss—that there was so much more to share.

From the moment you hire a dancer, you are emotionally tied to that person because you are extending an invitation that enables the dancer to celebrate his or her beauty. On the other hand, a choreographer must be generous and open enough to let that dancer go and pursue other goals. That hurts. Not many words were exchanged between Alvin and me when I chose to do Broadway. On the surface he was fine, he was encouraging. But underneath he was hurt.

But whenever someone leaves, there is always discovery. Within your ranks all of a sudden there is somebody you haven't seen for a long time, or a person in the background who needs to take a step forward and have a challenge. In this case, my leaving brought out Donna Wood. There is always a wellspring of talent that is part of the Ailey tradition and a part of life. Opportunities arise. Dancers are not replaced. They are unique and individual. It's just that someone else's uniqueness and individuality can also be seen and be shared.

I've been protected by people who acted as bumpers, softening the impact of obstacles in my way. Broadway was a real test period for me because there was no bumper. There was nobody for me to go to. That was a lesson in life. The only thing I could rely on was my faith in God. It was put to the test by my two years on Broadway. I had done a little acting a few years before in Ken Rubenstein's experimental theater. In his sparse version of *Romeo and Juliet*, I danced Juliet's psyche, while Ken's sister spoke the role. Ken was divine and became a good friend, though my colleagues from the dance world were less than enthusiastic about my time away from the concert stage.

My first year in *Sophisticated Ladies* was carried by my discovery of how much talent there was on Broadway. I knew that there were many people who tried to bounce back and forth between Broadway and the concert stage. But the kind of talent that you had to have to be able to jump in and do the same thing night after night was incredible.

At first, in Washington, D.C., we had line after line of dialogue and a vague story line. But gradually it turned into a revue. Part of the reason I think my co-star Gregory Hines is so happy about *Jelly's Last*

With Greg Burge and three-time Tony winner Hinton Battle in the sand dance from *Sophisticated Ladies*. *Author's personal collection*

Jam is that the show has a story. Most of the shows for African-Americans have been revues. Gregory told me how hard it was for an African-American man to get a Tony Award in a leading role; he had been nominated previously for his work in *Eubie!* and *Comin' Uptown*. Finally, ten years after *Sophisticated Ladies* he got one. Hinton Battle, another star of the show, has received three best supporting Tonys for his work on Broadway. I adore Hinton. What a beautiful dancer and very warm human being. He's a gift. And Phyllis Hyman, who could eat a hamburger before going onstage and open her mouth and sing like no one else. There was such an abundance of talent. Gregory was terribly supportive of me, but he has that sharp side to him you have to have in order to survive in show business. After all,

Broadway is dealing with millions of dollars—not fifteen thousand for a ballet—and the prerequisites are different. The stakes are higher.

One matinee, I came onstage behind Gregory and my heel caught in a hemline that had not been sewn on the skirt. First entrance, I went down flat. The wind was knocked out of me; I was hurting. Gregory did one of those eye things that he does, trying to make light of it. He helped me up and we kept going.

One of my fondest memories is having the Ellington band literally behind us, onstage, with Mercer Ellington conducting. Another is of the marvelous set by Tony Walton, Willa Kim's Erté-inspired costumes, and the choreography by Donald McKayle and Michael Smuin. Juilliard-trained Mercedes Ellington, the Duke's granddaughter, was also part of the cast. But there were so many changes! The challenge for me was to sing and dance at the same time, or just deliver a line while I moved across the stage. I took a few formal singing lessons, but what I came to rely on was the voice I had been singing with since I was a child.

There were constant edits, constant script changes at the last minute. But you're prepared for that; that's why you're a professional. I remember singing when I had bronchitis. One of the crew members came backstage and asked, "Are you all right?" I said, "I'm trying to sing over this bronchitis." I must have sounded awful. All those experiences added to my perspective and expanded my horizons. You learn an awful lot when you're working at that pace and also doing the same thing every night, which you understand is *not* the same thing every night. I don't mean literally. I mean when you go onstage and you're doing the same dances every night, as opposed to repertory, eight performances a week, if you lapse and think you are doing the same thing every night, meaning, "Oh, these are the same steps, let me just go on automatic," that's when things happen. That's when negative situations happen: you trip or forget a line. You really have to stay as crisp as you do when you are in a repertory ensemble and you're constantly challenged by the diversity of the rep. No song is sung the same way twice.

I think a repertory company like Alvin's is ideal because it is open-ended. You can constantly feed the repertory. For a company that has

In *Sophisticated Ladies*. *Photograph © Jack Mitchell*

a singular choreographer, once that choreographer goes, the transition becomes very difficult. You can resurrect many of the ballets from the past, but then you are eventually going to run out. But there are such classics in Alvin's repertory, the constant infusion of new works, that it's always a full meal.

*   *   *

With Alexander Godunov and Alvin. *Photograph by Rita Katz*

Though I had been out of the Ailey for a couple of years, when Alvin called, you always came back. Once an Ailey dancer, always an Ailey dancer. I came back for *Spell*.

Alexander Godunov had your basic blond-god look. He wasn't overdeveloped around the arms or the chest, but he had pumped-up legs. They were very well-defined, very well-formed, very hard legs. His dancing was very emotional, in the Bolshoi tradition. He had an overwhelming sense of self. At times, because I was so covetous of Alvin's attention, I'd be really on edge for that attention. But Godunov needed that attention more because he had never worked with Alvin.

When we rehearsed, I was in the mirror. I might have been a little uncomfortable in the rehearsals. He was so tantalizing to me that I couldn't fully concentrate. So, instead of focusing on where I was supposed to be focusing, I ended up in the mirror. And when we were working together and I messed up a step or I missed his hand, he'd say, "Stay out of the mirror." He said that to me a couple of times, and it's not *what* you say to me, it's *how* you say it.

Spell was a *pièce d'occasion*, done once and that's it. Randy Barcelo, the great Cuban designer of *For Bird—With Love, The Mooche* (which is being revised for our thirty-fifth anniversary), and *Opus McShann*, Alvin's last ballet for the company, created the bejeweled costumes.

CHAPTER 17

Vulnerability is one of my favorite words. The reason a dancer moves me onstage, beyond his or her technical prowess, is the sense of an inner passion, an inner challenge, a fear, almost. I ask dancers not to rely just on their *flawless* technique, which I write a little tongue-in-cheek because there is no such thing as a flawless technique. I don't care whom you're watching. You slow that film down and you're going to be able to see a person twitch a foot, move that fourth-position preparation for a pirouette. You're going to see that person adjust in some kind of way, because he or she is human, not a textbook, not a computer, not a robot.

I ask dancers to tap into that vulnerability, which is very difficult to do in real life. You see a lot of people in this world roaming around scared to death to open themselves up and show who they really are. As a dancer, you have the extraordinary opportunity to be in a controlled situation, which is the stage. You have a technique that is going to carry you through a performance, and beyond that technique you can really express who you are as a human being. That is wonderful. In what other arena, in what other venue, can you be this free?

Sometimes it takes a very long time for dancers to understand this or to be in a situation where they can express that freedom. In order to express that freedom, "This above all: to thine own self be true." My mother used to say that all the time. She loved quoting Shakespeare. She did it well, too. She always had the key phrases—the ones that can get me through the New York *Times* crossword puzzle or can flash through my mind and support me in a situation I know is going to be difficult.

Sophisticated Ladies gave me the income to buy a house in the country and escape the madness of doing eight shows a week. Donna Wood, Ulysses Dove, and Milton Myers used to come up, and we'd continue the legendary games of bid whist that began when I lived on Riverside Drive. I bought a couple of smokers and cooked hams and chickens and grew the biggest asparagus you've ever seen in your life. I got into cooking so much that I started a line of pies called "Jamison's Choice," which was a big success at Macy's. I had previously done some catering for Jacob's Pillow. I loved being in the country, but once the show closed, I didn't feel the same need for an escape. I had more tranquillity than I knew what to do with. When Alvin thought it was time to end my hibernation, he encouraged me to choreograph. Alvin knew what he was doing and worked doubly hard to get me where he thought I should be—at the Alvin Ailey American Dance Center.

Alvin gave me access to scholarship students. I started working periodically, about three weeks at a time. At that time, *Divining* was called *Oasis*. At home, I had been listening to percussive music, Olatunji or one of those very strange archival African recordings that they make. I imagine they stand out in the bush, in the dark, with long microphones, trying to get the "real" sound of the African people. It's one of those discs that you can get at Tower Records that's grouped under ethnic, "the bushmen celebrating the rain," or something along those lines. But I love percussion. It's always been "blood" to me. *Divining* became the first ballet that I choreographed, created in studio four on the eighth floor of our old building on West Forty-fifth Street.

During my fifteen years with the Ailey company I had learned over seventy ballets. Every step I tried to take as a choreographer on my own made me feel as though I'd always be borrowing from somebody else. Alvin helped me get over that by saying, "Do it and be true to yourself." I found that if I was as organic a choreographer as I was a dancer, then I could experience the same kind of growth.

The deeper the drum, the better the sound. *Divining* was a special experience because of Kimati Dinizulu and Monti Ellison, who helped to create the African-based score. During rehearsals I wanted to experiment with different rhythms and Kimati was so well schooled in them all.

When I felt that I had reached a certain point in the movement, I asked Kimati to come to the studio. He would, and then another drummer would join him. And then another, and another. By the time the choreography was half finished, I had five drummers.

Divining started out as a group dance without solos. It started out as a response to rhythm. There was no theme. Alvin came to see the student performance and said, "I'd like to have this for the first company." I was shocked. He suggested I use Donna Wood as a lead and I agreed. Donna created the persona of a strong leader. It seems that in each of my subsequent ballets, there's a strong female lead. *Divining* begins with runners going out into a virgin, unknown territory to make sure their leader can proceed safely. She then blesses the ground, checking out the spirits that are about, sensing the air, and making sure the ambience is right before she lets the rest of her people celebrate life.

Divining is mysterious, its title suggesting a search or quest. Titles have a tendency to tell you something about the work. I like the audience to come to a performance and get what they get out of it, and not have anything suggested by a title. It's the audience's work to see what they see in a piece. Your "job" in the theater is to come and enjoy yourself and be transported to another place. That is what the theater is about to me. That is what dance is about to me, and not some fixed idea about what the piece is going to be. When the performance starts, you'll find out what the piece is about. Take a chance. Open yourself up because you've got dancers in front of you who are giving you everything they've got. Your job is to receive the spirit.

It's a blessing to be able to transfer your inner thoughts and your emotions to other people, who then relay your message to an audience. I had that when I was dancing. I have knowledge and skill that I've developed over a lifetime of dancing. It's my obligation to give that back to other dancers. The first time I started choreographing was in the dark, in my living room, with the lights completely out, to some popular music on the radio. I put the radio on full blast and I started moving. I didn't know what it looked like. I didn't want to see it. That's how much I had to push myself into starting. I had to start in the dark.

The transition between dancer and choreographer was a vague transition. It's a different rush than I get dancing with dancers. The tension-release area is longer with choreography. With dancing, the tension happens before you go onstage. You do the performance, then you get the release. While creating a dance, the tension occurs when you are trying to get the movement correct in everyone, trying to have that exchange, but you don't get the release until the premiere—maybe.

Divining was announced as the first work I had done for a major dance company. But prior to that, I had choreographed a small ballet for the company that Mercedes Ellington and Maurice Hines had formed. That was in exchange for a ballet Mercedes created for me. It predates *Divining*. It was rather experimental, done once in Philadelphia.

In 1984 Maurice Bejart invited me to choreograph a ballet for his company. Each year he invited guest choreographers. John Neumeier had done his *Third Symphony by Gustav Mahler* with Béjart's company. He knew that I was working on my choreography for the Ailey company and asked me if I would do something. And I said, "Sure," not knowing what the timing would be like. My ballet *Divining* premiered earlier than expected, when Ailey dancer Gary DeLoatch was in a taxi accident and couldn't dance in *For Bird—With Love*, the ballet Alvin choreographed as a tribute to Charlie Parker. Two days later I had to get on a plane, fly to Brussels, choreograph *Just Call Me Dance* in a week on dancers I had never worked with before, and supervise its premiere. It was absolutely insane. I'll never do anything like that again.

Earlier I had worked out some of the ballet with Sarita Allen and Bruce Taylor. We went to Brussels and on the first day of rehearsal I wanted to show Maurice and the dancers which direction I was going in, so I asked Sarita and Bruce to do a pas de deux from the ballet. When they finished the pas de deux everybody applauded and then Maurice asked, "Do you think they can be in the piece?" I believe he had the feeling that his dancers could not "cut" the movement because it was too different and they didn't have enough time to learn *how* to do it. When he said that I was taken aback because it didn't dawn on me that that's what he was probably thinking. I said, "No. They're not doing this. You're doing this. That's why I came all the way over here."

We proceeded to teach, and to understand that this movement was not organic to them. They needed time and some of them were very young. Also, there was one American dancer who gave me the hardest time with his "attitude." It was just awful. I took him out and ended up with six people who really lent themselves to it. We did it and it was OK. It wasn't a great sensation.

I ended up taking some of that same vocabulary, had Ken Hatfield write additional music, changed the costumes, and put it on Mary Day's Washington Ballet. It's called *Time Out*. I wanted to do something that was frolicsome and light; red, white, and blue; fun and romantic. But light, because most of the pieces that I had done were very Sturm und Drang. It worked fabulously. They had time to learn it. Four weeks of rehearsals and classes and Horton technique. They did it well and then I put it on the Jamison Project and of course, they carried on!

Jennifer Muller commissioned my ballet *Into the Life* for her company, The Works. I thought, at the time, that many directors were hiring me just out of the goodness of their hearts, since I had no track record as a choreographer. My success had been as a dancer, which could sell tickets, but you just don't hire anybody because they can sell tickets. I hope not. You don't want to put your dancers through that.

Jennifer gave me the time to create and explore and to see what my mettle was. I wanted to say something but I didn't know how to say it. After *Divining*, Louis Falco came backstage and said, "You have enough movement in there for fifteen ballets. You'll learn." But that's usually what happens when you first start creating. You think you have to throw everything into it.

Into the Life's fourth section is a pas de deux called "One + One = One." My intention in this ballet was to say that in this life you're by yourself, period. You are born by yourself, with help from your mother, you come into this world by yourself, and you leave by yourself. In the interim, you are *still* by yourself, whether you're connected to another person or not. In the pas de deux the Brian Eno music and the movement were repetitive—something that I hadn't done before. At the end of the variation the two principals stand downstage, on the diagonal. The woman reaches out one way, and the man falls to his knees, then to all fours, taking small steps. The point is that they've missed each other by being so singular.

There was an unintentionally funny sequence in the third section where Ron Brown was supposed to be a preacher while his congregants testified behind him. As the David Byrne music played, one parishioner gave him a hard time. When the preacher left with the congregation, the difficult parishioner followed suit. The audience roared. I thought I was doing something deep and profound, but it came out funny.

The dancers "killed" themselves to do the million steps I had for them. They gave themselves over to me, which is all you can ask a dancer to do—to give themselves over to you and trust you. One rehearsal was interesting because there was a dancer I wanted to use who'd been suggested by a friend of mine as an assistant. I brought him in and on the first day of rehearsal I ended up in tears because he was rude to the dancers. They weren't getting the steps, and my assistant—a beautiful dancer who could do my movement exquisitely—told the dancers in the worst tone of voice that they did not know what they were doing. Then he said to me, "You're going to put up with this? You're going to let them dance like that?" I couldn't believe this was happening. All I wanted to do was remove myself for a while from the situation and go to the nearest window. I wasn't trying to cry, but tears just started welling up in my eyes. In the end, I let him go.

It can be difficult to understand my movement. Alvin told me it would be difficult to transfer how I move to other people, because I have such a unique, internalized way of moving. Jonathan Riseling knows how to do my movement without my having to say anything. If anything, I have to pull him back because it gets "slippery"; like Bernstein at the New York Philharmonic, it gets lush on him. I have to pull him back sometimes and give him dynamics. Leonard Meek, Nasha Thomas, and Renee Robinson are all good at it. It's an inner feeling, not an outer feeling. It's not a technician I need even though I need a dancer to be fantastically technical. It's an inner sense of movement that is indescribable.

I don't care if someone's a quick study or not, if he or she doesn't have an innate sense of how you move, then it won't work. It stops your creativity because you don't see the possibility of the step if the dancer cannot fulfill what your vision is. That was part of the relationship I had with Alvin. I could fulfill his possibilities of what a step could be. And if I couldn't fulfill his possibilities I moved to make whatever he gave me look exceptional, so that he'd have to say, "Ooh, I like that."

Alvin came to see *Into the Life* and was very supportive of what I was doing. Alvin had arthritic knees and it became very difficult for him to walk. We arranged for him to have a ticket that I thought would be in the orchestra, but there he was, way up top, having to negotiate all those steps. After the performance he came backstage. He loved me. The feeling was mutual. It's that simple, and that complex.

I work the way Alvin worked. He would demonstrate movement and I would "hit it." It's rare that you get dancers who can follow you or can pick it up a little bit. You have to know the dancers very well. One of the most painful moments is to get up, move spontaneously, then turn around to have the dancers look at you as if they didn't get any of what you just did. With Alvin, I would approximate what he was doing. If I couldn't remember, I knew how to *fill*. My *filling* was so good that even if I didn't do exactly what he did, Alvin accepted my movement. When Alvin choreographed he would get up, the music would go on, you would look at him and follow him at the same time. Then he'd stop, turn around, and look at you. You'd forget or you'd remember, but you still moved. Even if you weren't moving quite the way he was, he still might like the shapes that each individual had created.

I know several choreographers who work that way, and I certainly do that. It's the most frustrating thing if nobody can get what you're doing. Alvin always used to tell me, "Maybe no one is going to get what you're doing, because you're moving in such a special way." I refused to believe that.

I began to teach master classes at Jacob's Pillow in 1981, when my dear friend Liz Thompson became director. As creative as she is energetic, Liz had been a part of the Ailey family when her husband, Clive, joined the company. When she took over the reins of leadership, the Pillow was falling apart—the budget was in deficit, and archives were unattended, and the toilets didn't flush. "What have I gotten myself into?" she thought. But luckily for everyone she stayed for eleven years and brought the Pillow back to the prominence I'm sure Ted Shawn intended when he founded it in the 1940s.

The Jamison Project came together through the support of Jacob's Pillow and the collaborative efforts of Liz Thompson, Josie Stamm at Philadelphia's University of the Arts (which had recently become the home of the winter Pillow), and Sam Miller, who is now the president of Jacob's Pillow. I wanted to have a New York performance at the Joyce Theatre, essentially a one-night-stand. I wanted to explore the

With Liz Thompson, former director of Jacob's Pillow and steadfast friend. *Author's personal collection*

opportunities of getting a group of dancers together, for both my choreography as well as being able to commission works from others. We decided to develop it as a project, incubate it, and then determine its feasibility a year or two down the line. Liz Thompson came up with the name Jamison Project. We auditioned some dancers, and had our initial rehearsal period at the Pillow. Cynthia Wassell was working as resource manager for Jacob's Pillow at the time. Simultaneously, she became the Jamison Project's company manager. We did everything by telephone. She was keeping our books as well as the books for the Pillow. She's a terrific lady. When we needed a company manager for the road, Pat Jacobs joined us after our Joyce Theatre season. Keith Simmons became our stage manager, and the irrepressible Cassandra Scott our lighting supervisor. During one of many games of Scrabble on the road, Cass went to build on the word "show," adding the letters "i" and "z." "That's not a word!" we objected. "Showiz," she said, and we couldn't stop laughing.

Jacob's Pillow, in the Berkshire Hills in western Massachusetts, fulfills part of a student's studies with that missing element of nurturing that is not necessarily about technique, but gives you something that will also enhance you as a human being. The things we're talking about are not just about dance, but about life, about having the will and the confidence backed by knowledge and experience to take chances and make mistakes. If you're going to make a mistake make it a big one; don't be gray. And take chances, because the greatest achievers, the ones that have created their own niche, are the ones that have teetered on that line, have really walked an exciting tightrope. You become responsible for the steps that you take.

I began my association with Jacob's Pillow as a dancer in 1971, and as a master teacher ten years later. The qualities I look for in students are the same ones I look for in dancers, passion and will—how students stretch themselves, apply themselves, and how spongelike they want to be as learning instruments. You look for that same light and that same spark. If you're going to study with me, then you'd better come in with your head on and your heart ready and open and a body that wants to work.

For one or two weeks you give the students *Horton* technique, classes, and repertory. It's very difficult for the students to learn anything in that short period of time. Sarita Allen and Stephen Smith were my assistants in 1988. At the end of the two weeks, Sarita and Stephen organized the students into a performance using what they had learned up at the Pillow during their short stay. It made the dancers responsible as students and as dancers that they had to put together the entire evening's work. In that time, one of my talented students, Kris World, choreographed *Read Matthew 11:28.*

Liz Thompson and I sat together for the performance and knew immediately that *Read Matthew* was something special. When I decided to do the showcase at the Joyce Theatre, I added it to the Project's repertory. Former dancer and talented artist Andy Kay came up to the Pillow to begin his work designing new handpainted silk costumes for *Divining*. Betty Williams came up and pinned muslins on Jonathan Riseling while he stood rather patiently on the Pillow's outdoor platform.

We tried to coordinate a support staff. Edee Mezirow became immediately involved, and Paul Szilard was consulted. Paul, I believe, did not think this was a good step for me, and wanted more of a Judith Jamison and Friends, along the lines of Misha, Rudolf, and Cynthia Gregory.

As soon as we started the Jamison Project, Dr. Bernard Watson, the head of Philadelphia's William Penn Foundation, gave us a generous grant.

The Jamison Project premiered at the Joyce Theatre in New York on November 15, 1988. When the Jamison Project opened at the Joyce, Alvin was there, in the audience. We were rehearsing and building the costumes at the Pillow. Sam met with John Lucovitch, who at the time represented the Ailey repertory company, and it was decided that we should pursue alternate representation, rather than have John represent the new Jamison Project along with the Alvin Ailey Repertory Ensemble. Shortly after, Sam met with Sheldon Soffer. Sheldon represents Pilobolus, the White Oak Project, Bill T. Jones, and David Parsons and agreed to represent the Jamison Project.

Our repertory, at the start, consisted of *Divining*, *Tease*, *Time Out*, and *Read Matthew 11:28*. I then approached Garth Fagan for a ballet for the company. Garth sees movement in a totally unique way. I'd love to jump in his mind to see what he's projecting from in there. His vision is so different from everyone else's. I admire the way he incorporates diasporic movement into his work. There's Caribbean movement in his work that is very recognizable. I hate to categorize it because to me he is another form of dance. Garth gave us *Easter Freeway Processional*. The price for that was that he'd get to do a solo for me, but that was no price at all. *Scene Seen* was the last solo choreographed for me. Garth cares about dancers, not just his, but all dancers, and he cares

The original Jamison Project (clockwise from lower left): Rebecca Rigert, Jonathan Phelps, Wesley Johnson III, Adrienne Hurd, Michael Thomas, Antonio Carlos Scott, Jonathan Riseling, Tina Bush, Dee Anna Hiett-Washington, Sarita Allen. *Photograph by Michael Ahearn*

about their spirits. He can articulate spirit and he can also choreograph it.

For the 1988–89 Ailey season I was guest artistic associate. Alvin was not doing too well and he asked me to go out with him. We went on tour together. It was an interim job. Alvin's health was improving and of course I'd have done anything for him. But at the time, it was the Jamison Project—not the Ailey company—I saw as the instrument of my artistic goals.

I was looking to engage dancers who were great people and extraordinary dancers. I like to hire people who have something to share and can show the audience a reflection of themselves and a celebration of life so that when you come to the theater you're not seeing steps, but seeing something intangible that has to do with spirit. I see that as soon as I audition dancers or teach a class.

The company started out with ten dancers, and shortly after, we expanded to twelve and had only three weeks to rehearse and pull everything together for our first performance at Jacob's Pillow. It was an intense three weeks, a wonderful gala, and we were a sensation. But I forgot not to keep up the same kind of crazed intensity while I was rehearsing them for the next five weeks. I had dancers who loved what they were doing, and through their exhaustion, they grew. The Jamison Project was like working with a large family—twelve young people, and me, the thirteenth.

Tease was originally made on the Alvin Ailey Repertory Ensemble, with Dana Hash and Wesley Johnson in the lead roles, as well as Junius Backus, a wonderful dancer who played the devil character. This was in 1986. The next time it emerged was in 1988 in the Jamison Project. I was a different person, so it came out differently. It's about people who believe that beauty is skin-deep, and who get themselves in trouble as a result. *Tease* didn't come together the way I had planned. In my head I knew exactly what I wanted to see. I remember talking it over with my lighting designer, Timothy Hunter. It originally started with people at an art gallery opening, and what you're seeing is what they're really thinking. I remember telling young people during a lecture-demonstration that what's on the outside is not the truth. The most important part of a human being is what's on the inside.

I love dancers who hold on to their innocence. When it leaves, you can see it in their eyes and body language. It's marvelous when a dancer approaches movement innocently. And if you lose the child within, then you can't approach the movement the way I think it should be approached.

It's not about each performance. That is the last thing that I think about. The process is what is important to me, and before each performance you should have gone through the whole process of whatever it takes to get you onstage. That begins when you first walk in the door, whether you think it's a sacred place or whether you think it's just another place with barres in it and a floor. Your attitude from the beginning sets what the performance is going to be, regardless of the ballet. Whether the ballet is a hit or a miss is not important, it's your attitude when you first walk into the room that counts. It's a lesson I learned early from Marion Cuyjet.

In *Time Out* I switched Jonathan Phelps into the romantic pas de deux with Dee Anna Hiett-Washington, to whom I had always given the most punchy, most technically difficult things to do. I never saw her lyrically. She was wonderful. A marvelous innocence came out of J.P. that I had never seen before. I had seen only a quirkiness. The problem with switching roles in a large company is that people start claiming roles. That's why I always say that the dance is the most important thing. If you are not "right" for the part, you should be gracious enough to step aside and let somebody else do it. There were so few of us in the Jamison Project that if someone was injured there'd be very few replacements, so I decided to cover my bases and have the dancers become fluent in each other's roles. It worked beautifully.

Of the ballets I've choreographed thus far, *Forgotten Time* is closest to my heart. When I first heard the music—"Le Mystère des Voix Bulgares"—on a local university radio station in Philadelphia I thought it was North African because of the rhythms, the harmony, and the nasality. It pulled me in. I visualized a shower of many colors, and textures and rhythms that were both "hot" and "cold." The combination of wonderful dancers and wonderful music left me no choice but to create something beautiful. The idea of the dance is about support, love, caring, fall and recovery. In the ballet, you constantly see people fall forward and backward and then recover or have someone help them. To me, that's very much a reflection of life. You always want someone to be there when you need that help and support.

Forgotten Time shows my love of beautiful bodies, particularly male bodies, when I choreograph. I love the structure of a man's body. I was aware of that as a young person, though the full revelation came much later. For me, there's a tightness to the male form, but also a sensuousness and a looseness. I love that hard-soft juxtaposition within the same body. You get both sculpted contours and lyrical movement—it's like velvet.

When Ailey dancer Desmond Richardson comes onstage you notice his beautiful physique. What he does with that physique is extraordinary because his strength doesn't preclude his being able to float across the stage. Or Leonard Meek, who looks like a piece of Nigerian sculpture—with his strikingly broad shoulders and tiny waist—and moves lushly.

The lighting for all of my ballets has been designed by Timothy Hunter. I can tell Tim where I want light to come from and what feeling I want the light to possess and Tim will "hit it." There's very little explanation that I have to give him. His imagery marries with mine. The relationship that I had with Alvin as a dancer is very much the relationship that I have with Tim as a choreographer. He understands what I want to see. He will create a scenario that is phenomenal. I love the richness and the atmosphere he creates through the depth of his colors.

Most of Alvin's early ballets were designed with extraordinary lights, as opposed to scenery. That began as a budgetary problem. The light sculpts the stage. Nick Cernovitch and Chenault Spence were our early resident lighting designers; Tim Hunter lit Alvin's later works. Nick will always be remembered for *Revelations*. In addition to lighting Alvin's ballets, Chenault was also responsible for lighting Boito's *Mefistofele*, which I choreographed for the Opera Company of Philadelphia. He loved working with Alvin.

CHAPTER 18

Drs. William and Camille Cosby were friends of Alvin's, and have been generous friends of the company. Donald McKayle and I appeared on his television sitcom "The Cosby Show" in 1986, playing husband and wife. I had only one line, and when I was about to give it my all, my voice cracked. I thought it would be so easy to do, but television is a whole 'nother thing. It was a new arena.

Bill and Camille were the hosts of the Ailey company's Thirtieth Anniversary Gala in 1988 as well as our honorary chairs for 1992. Camille is a lovely, intelligent woman. George Faison staged the evening. Before the curtain went up, Dr. Cosby talked to all the dancers and listened as well. He's a good listener. He came onstage, during rehearsal, in a pair of colored tights and a wool cap, while every other man was standing around in a tuxedo. Dr. Cosby was wonderful. They're such a busy couple that when you call them and ask them to do things, and they respond favorably, it's wonderful.

In 1988 he produced, along with NBC, the Alvin Ailey television special, with a combination of old and new dancers, and all the kids from "The Cosby Show." George Faison staged it. We had the largest-ever cast for "I Been 'Buked." There must have been forty or more of us. It looked like a blossoming flower. The women wore their " 'Buked" dresses, but when I put mine on, I couldn't bear myself in it. I certainly wasn't my old dress size. I put on my black turtleneck sweater and my black tights.

Jimmy Truitte was in the center and danced the father figure. John Parks was on one side of him and Kelvin Rotardier on the other, two other men who had played that role. The performance was a gathering of the old and the new. Some veterans of the company—Miguel, Kelvin, and Carl Bailey—did excerpts from "Mean Ol' Frisco." Some of the older dancers were huffing and puffing. The classic early Ailey works are *hard* to do.

When *Cry* was danced at the gala I walked across the stage in the first section in a borrowed Donna Karan bone-white suit. That image worked well onstage and George tried to re-create it for television. It was well received by the critics; actually, the suit got more of a review than I did. That suit could have walked across the stage by itself. It was fabulous!

For the twenty-fifth anniversary, Sara Yarborough, Estelle Spurlock, Donna Wood, and I danced the last section of *Cry*. Alvin wanted me to dance with them, but during the technical rehearsal, I couldn't quite imagine myself doing it. I told him, "I'll just make a speech," but a half hour before the gala began, I changed my mind. Alvin had been asking me to do it for weeks, but I gave him so many reasons why I couldn't. I felt that I was too heavy, and I did not want to revisit the movement—I always had a problem going back to roles I no longer danced. When I finally told Alvin yes, I went backstage to ask each of the other women if they minded my sudden change of heart. Each welcomed me generously.

I introduced *Cry* rather solemnly, saying that Alvin had given me this piece and how it speaks of womanhood, the trials and tribulations of being a Black woman in contemporary society. I thanked Alvin very much, but I sounded very flat and very subdued. During the last crossover in the third section, I popped out of the wings and danced outside of the trio in my Michael Vollbracht silk gown. It was hand-painted with corn husks and corncobs, lots of material, a free-flowing dress. I remember going, "Well, I'm going to go out there and we'll see what happens." All four of us did the last crossover and the house went nuts. Everybody was beside themselves and all we heard was a wave of applause. People jumped out of their seats. The audience responded to all of us, and to the power of the piece.

A year or so later Alvin asked me to do *Cry* again, in costume. I just didn't want to do it. Once I've taken the glove off, it doesn't fit right when I try to put it back on. It happened again when I tried to revisit *Masekela Langage*. The circumstances were different. What motivated me to do it, to be that person, had changed. Five years later, I was obviously a different person. I could not draw from the person I was five years before. That's how much of my life I invest in roles—all of it. Therefore, if my life changes I can't go back and dig up what was once real to me.

Even though I had such a good time dancing the Madam in Donald McKayle's *District Storyville*, when I came back to the role after not having performed it for a few years, I was uncomfortable. I preferred to watch Donna Wood dance it, than to try and revisit it myself. *District Storyville* is a very theatrical, very funny piece, and one that Alvin actually danced in. It's a vignette about the young Louis Armstrong and how he had learned to play the trumpet by hanging out at the bordellos of Storyville, where, among other things, some hot New Orleans jazz was being created. There are some unique characters in the ballet, including the Madam, taught to me by Donny and Carmen de Lavallade. That role has gone through several metamorphoses. Donna, Carmen, and I danced a very contained Madam. Today, Donny McKayle has given Raquelle Chavis the license for a bawdier interpretation of the role. Linda Spriggs was incredible as Stingaree, and now Karine Plantadit wows them in that role. Donald created a new role for Marilyn Banks that was not in the original *Storyville*, because she's such a personality. We had as much fun rehearsing it then as the dancers today, because we got to portray characters and were given license to put ourselves in those roles.

There was an attachment of tulle hanging down the back of the

Madam's dress that was always lethal. It was as long as the dress and you felt as if you were going to trip over it. When you pliéd, it had its own dance going for it. It was always a problem and always something to think about. All I needed was to walk across the stage and fall on my face when I was supposed to be the Madam. There are certain dances where you can't fall, because there is no recovery, no way to convince the audience that the additional step was part of the choreography. If you fall, you fall. Thank God my Madam remained upright at *all* times!

CHAPTER 19

The women of Senegal carry themselves strongly as if they were the prow of a ship. They are the bearers of the history of their families. One of the ways Black people have maintained and passed on their history is through the oral tradition. In Senegalese society that generational history has to be passed on by the wife. She plays a very important role. It enables her to be free enough to do what she has to do, while remaining the woman that she is. Men and women help each other, but each has a separate role. In more experienced cultures, each person realizes the value of the other.

In Senegalese society nobody has the upper hand. The man and woman are on a par because they share important responsibilities in order to maintain the family, which is primary. When roles are defined, it helps clear the air. You're too busy doing what you're doing to "go at each other." If you have to go out into the field and get tonight's meal by picking it out of the ground yourself, you don't have time to sit down and think about what you don't have.

We *do* have time in Western civilization and we're pushed into situations where both men and women are constantly seeking more and better material goods. People who have been living in the older societies are concerned with food, clothing, and shelter. Their prerequisites are completely different.

My father hasn't recovered from my mother's passing and I don't think he ever will. She made it to fifty years of marriage, but she didn't make her seventy-first birthday, a week later. He still hasn't gone through her things yet. Her nail polish, her perfume, and her talcum powder are still on the end table near her side of the bed. Her clothes are still sitting in the drawers the way they were the last time she folded them. If my brother disturbs any of her things, my father gets very angry. The calendar on his wall stops in 1988.

She died at home. I was at her bedside about five seconds after she passed away; I had been in another room. She had been coughing nonstop. The doctor who was attending her had her trust, but he was not a specialist. I was trying to get her to seek a second opinion. I knew she was in a bad way, but she didn't want to go to the hospital. She was very much like her mother. "We put her in the hospital, and it was the worst thing we could have done," my mom said. "Terrible."

During the last year of her illness, I went home for a visit and she looked at me and I knew she wasn't well. But she wouldn't tell me she had cancer. There's that secrecy again; she didn't want me to know. From the day I was born until the day she died, she had to protect me. She put up with so much physical pain.

Only a year after my mother passed away, my father was at home trying to do some chore and I said, hoping to make things easier for him, "Why can't you do it this way?" He said, "I can't. This is the way she did it." Sometimes he slips and he calls me by my mother's name. I'll overhear him at church talking about her and he'll say, "My mother . . . my wife." It's extraordinary, I think, that two people could have been so close for fifty years. They became one.

I keep a snapshot under the glass of my desk, taken about the time Mom started not to feel well. They came to visit me in Connecticut and we took a drive and then a walk so I could take a picture of them by the pond. *Mom, Dad, my dog Kita, a small body of water, some clouds crossing the sky . . .*

Mom would put on a pretty good show, not just for me, but for everybody. When she died, the congregation of Mother Bethel was shocked; nobody knew how ill she really was. I didn't know how ill she was until I came home from tour one day. She used to like to spend time in the dining room and Daddy used to take the lounge chair from out back, wrap it thick in blankets so it would be comfortable for her. When I saw her wrapped up in the chair, I got the clue that something was wrong. That's when Dad told me that she'd gone to the doctor for tests, and that she had cancer. "Where?" I asked him, but he said he wasn't sure. I never got a really clear report from her doctor. I couldn't get him on the phone or see him in person. And my dad was being pretty vague about the facts.

My brother got hysterical when he came to visit and saw her wrapped in the lounge chair. He told me that he thought she was going to die. "She's not going to die," I told him, but still in the back of my mind, this time I knew she had the look of death. I looked her right in the eye and I knew.

I thought back to the time I was seventeen, and the police brought Mom home because she had had a cerebral hemorrhage and had fainted on the trolley. I brought her upstairs to her bedroom, even though she insisted that she was fine. I called my father at work and he returned immediately. By that time, Mom had fallen into a coma, and her breathing had become irregular. When we could not wake her up, we called the ambulance.

Then, I wasn't scared. Mom was not going anywhere, she was not going to die. A few weeks later she returned home and our house returned to its normal rhythm. Years later I learned that she was sicker than she would admit. She used to get frequent headaches, but my mother pushed on. It's very much like some dancers: if they have pain, they don't tell anyone and continue trying to work through it. Mom was very much that way, so I never really knew how sick she was.

*   *   *

At the time of her last illness I was smack in the middle of my work with the University of the Arts and the filming of the PBS special "The Dancemaker: Judith Jamison." The show's intention was to document the "creative process," so the camera was everywhere. I lost my mother but the camera kept rolling. Her spirit never left. I still have the last letter she wrote to me when *Mefistofele*, the opera I choreographed for the Opera Company of Philadelphia, premiered. She couldn't go to the opera, which was unusual. Then I knew she was really going to go because she would always appear at what I was doing, no matter how she felt. I remember Robert Montgomery Scott, the head of the Philadelphia Museum of Art, begging me to have her attend. They had met before and he was anxious for her to see the opera. To me, she wrote a beautiful letter saying she wished both she and Dad could attend "because this is yours and my and Dad's premiere," how much they loved me and how much I had done for them.

She continued her journey. Mom died at about one o'clock in the morning. I had to follow the ambulance, and I bypassed the hospital because I was used to taking a certain route. I didn't realize it for about two minutes that I wasn't going to the hospital. I finally took my father home and I didn't know what to do so I cleaned my room. I made the bed, put things in order. I didn't sleep.

My regime was to go to the Y on Fifty-second and Chestnut first thing in the morning and swim laps. Before I would lap I'd do a floor barre. At 6 A.M., I got in my Chevy Blazer and drove to the Y. I did my exercises, lapped in the pool. Somebody asked me how I was and I said, "My mother died." She died on the sixth and on the ninth we buried her. That day I got on a plane to Boston to judge a choreographic competition with Liz Thompson, Bruce Marks, the director of the Boston Ballet, and Bill Como, the late, great editor of *Dance Magazine*. I remember Bill asking how I was and my saying, "I buried my mother this morning." My words came out devoid of feeling because I was in a state of shock. Bill said to me, "Keep being tough as nails." But I didn't feel tough at all. I felt my usual shut-down self, the way I used to get before a performance, or in a situation where I was shocked.

I was surrounded by friends, but when somebody dies, you're completely alone. Nobody can die for you; you've got to die for yourself. And in that moment you feel the vacuum. It's a total vacuum and nobody can enter that space. When it's on the opposite foot, what do you say to someone whose lover has died, or best friend? "I'm sorry. They were a good person." It all sounds so contrived. It's all been done on late-night television. I figure all you can do is *feel*. That's all I can do. I'm at a loss for words when somebody passes away.

After we buried her, I wanted to cook my dad something that she used to cook. My father loved her macaroni and cheese and I looked all over the kitchen for the recipe but I couldn't find it. I picked up a store-bought box, made it, but it was awful. I couldn't serve it. I threw it out.

CHAPTER 20

Alvin died one year later on December 1, 1989. Seven months earlier, while I was with him on his last U.S. tour, he had asked me to take over the company. I said yes, of course. He had always tried to prepare me for some kind of leadership role within the organization. If he had to make a speech, but couldn't go, I'd make the speech in his place . . . or accept an award, or run a rehearsal. Several of us were doing that, not just me. He gave me the confidence to know that I could step in for him. I think he was guiding me in certain directions to represent him, and then, ultimately, extend his vision and see a horizon that he made possible. Alvin felt, in his heart of hearts, that I should be his successor, even though I was running the Jamison Project. For six months I ran both companies at once.

I was appointed artistic director of the Alvin Ailey American Dance Theater on December 20, 1989. It was a very traumatic experience to have Alvin pass away on the first of December, with the New York season beginning on the sixth, but it was quite a performance. The dancers danced like I had never seen before. It was an absolute

testimony to the spirit of a man who had given us so much, that generosity and commitment, the joy of movement, the genius, and the wanting to share not just with dancers, but the world, what it was like to celebrate life through movement.

It was remarkable to see five thousand people at Alvin's memorial service at the Cathedral of St. John the Divine, on Manhattan's Upper West Side. We all thought we'd *known* Alvin intimately. There were people looking around saying, "Who's that? I've never seen them before." But they knew Alvin as well as I knew Alvin. He had so much to share with everyone and he'd made each of them feel so individual and special to him. He did that with audiences all over the world, and especially with the dancers in his company. They understood that they could not possibly participate in the Ailey celebration of dance without being complete individuals, without being whole human beings, without digging deep into their inner self and finding out who they were so that they had something to share with the audience. That's what distinguishes an Ailey dancer.

Everybody thought, "I knew him better than anyone else in the world." The truth is that we all knew Alvin. He made us all feel, individually, like we had a personal connection. Duke Ellington, I'm told, was the same way. That's why five thousand people showed up at St. John the Divine. Alvin had many, many lives and many experiences with people outside the dance world. I didn't know them. I had never met them. They all thought they knew Alvin well. They did, and loved him.

I wanted to touch his face one last time before he was buried and I was shocked at how cold, how wooden his skin felt. I got to thinking how Alvin had changed over the years, both physically and emotionally. In the early eighties, Alvin's moods had become public knowledge—he had been diagnosed as a manic-depressive and needed lithium. At that time, he wasn't in control of his emotional life. One day he walked into the office and fired most of the staff. When he left, Bill Hammond hired everybody back.

It took much persuasion to convince Alvin that he needed to be

Alvin Ailey and his mother, Mrs. Lula Cooper. *Photograph © Jack Mitchell* hospitalized. He didn't want to go. I don't think he realized how self-destructive he had become, and how a chemical imbalance could be treated with proper medical care.

I look back on the day when we stood in the lobby of the Forty-fifth Street studio to tell Alvin that he needed a doctor. We told him how much we cared about him. I said, "Alvin, you know we love you."

"Love me?" he answered.

He spent his last days in the winter of 1989 at Lenox Hill Hospital. I had never seen him so thin. God needed to release him from his pain. When he passed away, Mrs. Cooper, Sylvia Waters, Chaya, and I watched as he took his last breath. It seemed to me he held on to that breath and never let it go. He inhaled and never exhaled.

Somebody must have leaked word about Alvin's death because we were told that members of the press were in the lobby. I don't see how they could have been there that quickly, otherwise. We were able to leave the hospital by a side exit.

I don't feel as though I'm standing in anyone's shoes. I'm standing on Alvin's shoulders. The horizons become broader. He was an individual. However, we shared the same spiritual traditions. That's why I stayed with the company for fifteen years: we were walking in the same path, that's why we had such a special connection.

I'd been steeped in the way the Ailey company functions and had been to a certain extent embraced by those who had been in the organization for a certain period of time. But there are changes. The biggest change is that I cannot call Alvin on the phone and chuckle for half an hour, or get together and reminisce about things that happened a long time ago or things that happened a minute ago. And I can't give him a hug, or look into his eyes. I miss Alvin physically. I miss his physical presence. However, his spirit carries me forward and I pray that it carries all of us forward.

When I came to Ailey in my new position, I gave a speech to the dancers saying that I didn't expect them to shift their loyalty to me just because Alvin had appointed me artistic director. I pointed out that I came with a history of doing his movement well and understood what he was talking about.

My first day of being artistic director of the Alvin Ailey American Dance Theater was not as memorable as one might think, because I never really left the organization. Before the official first day, it was announced to the company at a studio at City Center. I had come into the fourth-floor studio and Bill Hammond announced to the company that I was going to be named artistic director. There was applause, yelling, and screaming. The dancers were excited. I think that they were a little nervous. No one knew that Alvin had designated me. Initially, the Board had to go to Alvin and ask him who was going to take over.

I don't think anybody thought that the company was going to stop. There was going to be continuity, regardless of whether it was through me or somebody else. Besides, you don't abandon anybody that's stuck with you through thick and thin and had the genius to create an entity that is letting you be totally free.

For our opening night on December 6—five days after Alvin's death—I wore a white suit and was told by Chaya that in Japan, mourners wear white instead of black. At the end of the performance, after *Revelations*, we brought Alvin's photo from the memorial service onstage. All the dancers came back onstage, each one carrying a flower. Some laid their flower beneath the portrait, some held their flower. The dancers were crying. The audience was applauding. It was a meeting of opposite emotions.

It wasn't a feeling of tears, because there was a sense of relief that Alvin was finally out of his intense pain. He had been hurting so bad. I remember telling Donna that Alvin needed to take that next step and walk through that Door.

There was a vacuum onstage, but there was air. It was that bubble, that controlled space that surrounds us every time the curtain goes up. It very much felt like a space that Alvin was in control of, still. I felt so drained that I had no emotion left, except maybe to hold somebody's hand or try to pat someone on the back. By that time some of the dancers were unable to accept comfort. There was no comfort zone. The pitch is so high when you finish a performance—the dancers are so way up and way down at the same time. Everybody was having their own private grief in front of the entire City Center audience. That's a performer's life.

I'm always careful when I hire young dancers for the Ailey company—it's such a "high." They need to come in with a generous self-confidence in order to really go over the edge. They've got to come in that way, otherwise they'll get run over. There is such power and speed and technical prowess out onstage that you will literally get run over. Emotions run high.

First day, when I had a meeting with the dancers I told them, "If you feel you are a victim in this company, that people are putting pressure on you to do things you don't want to do, please leave. If you cannot remember why you're dancing in the first place, then please leave. This is a shared gift that we have, and everybody wants it to continue, so let's try to keep it going that way." I've always said, if you are not happy in your situation, don't be a victim. Get out.

I held one of my early rehearsals with the company to clean up *Revelations*. The purpose was not to change the ballet, but I wanted to go back to some of the old things that we used to do. I didn't expect the dancers to do it exactly the way that Alvin had us do it. *Revelations* is supposed to be in constant metamorphosis always, like *Swan Lake*, which people don't dance today the way they did in the last century. But I wanted to bring back a feeling of religious fervor I thought was missing. I started breaking down *Revelations* in sections and rehearsing specific details, such as the way the head should be held and the way the hand should be held, how the torso should respond to a certain bounce in the knees in deep plié. I called the women together to rehearse "The Day Is Past and Gone," to align their heads and arms and make sure everybody was over in flatback. I'm a detail person and I love the freedom of being precise within movement, being definitive with whatever you're doing.

Revelations. Photograph © Jack Mitchell

This was not precision drilling, but attention to detail. If it's a Horton flatback, then you should be in flatback, not halfway up or halfway down. It wasn't easy, because I didn't have the luxury of time I'd had with the Jamison Project. Now I had to contend with five-minute breaks every hour. Back when I was dancing, you went straight through until you got it.

And I was working with a whole new, younger generation—one who was that much further away from experiencing what Alvin experienced. I had grown up in a church in Philadelphia with people who were born in the South; I come from that tradition. Alvin didn't have to sit down and tell me what *Revelations* was about. When I was teaching "Rocka My Soul" the other day, just to refreshen it and make it tighter, I looked around to see dancers who were barely twenty-one. These young people were old enough to be my children. I told them to go to church to experience what it was like. You almost can't talk about it but I do have to talk about it to give them the imagery to understand that they're not just fanning a fan. These women are steeped in dignity and pride and spirituality and have the Holy Ghost. They live in a tradition of being able to say, "Glory be to the Father and to the Son," and know what it means.

Of course, getting the young dancers to understand all that is a lot easier with live music. All of a sudden, with a real choir in the pit, they can *hear* it. This happened in Baltimore, with the Morgan State University Choir, and at one point I turned around and stopped the dancers and said, "Now you know what I'm talking about." It all came from the essence of the music, its beat and its rhythm and the words. There is something so alive and active when live music happens. I didn't have to explain to them; they could hear it. In the chords of the spirituals, in the singing, in the feeling of the lyrics. I wish we could afford to have more live music than we do.

Before I worked with the Ailey Board of Directors, I felt some concern: The Board of the Jamison Project had been so family-oriented, so grass-roots, that I was afraid I would miss the familiarity of having friends like Nancy Kalodner in my vision. Nancy's petite, but what a powerhouse! She lectures all over the country on real estate, and in 1992 was named Realtor of the Year in Massachusetts. She's always very open about her house, a few miles from Jacob's Pillow, which architect and interior designer Philip Smerling designed and built. It's at the top of a hill, with a single dirt road that only one car at a time can manage.

For six months I was going back and forth between the Jamison Project and the Ailey company. I couldn't have done it without my assistant, Pat Jacobs, who coordinated my schedule, even when I forgot which company I was catching a plane to meet.

The Jamison Project gave its last performance at the Annenberg Center in Philadelphia. I can still hear the emotion in Keith Simmons's voice as he announced the cast changes to the audience shortly before the performance . . . for the last time.

For the Jamison Project I had changed the lead in *Divining* from a woman to a man—Antonio Carlos Scott. And for the last performance of the Project, I had all my leads out onstage at once: Carlos, Lydia Roberts, and Karine Plantadit. It was magic.

The Jamison Project was an extraordinary group of people who worked well together. I think that's why it was painful for everybody to break up. But there was no way I could have refused Alvin. It was a heart decision, not a head decision.

One of the hardest experiences in my life was firing five dancers. I hated doing it because I think it puts a rumble through the entire organization, a sense of instability, which is not something dancers need more of. There were a few Ailey dancers whose resistance to me showed in their attitude in rehearsal, in their reluctance to take corrections. Alvin had left me a list of those dancers, whom he had not wanted in the company in the first place. There are dancers in the company right now who if Alvin had had his way would not be in the company. Alvin was good at predicting what he knew wasn't going to work, and perhaps I'm just being stubborn thinking I can make it all work. Unfortunately, some of those people I had to let go and some of them I kept. And some that I kept I had to let go, eventually. I gave them a chance not to be what he had told me they were going to be and they just dug their rut a little bit deeper, without even knowing it.

What I did was get the shape of the company that I wanted—who and what I wanted to see and feel. There's a different feeling each time someone is not there, which is a justified feeling, a marvelous, valid feeling. Everything has to change anyway. Everything has to go through metamorphoses. In the general picture, dance has to change.

You always miss uniqueness. People are irreplaceable because of their total uniqueness, and it's particularly evident and obvious in the Ailey company with personalities that are indelibly impressed on your heart. The legacy that they leave is untouchable. You can remember them beautifully. You can remember them fondly. You can remember them with great love, but your eyes have to be open for the next discovery that continues the lineage that's been going on since the first man stepped out on the continent.

Part of the fabric of the Ailey company is that the dancers' lives are an integral part of what goes on onstage. There has to be care taken with those lives, and when it comes down to evaluations of their dancing, what you're really talking about is their lives. When you fire somebody you're shattering his or her life and life's work. As much as I love the power of my position, that's not part of the power I like.

Alvin understood people so well, which is one of the reasons he was a great choreographer. I don't know if I have that sense of knowing people as quickly and as thoroughly as Alvin did. I can speak easily to crowds, but working one-on-one is harder because you really have to *listen*. I feel negligent when I'm out on the road and I haven't talked to every single dancer as much as I'd like to, or I'm back in the office and I'm trying to do everything at once. That's the difficulty of it, the people part of it, because this organization is about people who have special gifts.

Part of Alvin's inner pain was that people would hurt him so badly, without even knowing it. I'm sure I hurt him many times when I was performing. I can remember taking a certain attitude in a rehearsal when he needed me to do something extra in order to see it, and I'd make some kind of excuse not to do it. Sometimes he needed me to shine and I needed some buffing. It's minor, but that kind of thing can hurt. It's difficult when twenty-two different people need stroking all at the same time, because you have to juggle all that emotional baggage. You can't respond to it angrily. You cannot turn around and say, "Now look . . ." We can't do that because everybody has to go through what they have to go through. As a professional, you know that when the curtain goes up you have to be on, be able to deal with any emotional stress that might have built up. That's what separates the professional from the amateur. You're going to use whatever detrimental emotions or whatever good emotions you have; whatever's gone on during the day, you're going to use. Just as Alvin had to, I have to sit there and deal with it and then love them unconditionally because I've hired them to get out onstage and be the dancers they are.

As an artistic director, that's very hard for me to do. I'm very emotional. I want to lash back. I want to come back at the person. But I can't do that because what I'm running is bigger than myself. I have to take the good, the bad, and the ugly and see it on a much larger scale. The end result is that human beings are acting like human beings. Fortunately, the Ailey dancers have always been able to use whatever is not working for them emotionally, bring it onstage, and have it flower into something beautiful.

If something is working the way I want it to work, it goes to my heart. What releases that feeling is when the curtain goes up or there's a rehearsal that's extraordinary or when I see a dancer all of a sudden make a discovery, take an inch forward toward blossoming, toward flowering, toward growing. When I see dancers take that next step, it erases everything that just went before. As with Alvin, all that is churning inside me. It's part of the job description, except it's not written down.

It's all revisiting me now. It's all one big circle. I was tickled recently in rehearsal to see one dancer's leg warmers slip halfway down her legs. She shouldn't have had them on that loose in the first place. All of a sudden, working with the rest of the group, she took one leg warmer off and threw it out to the front, exasperatingly. She continued to dance full out and then the other leg warmer loosened further and had to be tossed off. All that was nothing but attention-getting stuff. You don't start out with leg warmers you know are going to fall down. At first I was annoyed, and then a smile came to my face because I recognized that this person was just trying to get a little more attention, that this was the only way she could. Ten years ago I would have been very angry. But from what I hear, I must be maturing.

It's hard sometimes to listen. I'm a talker, but it's very important that I hear my dancers. Unlike Alvin, however, I'm not one who wants to know everything about their private lives. But I am concerned that the dancers' lives are not traumatized by their dancing and that they are *living* their lives. I need to listen to what the dancers are saying onstage as well as off.

During our 1990 European tour, my first as artistic director, I sat down in front of all the dancers and made a speech about how we should treat each other and how we should be nice to each other because you go through times where everybody gets edgy. It's so hard to be on the road as often as we're on the road and do the work we do on the stage. As a family, in close proximity, there are moments where things really get grating. This was one of those moments. And so, I sat everybody down and tried to dispel the negativity.

It was a bombshell. Whatever anybody had been holding in came out at that meeting because I hadn't been listening. I had thirty people in front of me letting out whatever they needed to let out. It was like the biggest therapy session you've ever been to and I was the listener. It was very informative. One dancer said they all needed more of my attention. Another dancer said very coolly, "I don't need her approval." Of course, it was a dancer who needed a lot of that. There's a persona that's put on in front of your peers and another persona when you're one-on-one. They needed to get all that off their chests and at the end I said, "Please, my door is open." About four dancers out of the thirty raised their hands to come and talk to me. In my dressing room they said they were sorry for what happened. It was rough, but I wasn't sorry—it had been a real learning experience for me, part of my growth as a human being.

It's always a great lesson learned to listen to people before there is turmoil. But that can't always be done. As the leader, I have to be able to sit there and have the finger pointed at me and the rotten eggs thrown at me. I went through this with Alvin where we did the same thing to him. Everything that I've ever been through with Alvin is revisiting me. *Everything!*

When I started to choreograph, Alvin kept saying to me and I kept saying to myself: "All I have to do is transfer intimacy to another dancer." But for that, you need trust. With Alvin, if there was a step I didn't want to do, my body language made that clear. Alvin knew, but he'd still give me the step anyway. That's what I loved about Alvin. He'd give it to me anyway.

I recently hired dancers who were trained in the Ailey American Dance Center, under the directorship of Denise Jefferson. They graduated into the Repertory Ensemble, under the direction of Sylvia Waters, stayed for a year or two, and now auditioned for the first company and were accepted. All of that is a part of Alvin's vision. It's not just the fact that the first company is exemplary and unique because of its diversity as far as dancers and choreographers are concerned. But the whole system works from the school to the second company, which constantly feeds the first company with new dancers.

Dancers are from all over the world. I get telegrams from people on the road asking about auditions. People are very excited about being with us because of our nature as a repertory company, and also because of one man's vision.

I think God gives us extraordinary people, like pure drops of gold, every now and then so we know how special and how talented they are. When the special ones come along, it's pure talent, pure passion and commitment. All of that is right there as soon as they take their first step in the audition. You can see their love for dance and their gift for it.

Dance is a totally committed art that is so hard to do. It requires many hours and much sweat. If you don't love what you're doing and if your goal is to make money, you can forget it. There's a commitment, as a choreographer and as a dancer, to be true to yourself and be true to your audience.

Alvin was a choreographic genius because of the accessibility of his dances, their capacity to totally absorb the audience. All of a

With Masazumi Chaya and Donna Wood. *Photograph © Jack Mitchell*

sudden you're clapping along with *Revelations*. Alvin understood theater, props, costumes, and lighting. He knew how men would react to situations and he knew how women would react to the same situations. People are always interacting with each other in his pieces and there's a warmth and a caring that are accessible. Once an Ailey dancer, always an Ailey dancer. One does not detach oneself from such a great mentor and influence, in life and in the dance.

Alvin might offer words of reassurance when we were about to go onstage: "You're in command of the stage . . . enjoy yourself." Some people needed that, what I call overnurturing, but that takes a *lot* of time and Alvin also knew who *not* to waste his time on. I find the same thing when I'm working. I know whom to stay away from and whom to encourage. Alvin always used to say, "Everybody hears a different drummer." The same vocabulary is not going to produce the same exact movement from each dancer. You have to get the dancer to go beyond technique, into the spirit. I tend to give dancers the space to go home and do their homework. I can't lead them around and say, "Yes, that was wonderful" or "No, that was terrible." Nothing is that black and white, nothing is that concrete.

I can deal with a dancer's doubt—up to a point. However, I've got twenty-nine other people to worry about, plus a staff, plus I'm trying to raise money, and yes, I'm trying to choreograph ballets. Renee Robinson is an exquisite dancer and had a tendency to doubt herself. She can be so analytical about how she moves, and then the curtain will rise on a performance and she'll explode out of the wings and dance magnificently, as usual.

She never said, "I can't," and I never had any doubts about her unique talents. I will take time out for those people who I think are worth it. If I don't, it's because I can't do anything more *at the moment*. I will wait for another window of opportunity to help. I always believe that dancers must trust that they are growing, even if they have a bad day, or a bad performance; that the experience is just a springboard to help them get someplace better.

Dancers have to go "over the edge" onstage. It's no place to be safe. What's the point? What are you waiting for? The stage is the perfect arena for you to let out all the stops. I told one dancer who was timid in his attack in a particularly powerful role, "Just throw caution to the wind and, within the context of the movement, get as large as you can. Punch it instead of stepping into it carefully," I told him. Later he gave a performance where he threw himself all over the place. I came backstage and said, "Now I can tell you something. I can always pull you back, but if you don't give me anything, I don't know what to tell you because you won't get my *attention*. I'll sit in the audience and ignore you."

He's had a complete improvement. If you haven't pushed beyond what you think is "sane," then I can't help. If you haven't been "deranged," then I can't help. To do what we do, you have to be slightly "imbalanced." To do what we do with our bodies . . . it's like being an actor. I was called to Albany with Colleen Dewhurst and half a dozen other celebrities to testify before State Senator Goodman to help save part of the New York State Council on the Art's budget. Miss Dewhurst said, "An actor takes a chance of making a complete fool of himself." That's where you have to subjugate that ego, but use it to go over the edge. And that's when a director will tell you too much or too little, or do this or do that, but you've got to give the director something to work with.

I think actors have a more difficult situation because words are ambiguous. Dance can go "straight to it." You do an arabesque, it's an arabesque—period. And you do it with abandon or you don't do it at all, unless you're directed otherwise. But I don't know what to do with you unless you take it over the edge. You have to come in here *kicking*. You have to come in here *dancing* with all your potential. If you're not in contact with the child you once were who wanted to dance, if you can't remember why you wanted to dance in the first place, then why are you doing it? You must come to dance with a vulnerability and with an open mind.

I find that young dancers are especially vulnerable in thinking that if they don't have a certain role or if things are not going well in their lives that they're stagnating, that they're not growing. They don't realize that sometimes you're not in control of that growth. The only thing that you can be is ready, prepared for the next step. To me, there's never an arrival, but you are constantly rising regardless of whether it's within your concept of what you're doing or not. It's all in recognizing that there's something bigger than you going on.

Not that long ago, images lingered; now they fade quickly. It's a fast-forward life due to the economy, due to the life of a dancer and how long it's *supposed to last*. Today, with television and faxes and all things fast, he or she is anxious to move on to whatever is next. The latest stars on MTV are ten and eleven and wearing their clothes backward, though they're moving twice as fast. It's a fast world. All those variations contribute to the positive aggressiveness of dancers and choreographers—the you've-got-to-do-it-*now* mentality. A lot of the incentive is for people to take a master class and write on their résumés that they studied with me.

Rift, my first ballet for the Ailey company, did not work for me. I don't like working under pressure. I don't like having only thirty hours of rehearsal. People used to take a year to create a ballet. When we did it in Miami, toward the end of the tour, the dancers pulled it "out of the hat." They were brilliant. They were open to my frequent changes, always giving new movements a chance. Nona Hendryx wrote wonderful music. There are times when you don't have anything going on in your head, but you're supposed to produce a piece. I know people who can churn it out left and right, but I'm not that way. *Forgotten Time* took four months to do, though certain sections took only a few days. I had the luxury of time to be able to contemplate and change and see what looked good on people's bodies. *Rift* was choreographed during my second year as artistic director, when I was *supposed* to know all my dancers. I take no liberties in saying "my dancers" because Alvin made sure I understood that before he died. On his deathbed he said, "You make sure you remember these are your dancers."

On and off to this day, it's hard to grasp that. Now there are some Jamison Project dancers in the Ailey company, and they've taken well to the Ailey organization: Tracy Inman, Jonathan Phelps, Karine Plantadit, Lydia Roberts, Antonio Carlos Scott, and Michael Thomas. Some of them left for various reasons. It's getting to know your dancers, what works on them. That second year, and even today, I am still in the shock of Alvin's death because I never really grieved over Alvin not being here, because I haven't had time to. And I don't mean wailing, but I'm still carrying a space inside me for Alvin.

Alvin's vision is clear to me. I am the catalyst, the conduit in this situation, and the one who is responsible for continuing that legacy. One + One = One.

* * *

Receiving the Frontrunner Award from the Sara Lee Corporation in 1992 enabled me to donate money to a women's organization—I chose the dance group Urban Bush Women. Artistic director Jawole Willa Jo Zollar founded the company in 1984. Since then, she has received three Choreographer's Fellowships, two Inter-Arts Program Grants from the NEA, and a fellowship from the New York Foundation for the Arts. Jawole has created her own unique movement vocabulary. I hate to call it "postmodern Dunham" because that's only part of it. Jawole incorporates Haitian *yonvalou*, plus an African way of undulating the torso, with modern movement. It's quite a combination. It's something you can or cannot do—it has nothing to do with color. It's the music within your body, which is colorless.

Jawole gave us her 1988 ballet *Shelter*, with its texts "Belongo," by Laurie Carlos, and "Between a Rock and a Hard Place at the Intersection of Reduced Resources and Reverberating Rage," by Hattie Gossett. The ballet is about global homelessness. The words say, "Where we gonna go? What we gonna do?" It is about women who *must* support each other. When Jawole worked with the twelve women of the Ailey company to form two casts of six dancers, it was a beautiful exchange of spirit.

There are so many African-American women who are accomplished, but you turn on the television and you don't see them. You don't see documentaries about African-American men and women who have risen to prominence in the fields of science, education, business, or law. You turn on the television and you see Black men getting arrested every five seconds. I felt very blessed to win a Candace Award from the National Coalition of 100 Black Women, and to be, at various times, in the company of Cicely Tyson, Toni Morrison, Maya Angelou, Susan Taylor, Alice Walker, Jewell Jackson McCabe, and Johnnetta Cole, the president of Spelman College. I met Dr. Mae Jemison, the first African-American woman astronaut, who is also an M.D., a dancer—and stunning. She honored the Ailey organization by taking a poster of the company with her into space, *where no dance company has gone before* . . . Here are a few examples of powerful bulwarks of

African-American femininity, who combine strength, intelligence, and beauty. It is phenomenal to be in the presence of women for whom I have always had a great deal of respect.

There is a lineage of strong Black women who have influenced me all my life, including my grandmother, my mother, Marion Cuyjet, and Carmen de Lavallade.

Sometimes in your life when you feel that you are mentorless, you have to go look for one. Most people when they're older say, "I'm all grown up now. I don't need one." But you do. You need one all of your life. I'm always telling young people that they have to keep their eyes open. Their homework is to go and look for people who will be supportive and care about their long-range direction in life. I admired Alvin's ability to create his own agenda. You create your own agenda. If a door shuts, a window will open.

You need to fill yourself with knowledge. You need to get an education because we all cannot be performers; we all cannot be on a stage dancing. There are very few people who get a chance to do what I do. It's possible that if you want to dance, you will do it. But life is so rich and so full there are many things creatively that can be done. Writing, for instance, or being a doctor or a lawyer. Being whoever you are, fully, is the most important thing so that you will be able to contribute something positive in your life.

There's more to life than what is thought of as stereotypical beauty. When you're looking at yourself in the mirror you have to remember that that image is only a part of you. *The you is inside*. If you have any kind of brain at all, any kind of sense of self, you realize how unique that is. Nobody can be you. Uniqueness needs to be celebrated. There's only one of you. You're totally and absolutely individual. Sometimes that's hard to realize. We get bogged down by so much input from the outside world, and when we let outside influences define us, it becomes problematic. Self-definition is very important. You define who you are by actions, by what you do with your life.

You must spring from honesty. What makes the Ailey company so special is that it's filled with dancers who are people first, who happen to have the gift of dance. They are in touch with the honesty of who they really are and I insist that they remember why they wanted to dance in the first place. You need to back up and figure out what happened to that innocence and excitement that turned you on to do what you do. If you can remember that, you're in business because you'll just rekindle the flame.

That's why we do outreach in the schools, and have miniperformances to turn our young people on, not just to dance, but to *life*. I ask Leonard Meek and Renee Robinson to be the moderators of the miniperformances. They introduce the ballets, discuss the company history, and talk about themselves a little bit. The age of the audience determines our program. We can dance for only fifty minutes because it usually has to fit into one school period. This year we presented Louis Johnson's *Fontessa and Friends* and excerpts from *Revelations*.

Alvin was interested in the ability of dance to change the lives of young people. If one performance can turn on a young person's creative light, think of what we can accomplish during a few hot weeks in July and August. Ailey summer camps, directed by former company member Ronni Favors, originated in Kansas City, Missouri, five years after our initial affiliation there, and have made it possible for others—in New York and Baltimore—to spring from its success. Ronni interacts beautifully with young people. All of the camps teach tap, Dunham, and ballet. Students also learn about music in a class where they make their own instruments, and learn how to write in a creative writing class that encourages them to keep a journal as well as write poetry and other prose. After the summer, there is a structured follow-up. There is a caring. When we later run into the same young people that participated in the camps, they are still able to benefit from the change. They are still struggling to apply themselves and to incorporate the kind of groundwork we left them with—to be responsible for their lives and to understand that they have a "light" inside.

When you see Ailey dancers like Andre Tyson and Elizabeth Roxas walk into a room, just by their presence and the way they carry themselves, they're already making a statement about how they're taking responsibility for their lives, what they're committed to, what they love doing, and what kind of passion they have. They've made a statement even without words. You must care for yourself before you can care for others. Young people get to see that kind of positive presence even before they see Liz and Andre dance. That's where they get the chance to challenge themselves, because the children don't walk in saying, "I can't wait to do this." Some of them walk in maybe not even wanting to be there at all. But none of them want the camp to end, because they've had such an enlightening experience.

Some children come in energized and are able to meet people who can help them direct that energy. They've been given the incentive and the opportunity by someone named Alvin Ailey, who said there should be camps that involve dancing as well as speaking, learning to write, and how to get along with your peers. It's all incorporated. It's similar to my experiences as a student with Marion Cuyjet. There was a complete world inside her school, including the tea dances. It was a microcosm of society that taught us how to get along with people, taught us the right manners and courtesies, taught us hard work.

In 1977 we danced at our first presidential inaugural gala, for Jimmy Carter. Shortly after, we danced for President and Mrs. Carter at the White House. During rehearsal, I hit my hand on the wings and Rosalynn Carter sent me downstairs to the infirmary. It was just a little bruise. When we danced *Revelations*, my umbrella hit the chandelier! I had previously been invited to dinner by President and Mrs. Ford. There's a big difference between going in the front door of the White House as a guest and going in the back door as an entertainer. Mrs. Ford had been a student of Martha Graham's in the 1940s, when her name was Betty Bloomer. Her enthusiasm for our company brought her to one of our performances at City Center. Though she had stopped performing many years before, when she came backstage and we posed for pictures, she could still "hit the line" like any professional dancer.

In 1993 the Ailey company returned to Washington, D.C., to dance on the eve of President Clinton's inauguration. Michael Kaiser, our executive director, Calvin Hunt, then the production stage manager, and I arrived on Saturday, January 16, 1993. I had arranged to rent a van from the local rent-a-car, but when we arrived for the pickup, there was no van. Calvin arrived ahead of me but was still last on the line. There wasn't a single van that Saturday morning. I told the woman behind the desk, "We have an inaugural to do!" And she gave me one of those "so what" looks. If they didn't have any vans, they didn't have *any* vans. We took my leased car.

For some reason, Calvin's license did not go through as a supplementary driver. That meant I had to do the driving. Calvin and I picked up Michael at his apartment and the three of us went to the studio. We piled in seven wooden stools for *Revelations*, fourteen costumes—vests, shirts, pants, skirts, tops, hats, fans—shoe bags, and a steamer for Denise Soteras, affectionately called "Zorba," the head of wardrobe. We packed all that into a Chrysler Imperial, with stools poking out from every direction. It was ridiculous. For our first stop, we had to unpeel ourselves from the car and trust that what we had adjusted to get out, we could adjust again to get back in.

It was just so totally packed. It reminded me of the days that I was so happy I wasn't a part of—the "station wagon days" where everything was piled in. At least we had buses during my era. At first there were ten dancers, then twelve dancers, then fifteen dancers, so it started getting a little tight, and we were carrying around more and more ballets.

We had an open dress rehearsal for twenty thousand people, at the Capital Center in Landover, Maryland. They had written in for tickets. The only requirement for admittance was canned goods for the homeless. I had to restage *Revelations* because we were performing in the round and the dancers had to enter from the audience. I turned the men upstage in "Rocka My Soul," so that the entire audience had a chance to look at them. The dress rehearsal was much more comfortable than the gala performance, when there were twice as many people backstage and the theater was tense. Trailers had been driven into the backstage area and then curtains put in front of the trailers to hide them. Paper signs were pinned to each curtain, including Barbra Streisand, Michael Jackson, Barry Manilow, and Aretha Franklin. Goldie Hawn and Sally Field introduced us.

Everybody was nervous when the *future* President showed up, including the Alvin Ailey American Dance Theater, who told me they were nervous the next day. It was very impressive. I didn't have to worry about going onstage and dancing. I was so proud of the dancers because we were the only dance company that had been invited, representing dance in the United States.

CHAPTER 21

JUMBY BAY, ANTIGUA

An angel came and visited me today. I was trying to read a biography of Adam Clayton Powell when the maid came in and started singing in a wonderfully high, squeaky soprano. I couldn't understand her at first because of her accent. There was no pretension. She was just doing her work, but when I started to crave a little quiet I suddenly heard "Precious Lord," "The Lord Is My Light and Salvation," and "His Eye Is on the Sparrow," which my mother loved to sing: I sing because I'm happy . . .

It touched my heart because it reminded me so much of my mom that it brought tears to my eyes. I marveled at this for a minute and then turned to her and said, "You know every verse, don't you?" I was more familiar with the chorus, but she knew all the verses and sang every one of them in a soprano that was otherworldly. When she finished the room, she left and headed toward the palm trees, in the direction of the ocean, still singing. You never know where angels are

going to come from. All blessings come to you from unknown and
unexpected places. I accepted that and had a beautiful day.

In the morning I fall out of bed, get on my knees and say, "Thank you for another day," then I do my floor barre. Then I have a cup of coffee. My stereo turns on automatically at six o'clock. If I'm on schedule I run out to get the newspapers and come back and read them; if I'm late I bring them with me to the studio. Sometimes there will be a breakfast meeting, or a meeting with Paul Szilard, or Calvin Hunt, or Molly Browning (our director of marketing), or Sharon Luckman (our development director). There can be a meeting with a foreign impresario or a call to Garth Fagan to discuss his new ballet for the thirty-fifth anniversary, a visit to the Ailey camps, and, of course, choreographing a new ballet, rehearsing repertory, trying to meet with my dancers, doing interviews for television and print, helping to arrange photo calls, observing classes in the Dance Center, meeting with potential choreographers, watching videos of potential ballets for the company, meeting with Michael Kaiser about our five-year plan, and consulting with my associate artistic director, Masazumi Chaya, who is a constant source of strength. His enthusiasm, and the fact that he's so good at what he does, make my "job" easier.

One can see a dancer a mile away, and I'm not talking about someone who waddles down the street carrying a dance bag . . . but there is an aura about that person. Someone like Chaya has an innate sense of what dance is, and it becomes obvious when he has to reconstruct a revival such as *The River*. I look at old tapes of him moving and I see him moving today and demonstrating those things as only a true artist can.

Donald Byrd choreographed *Folkdance* in 1992 for the four senior members of the company: Dudley Williams, Sarita Allen, Marilyn Banks, and Gary DeLoatch. Unfortunately, this was Gary's last appearance with the Ailey. He passed away in the spring of 1993, but will always be remembered for his outgoing personality and huge gifts as a dancer.

I was one of the last in the company to see him. While I was at the hospital, a priest came in and gave Gary his last rites. Gary was not Catholic. He said all the prayers—you name it, he said it. It was the opposite of Alvin. While all that was happening to him, Alvin wanted happy music.

But through it all, Gary was still entertaining. He could barely speak, but he was an entertainer, and there he was on his deathbed, entertaining. The oxygen mask was over his mouth and you could barely understand him. His cousin and friend Stephen Smith were there. Gary's eyebrow would go up every once in a while in a familiar Gary expression of "I'm still here." He knew that drugs were "taking him out," but he was still coherent. I wasn't there when he died; I understand that he was very peaceful.

Gary loved Alvin so dearly and I think Alvin saw in Gary a younger version of himself, particularly when he created the ballet *For Bird—With Love*.

So many people dwell on negativity and I've survived by ignoring it: it dims your light and it's harder each time to turn the power up again.

I try and read a chapter of the Bible every day, which brings with it a kind of stability. There's a verse I typed into my Sharp Wizard organizer from Ephesians, chapter 2, that I titled "Faith and Grace": "For by grace are ye saved through faith; and that not of yourselves; it is a gift of God: Not of works, lest any man should boast. For we are his workmanship, created in Christ Jesus unto good works, which God hath before ordained that we should walk in them." There's God's grace and the faith that you have in Him. Faith in man is different. God is a constant, man is ephemeral. The kind of faith I have in God is constant. Alvin was not a god. He was a man and came with the frailties of a human being. I learned as a child that you do not have the same faith in man as you have in God. I trusted Alvin with my entire being—the faith of a dancer trusting a choreographer.

I've always believed that my life has been predestined; all I've had to do is be prepared. I remember believing that I had a special connection with God; all of us do. Since I was a child there has been an awareness in me and I don't know if it came from my parents or what. I think I was born knowing that I had a special relationship with whoever put me on this earth. It wasn't always that clear-cut, but it was in the back of my head. I couldn't see it all the time but I had great faith that God had great grace. If I didn't know what was going on, He certainly did.

That's very much how I feel about Alvin. The reason that I was with the company for fifteen years is that I maintained my faith. Alvin was just the conduit of God, as we all are. He was predestined to be on this earth running this company and I was predestined to join the company the way I did. So that some things that are shocks to other people are not shocking to me at all. For instance, coming into this company and being the artistic director. The shock was that he wasn't there physically anymore. When he asked me to assume the position, I just said yes. Everybody else was saying that the transition would be so difficult, but no, that's not the way it was. I'm basing my head on "this is the way it's supposed to be. I'm here. It's not supposed to be any other way."

Dance is about never-ending aspiration and Alvin expressed that through movement. It didn't necessarily come out of despair or some deep, dark place. It came, more often, from the idea that no one is ever finished, that there is always something to aspire to. It was Alvin's genius that he could give you that image. Everybody around the world understood what he was talking about.

Alvin always used to say that you are on a mountaintop by yourself, words I couldn't fully appreciate until he named me artistic director of the company. The down side of being artistic director is separation from people: people who relate to you differently as an artistic director than they would if you were still a dancer. When I first became artistic director, there were people I had known for years who suddenly acted completely differently toward me. After *Cry*, I was still a family member; I was still dancing. Now I'm not, although I'll always be a dancer. As artistic director, I have to make decisions that I didn't have to make as a dancer. Only I can make those

decisions—that's what puts you on a mountaintop by yourself. I have to be very private about the decisions I make. That separates me in a way. It's like being a parent. Parents cannot just be buddies. They're in charge.

I think that's part of the problem with kids that go in the wrong direction today. They haven't had the kind of figure who says, "This is the way it's going to go." There's that separation: I love you to death and will do anything for you, but I'm running it.

It's so delicate. What you are dealing with is someone's intangible spirit that becomes manifest onstage. And then it's gone. You can't mess with it. You've got to nurture people individually. With some, you "jam it" home; with others, you walk around them gently. You've got to figure out the combination of each personality. The same combination does not unlock everybody in the same way. You've got to be attuned to what each person needs.

I'll always be a dancer; I was born that way. I've never stopped. That's what I was supposed to be doing in life. I'm still connected through my choreography. Dancing is a gift. You're supposed to do it; it's like breathing. And if you're supposed to do it, you know it, and you pursue it. I always tell a young dancer who comes to me for advice and asks, "Should I be a dancer?"—if there's a question in your mind, then the answer is no. Don't do it. It's a commitment inside. You already *know*.

I always tell young dancers they've got to learn it all, to keep an open mind because it keeps you alive. There's a phrase I've heard— "to dance is to live, to live is to dance." I wonder, how are you going to bring full meaning to your performance if you don't know anything about life? How are you going to bring it to the stage if you don't know anything about life? It's not all-consuming, you've got to live, but when you get into that studio you've got to bring your entire self there.

I love teaching energetic, enthusiastic people who openheartedly

The classic Jack Mitchell portrait. *Photograph © Jack Mitchell* receive. Choreography is a reciprocal moment in the studio . . . an exchange of spirit. To me, it's very religious what happens between a choreographer and a dancer. It's like a marriage. You must understand each other in the moments you're in the studio.

I hope I am a continuation of Alvin's vision. He has left me a road map. It's very clear. It works. The support system here is incredible; the staff, the entire organization, work well together. All of this was in place, which makes my job so easy. If his vision hadn't worked, I'd be going, "We need to change this or we need to change that." But it works. I was a part of it working in the past and I'm an extension of it continuing to work into the future. The dancers are the visual manifestation of a vision that works.

I have people with me who do the work of ten people. In these difficult financial times it's necessary to keep things at the highest possible level with the smartest people around, who really enjoy what they're doing. Everyone here has the same passion you see when you see that dancer onstage.

Alvin said that you entertain and you educate. You show people that dancers are not just bodies onstage doing steps. Alvin wanted to have something deeper going on than the magic that happens onstage, so we started doing residencies in the school systems. Our dancers understand that this is a two-way street. They're not just sharing their gifts onstage. When you teach a child, it helps *you* to remember that at one point in *your* life you didn't know your left foot from your right. It brings a certain humility.

There's only one of you on earth. Isn't *that* wonderful? You should be able to celebrate that fact and you should be able to share it. What we try to convey to young people is that there is not a pomposity about accomplishment, but there should be a generosity about it. Yes, feel free to make mistakes in class and stumble in class, but learn your craft. Learn the craft of knowing how to open your heart and how to turn on your creativity. There's a light inside of you.

In *Mary Lou's Mass*. *Photograph © Jack Mitchell*

You don't have to be five feet ten to be a dancer. Don't let what your body does define what you can do. Think of movement as much bigger than what your body says you're limited to. Your hand can go into the depths of your heart to pull out what you need to communicate with another person. I made a career not on how high my legs were but on how high you *thought* they went. Dance is bigger than the physical body. Think bigger than that. When you extend your arm, it doesn't stop at the end of your fingers, because you're dancing bigger than that; you're dancing spirit. Take a chance. Reach out. Go further than you've ever gone before.

Dance from the top of the head to the bottom of your feet. There is no step that is not justified. Even when you're stationary, you must be moving and alive. Even static sculpture has movement. You may be standing still but you're moving. Energy is coming out. And for that you have to be alert. Every single step has value, has justification. Be clear—it's the only way to bring forth the honesty in the movement.

If you lose the step, turn inside. When you get lost, focus. Believe that the gift is in you. Accept it. If there are mistakes, so be it. God is in you. Let your light shine . . .

JUDITH JAMISON'S CHOREOGRAPHY

Ballet–Premiere	Music	Costumes	Lighting
Divining 1984 (Alvin Ailey American Dance Theater)	Kimati Dinizulu Monti Ellison	Masazumi Chaya (Ailey) Andy Kay (Jamison Project)	Chenault Spence Timothy Hunter
Just Call Me Dance 1984 (Maurice Béjart's Ballet of the 20th Century)	Ken Hatfield	Sarita Allen	
Time Out (Washington Ballet) 1986	Ken Hatfield	Sarita Allen Dean South	Tony Tucci
Time In 1986 (Ballet Nuevo Mundo de Caracas)	various contemporary	Sarita Allen	Pamela Cooper
Into the Life 1987 (Jennifer Muller/The Works)	various contemporary	Sarita Allen Dean South	Ken Tabachnick
Tease 1988 (Alvin Ailey Repertory Ensemble)	various contemporary	Duane Talley	Timothy Hunter
Forgotten Time 1989 (Jamison Project)	"Le Mystère des Voix Bulgares"	Judith Jamison Ellen Mahkle	Timothy Hunter
Rift 1991 (Alvin Ailey American Dance Theater)	Nona Hendryx	Kathryn Simon	Timothy Hunter
Hymn 1993 [Him] (Alvin Ailey American Dance Theater)	Anna Deveare Smith (libretto) Robert Ruggieri (music)	Toyce Anderson	Timothy Hunter

THE ALVIN AILEY AMERICAN DANCE THEATER
35th ANNIVERSARY 1958–1993
Founder—Alvin Ailey
Artistic Director—Judith Jamison
Associate Artistic Director—Masazumi Chaya
Executive Director—Michael M. Kaiser
Artistic Director, Repertory Ensemble—Sylvia Waters

COMPANY MEMBERS
Sarita Allen   Marilyn Banks   Roger Bellamy   Cubie Burke
Raquelle Chavis   Duane Cyrus   Gary DeLoatch (deceased)
Linda-Denise Evans   Bernard Gaddis   Danielle Gee
Dana Hash   Tracy Inman   Michael Joy   Vicky Lambert
Aubrey Lynch II   Deborah Manning   Leonard Meek
Jonathan Phelps   Toni Pierce   Karine Plantadit
Troy Powell   Dwight Rhoden   Desmond Richardson
Lydia Roberts   Renee Robinson   Elizabeth Roxas
Matthew Rushing   Antonio Carlos Scott   Michael Thomas
Nasha Thomas   Andre Tyson   Melissa Vaughan
Desire Vlad   Dudley Williams

THE ALVIN AILEY AMERICAN DANCE CENTER
Director—Denise Jefferson
Artistic Advisor—Judith Jamison
School Administrator—Kathleen Connolly
Business Manager—Diane Grumet
Financial Aid Administrator—Salley LeLong
Foreign Aid Advisor—Joanne Ruggeri
Registrar—Rachid Kerdouche

DEPARTMENT CHAIRPERSONS
Ballet—Celia Marino
Horton—Ana Marie Forsythe
Dunham (Afro-Caribbean)—Joan Peters
Jazz—José Meier
Graham-based Modern—Jeanne Ruddy
Ballet—Walter Raines (chairperson emeritus)

OVERLEAF

In *Cry. Photograph by Herb Migdoll*

INTERVIEWS

Delores Brown Abelson
Michael and Annie Ahearn
Clive Barnes
Mickey Bord
Michael Brenner
John Butler
Masazumi Chaya
Lili Cockerille Livingston
Marion Cuyjet
Carmen de Lavallade
Agnes de Mille
Ronni Favors
Allan Gray
William Hammond
Geoffrey Holder
Timothy Hunter
Patricia Jacobs
John Jamison, Sr.
John Jamison, Jr.
Doris Johnson
Louis Johnson
Martha Johnson
Michael Kaiser
Nancy Kalodner
Andy Kay
Sam Miller
Milton Myers
Joe Nash
Joette Pelster
Jonathan Riseling
Ken Rubenstein
Josephine and Earl Stamm, Esqs.
Paul Szilard
Clive Thompson
Liz Thompson

James Truitte
Cynthia Wassell
Sylvia Waters
Mrs. Allie Whetstone
Patricia Wilde
Beverly Williams
Billy Wilson
Donna Wood
Sara Yarborough

SELECT BIBLIOGRAPHY

Balanchine, George, and Francis Mason. *101 Stories of the Great Ballets*. New York: Anchor Books/Doubleday, 1989.

Chujoy, Anatole, and P. W. Manchester, eds. *The Dance Encyclopedia*. Rev. ed. New York: Simon and Schuster, 1967.

Long, Richard A. *The Black Tradition in American Dance*. New York, Rizzoli International Publications, 1989.

White-Dixon, Melanye P. "Marion Cuyjet: Visionary of Dance Education in Black Philadelphia." Ph.D. diss. Temple University, 1987.